CONFISCA[TION]
A Practical Gui[de]
Confiscating Crime Proceeds

AUSTRALIA
LBC Information Services—Sydney

CANADA and USA
Carswell—Toronto

NEW ZEALAND
Brooker's—Auckland

SINGAPORE and MALAYSIA
Thomson Information (S.E. Asia)
Singapore

CONFISCATION
A Practical Guide to
Confiscating Crime Proceeds

Lesley Thomson

W. GREEN/Sweet & Maxwell
EDINBURGH
2000

Published in 2000 by W. Green & Son Ltd
21 Alva Street
Edinburgh EH2 4PS

Typeset by LBJ Typesetting Ltd of Kingsclere
Printed and bound in Great Britain by MPG Books Ltd,
Bodmin, Cornwall

No natural forests were destroyed to make this product;
only farmed timber was used and replanted

A CIP catalogue record for this book is available from the
British Library

ISBN 0 414 012 976

W. Green & Son Ltd 2000

PREFACE

The aim of this book is to provide a handbook for use by those involved in confiscation cases at all levels. In addition, it is hoped that it will be of particular help to those coming to the subject for the first time. I have dealt with confiscation practice as it currently stands including its restricted operation for non drug trafficking cases as a result of the *Adamson* decision.

The book draws on my personal experience in confiscation cases during a three year secondment to the Confiscation Unit at Crown Office. However, any views expressed in the book are my own and are not binding on any government department or other body. Any reference to Crown practice in the book refers to cases already heard in Court. I alone am responsible for any errors and omissions.

I am particularly indebted to my two friends David Bruce, CA and John Duvoisin, CA for contributing Chapter 5 and the model computation in Appendix 2, style III. Without their assistance and guidance in the proper application of accountancy principles to confiscation practice, this book could not have been written. I would like to thank the staff at W. Green & Son Ltd for all their help and assistance.

Finally, I would also like to thank my two sons, Andy for helping with the proof reading and Stewart for keeping quiet while we were doing it.

I have tried to state the law as at November 25, 1999.

Lesley Thomson
Glasgow,
December 1, 1999.

Contents

Chapter 6 The Prosecutor's Statement and Answers

Chapter 7 The Confiscation Hearing or Proof

Chapter 8 Enforcement of a Confiscation Order and the Use of Administrators

Chapter 9 Miscellaneous

Table of Cases

Table of Statutes

Table of Statutory Instruments

CHAPTER 1

CONFISCATION—WHAT, WHY AND WHEN?

This book seeks to explain, in a straightforward manner, how **1.01** the law relating to asset confiscation currently operates in Scottish courts. It is intended as a practical guide to assist the practitioner in finding a way through what at times can be extremely complicated legislation covering both criminal and civil courts and the fields of law and accountancy.

CONFISCATION—WHAT IS IT?

What is meant by asset confiscation? In Scotland it is the power **1.02** to confiscate the proceeds or benefit of crime, *i.e.* to remove the proceeds or benefit derived from crime from any convicted offender and to return him to the same financial position he would have been in had he not become involved in criminal activity. In Scots law, asset confiscation is distinct from forfeiture which denotes the removal of property from a convicted offender when that property has been used in the commission of the crime itself.

Accordingly, in Scotland, asset confiscation is not the removal of specified items, as is the forfeiture of property. Rather, it is an order to pay a sum of money within a fixed period of time, the sum being calculated with reference both to the proceeds or benefit made from crime and to the assets left. This approach is in line with both English and European law.

CONFISCATION—WHY?

The reasoning behind the legislation is based on punishment **1.03** and prevention. The punishment element is obvious. As a preventive method, the aim is to ensure that whenever the sentence of the court has been completed, normally a sentence of imprisonment, the offender does not have access to funds whereby he can commence his criminal activities anew. In addition, Scottish confiscation legislation has certain practical effects, such as:

(a) it aims to show that crime does not pay (it seems to appeal to the general public that convicted criminals can no longer live luxurious lifestyles on their release from prison, and indeed that their families are unable to live in such a fashion while their relative is serving his sentence);

(b) it takes "bad money" out of circulation. There seems little doubt that money made, for example, from drug trafficking is used to fund diverse criminal enterprises;

(c) it boosts government funds. Neither individual police forces nor the procurator fiscal service nor any other enforcement agencies are financial beneficiaries, the money going instead to the consolidated fund at the Treasury in the same manner as collected fines. The Scottish system does not follow the American example of confiscation where the property then goes directly to the enforcement agency itself, leading, perhaps understandably, to criticism of cases being revenue-led and agencies being accused of case targeting on the basis of available assets rather than the level of crime;

(d) theoretically, strong confiscation legislation should act as a deterrent in not only punishing the crime and possibly persuading like-minded would-be criminals to reconsider embarking on that course, but also in removing the "reward" element from their actions. In practice, though, it may lead to some offenders seeking more effective methods in the concealment of their criminal profits within the financial system.

It has to be remembered that the legislation is very wide-ranging and is often perceived to be somewhat complicated by practitioners since it departs from "normal" criminal principles in the sense that the court is able to consider a longer period than that covered by the crime itself and, in practical terms, the onus is on the convicted offender to explain where his assets came from. (How the legislation deals with this is dealt with in later chapters.)

CONFISCATION—WHEN?

1.04 Scottish confiscation legislation is found mainly in the Proceeds of Crime (Scotland) Act 1995[1] with some provisions in relation to drug trafficking found in the Criminal Law (Consolidation) (Scotland) Act 1995.[2]

---

[1] (c. 43) (hereinafter referred to as "PCSA 1995").
[2] (c. 39) (hereinafter referred to as "CLCSA 1995").

A confiscation order is an order to pay a fixed sum *after* a person has been convicted and *after* confiscation proceedings have been concluded. The offender is normally given a period of time in which to pay that sum which is payable to the court and treated, in practice, like a fine. Whilst the aim of the order is to remove funds generated by criminal acts, the fixing of the figure to be confiscated does not always relate solely to the crime the conviction represents. Rather, there are assumptions within PCSA 1995 which allow the court, in certain situations, to take account of proceeds or benefits over a six-year period prior to the date of the crime before the court. (See below, Chapter 4.) Put simply, once an accused satisfies the criteria laid down in PCSA 1995 and is the potential subject of a confiscation order, his crime acts as a trigger to allow the full confiscation rules to come into play. This novel legal concept has been difficult for practitioners to digest because it means that once an accused has been convicted of a "confiscation crime", the circumstances of some crimes, usually drug trafficking cases, may have very little obvious link to the confiscation proceedings other than to act as a "start button" to initiate them. (See the example in Appendix 1.)

It is important to remember that there are two separate types of "confiscation crimes", namely:

(1) drug trafficking; and

(2) "all crime".

These are treated separately under the legislation and, at times, different rules operate.

An important aspect of the legislation to bear in mind is that the upper limit of a confiscation order, no matter the type of crime, is the lower of (a) the proceeds of drug trafficking or the benefit from the crime and (b) the amount which might be realised at the time the order is made. In other words, the court cannot recover any more than is left. The amount which might be realised is simply what the court determines truly belongs to the offender, no matter in whose name the property may be. This is known as his "realisable property" and includes gifts and implicative gifts to others. (See below, Chapter 4.)

Put simply, a confiscation order cannot be made by the court for an amount greater than an accused person's realisable property (*i.e.* the assets truly belonging to him) at the date of the making of the order. For example, if a drug trafficker can be shown to have made £100,000 from drug trafficking over the previous six years, but the only assets left are a car valued at £5,000 and a house with £20,000 equity, then the confiscation order will be for the lower figure of £25,000, being the value of the assets remaining, but there will be a finding in fact to the effect that there are proceeds of £100,000 from drug trafficking. Matters do not necessarily end there, however, as PCSA 1995 provides a method of returning to court to have an order increased within a period of six years if currently hidden funds come to light. These matters are covered in more detail in later chapters.

Basically, therefore, confiscation was introduced to punish and prevent; proceeds of crime are removed from the criminal, his associates and family; and government funds are increased by crime proceeds and put to a better use, thereby helping to satisfy the old adage that crime does not pay.

When can the legislation be used? Before April 1, 1996, a confiscation order was competent only when a person was convicted in the High Court or remitted there for sentence from the sheriff court in relation to the drug trafficking offences listed in section 1(2) of the Criminal Justice (Scotland) Act 1987.[3] There are a number of offences listed, but in general the most common offences which triggered confiscation proceedings were sections 4(3)(b) and 5(3) of the Misuse of Drugs Act 1971.[4] From April 1, 1996 the legislation was extended to include drug trafficking and "all crime", as defined below. The author has endeavoured to deal with the two areas separately where appropriate.

Drug trafficking

1.05   From April 1, 1996 confiscation powers were extended to the sheriff court, and in terms of section 1 of PCSA 1995, in respect of any drug trafficking offence where:

> "(a) the accused is convicted whether in solemn or summary proceedings; or
>
> (b) in the case of summary proceedings (without proceeding to conviction) an order is made discharging him absolutely,
>
> the court, on the application of the prosecutor, may make an order (a 'confiscation order') requiring the accused to pay such sum as the court thinks fit."

[3] (c. 41).
[4] (c. 38).

Although the section applies to an offence which can be on indictment or on summary complaint, where it relates to summary proceedings it must be an offence punishable by a fine of an amount greater than the amount corresponding to level 5 on the standard scale, or by imprisonment for a period longer than three months, or by both fine and imprisonment. Confiscation applies, then, where the accused is facing more than a three-month sentence or a level 5 fine. What matters is that the court has the power to impose the sentence, not that the sentence has been imposed. It follows, therefore, that confiscation proceedings would be competent where, for example, an accused is prosecuted for a contravention of section 5(3) of the Misuse of Drugs Act 1971 for a Class A drug at summary level and is facing imprisonment of 12 months. In effect, therefore, the small-time dealers whose offences do not merit prosecution on indictment can still have their proceeds from drug trafficking and remaining assets targeted by a confiscation order.

As an example, Mr A is a small-time trafficker who is convicted of possession with intent to supply of one deal of heroin, a Class A drug, the offence being committed at one point on one day, and he is sentenced to eight months' imprisonment and is then subject to a confiscation order. He is found to have £3,000 in a building society account, a car valued at £4,000, a boat he gave to his girlfriend, valued at £7,000, and a flat in Troon in his mother's name, but paid for by him, and valued at £30,000. As such, he would appear to be a likely target for confiscation proceedings. If Mr A's finances are analysed over the preceding six years, as allowed under PCSA 1995 (see "The confiscation assumptions" in Chapter 4 and the financial analysis in Chapter 5), and his drug trafficking proceeds figure comes out at about £50,000, then all the assets could be viewed by the court as his realisable property and a confiscation order made, equivalent to the value of the money, the car, the boat and the flat, *i.e.* £44,000. The method used by the court to take into account assets which are in the names of others but which truly belong to the accused is to be found in the statutory provisions relating to implicative gifts (see "Implicative gifts" in Chapter 4).

The types of drug trafficking offences to which section 1 applies are defined in section 49 of PCSA 1995, which section also includes a definition of drug trafficking. Specific reference should be made to the section, but offences include the most common charges for confiscation proceedings, namely sections

4(3)(b) and 5(3) of the Misuse of Drugs Act 1971 and section 170 of the Customs and Excise Management Act 1970.[5]

It should be noted that possession of a controlled drug in terms of section 5(2) of the Misuse of Drugs Act 1971 is *not* a drug trafficking offence.

Section 1(5) of PCSA 1995 deals with the fixed sum payable by a person who has been convicted of a drug trafficking offence. As stated above, this is an amount not exceeding the value of the proceeds of the drug trafficking itself, or the offender's realisable property, whichever is the lesser.

However, it has to be borne in mind that the court assesses the value of the accused's realisable property *at the date the order is made*, so up-to-date valuations for cars, houses, jewellery, etc. will always be required.

"All crime" (from April 1, 1996)

1.06   It is convenient to refer to offences under PCSA 1995 which are not drug trafficking offences as "all crime" offences, which is the term used hereinafter. Because the rules differ, "all crime" itself is split into two categories—"single crime" and "double crime".

Section 1 of PCSA 1995 states that confiscation is competent in respect of any offence where:

> "(a)   the accused is convicted in either solemn or summary proceedings, or
>
> (b)   in the case of summary proceedings (without proceeding to conviction), an order is made discharging him absolutely."

Additionally, the same rules apply as for drug trafficking in that the accused has been prosecuted at either solemn or summary level, provided that if the offence is prosecuted at summary level then it is punishable by a fine greater than the amount corresponding to level 5 on the standard scale or by imprisonment for a period longer than three months or by both such fine and imprisonment. Some of the offences which carry an enhanced summary penalty are trading standards offences, environmental offences, health and safety offences and common law offences of dishonesty where the accused already has an analogous previous conviction. (It should be noted that terrorist offences are specifically excluded and are dealt with in different legislation.)

[5] (c. 2).

Section 1(4) of PCSA 1995 provides that a confiscation order can only be made in "all crime" cases where the court is satisfied that the accused has benefited from the offence. This provision should be read along with section 2 which defines "benefit" and provides for certain assumptions in both "single crime" and "double crime"-type cases.

According to section 1(6) of PCSA 1995 the fixed sum which a confiscation order requires an accused to pay in an "all crime" offence is an amount not exceeding the lesser of:

"(a) the amount of the benefit—

    (i) from the commission of the offence; or

    (ii) where section 2(4) of this Act applies, from the commission of the offence and any other offence, not being a drug trafficking offence, to which this part of this Act applies; and

(b) the amount that might be realised at the time the order is made."

Section 2(4) of the Act applies where a confiscation order is sought either in respect of two or more offences or where the offender has been convicted of at least one other offence to which the Act applies during the period of six years immediately prior to the institution of proceedings. In simple terms, therefore, the upper limit of a confiscation order in "all crime" is the benefit from the crime or the amount which might be realised, whichever is the lesser, although what constitutes "benefit from the crime" depends on whether section 2(4) applies and what exactly that section means.

"Single crime"/"Double crime"

Therefore there are really two separate types of "all crime" **1.07** situations, either:

(a) where the Court is dealing with one crime whether on a summary complaint (provided the maximum sentence imposed could exceed the normal summary maximum) or on indictment, this is known as a "single crime" case; and

(b) where the Court is dealing with more than one crime this is known as a "double crime" crime.

These can arise in two ways under section 2(4), where either the accused faces two crimes on the indictment or complaint and the confiscation order is sought in respect of both offences; or during the relevant period of six months prior to the institution of proceedings (but not before the commencement date of the Act, April 1, 1996) the accused has a previous conviction to which the Act applies.

1.08   Prior to the case of *Adamson v. H.M. Advocate*,[6] it was thought, by the Crown at least, that in "double crime" cases the court was entitled to use the same type of financial analysis to calculate benefit as that used to calculate proceeds in drug trafficking cases. In other words, the application of sections 2(4) and 2(5) of PCSA 1995 was to the effect that the Crown could invoke the confiscation assumptions, as outlined in Chapter 4 below and assess the accused's "benefit" by means of analysis of his assets and expenditure in the preceding six years without linking the analysis to the crimes of which he had been convicted. That approach was in fact adopted by the sheriff in making a confiscation order against Adamson (see Chapter 8 below). He stated that: "Parliament must have had it in mind that a criminal with convictions for two or more offences should be liable to confiscation procedures in relation to past activities which might no doubt be incapable of proof by the Crown." However, the Appeal Court in the *Adamson*[7] case, *per* Lord Sutherland, rejected the Crown's position on sections 2(4) and 2(5) in relation to criminal conduct and stated that it was not "at all clear that Parliament intended the sort of regime which applies in drug trafficking cases should also be applied in non drug trafficking cases." The court quashed Adamson's confiscation order which had been based on a benefit figure after looking at his assets built up over a six year period. The door now appears to have been closed on the view that in "double crime" cases the Crown can use confiscation to obtain the assets of criminals who have been engaged in a course of criminal conduct. There is no doubt that PCSA 1995 was poorly drafted in relation to the use of assumptions over a six year period to calculate benefit by means of sections 2(4) and 2(5) which, perhaps significantly, were introduced very late in the progress of the Act's passage through Parliament. It would be expected therefore that if Parliament did intend PCSA 1995 to be used

---

[6] High Court on appeal, October 20, 1999, unreported (Appeal No. C434/99).
[7] *ibid.*

for confiscating the assets of career criminals in the same way as drug traffickers, as is now common in many other countries, the position in *Adamson* will be reversed by legislation in the near future.

The present position then is that there remain two categories of all crime cases. However, once the investigative/restraint stage is passed, there is very little practical difference.

The easiest way to see how confiscation applies to all crime cases is to consider some examples.

Mr A is convicted of embezzlement of £9,000 on October 31, 1999. He committed his offence on October 31, 1998. He owns a house with equity of £5,000, two cars valued at £10,000 and has £3,000 in the bank.

Example A: Mr A has no previous convictions and appears on a **1.09** summary complaint. In this case, confiscation does not apply as the maximum sentence Mr A faces is three months (a "non-confiscation" case).

Example B: Mr A has a previous conviction for robbery in **1.10** October 1995 and appears on a summary complaint. In this case, confiscation does apply as Mr A faces a maximum sentence in excess of the normal summary maximum. A confiscation order could be made for the sum of £9,000 being the benefit Mr A got from his crime. His previous conviction is only relevant as it means Mr A faces a sentence of more than three months. It is not relevant in the benefit calculation as it occurred before PCSA 1995 came into force (a "single crime" case).

Example C: Mr A has a number of previous convictions, **1.11** including one for theft of £10,000 after April 1, 1996, He appears on indictment as a result of his record. A confiscation order could be made for the sum of £18,000 as this is the value of Mr A's realisable assets. The court would also make a finding in fact that he benefitted from his crimes to the extent of £19,000 (a "double crime" case where the benefit is linked to two crimes in the preceding six years).

In example C, the benefit remains straightforward but now includes the benefit from his previous conviction as he has committed a further crime and has assets available to pay a confiscation order. However, the position changes depending on what Mr A has done with his ill-gotten gains, as follows.

If, however, Mr A having embezzled £9,000, he puts that money into shares which increase in value by £9,000, then the benefit from the commission of the offence would properly be seen to be £18,000 and any confiscation order would be for that fixed sum. In that situation, there would be benefit to all except the criminal if the judge decided to make a compensation order to the complainer and a confiscation order for the increased benefit remaining of £9,000.

As in drug trafficking cases, the Court assesses the value of the accused's realisable property at the date the order is made, so up-to-date valuations are required.

Drug Trafficking and "All Crime"

1.12   In both drug trafficking and "all crime" cases the Crown's application for a confiscation order is made in solemn cases when moving for sentence and in summary cases following the conviction of the accused (section 1(7)).

The important difference between "all crime" and drug trafficking cases is that as soon as an accused is in a drug trafficking situation, then the Crown is able to use the full powers under the Act and the six-year assumptions can be invoked.

In relation to both drug trafficking and "all crime" cases, a confiscation order is regarded as a sentence and the confiscation proceedings are part of the sentencing process. As with other decisions regarding sentencing, it is at the discretion of the presiding judge whether to make a confiscation order at all, and if an order is made, for how much. The only mandatory aspect of the process is that the judge cannot make a confiscation order for an amount which is more than the accused has been found to have left, no matter how much money went through his hands at an earlier stage. Perhaps that illustrates one of the few flaws in the legislation in that those criminals who spend their "criminal money" as soon as they can on non-tangibles, such as drink, drugs and holidays abroad, can still have the benefit of their ill-gotten gains, at least in the short term.

CHAPTER 2

INVESTIGATIVE POWERS

Confiscation will only be able to operate successfully where the **2.01** Crown has reasonably accurate information about the accused's financial position. This information is required not for the purpose of proving the crime itself, although in some cases there may well be an overlap, but to show the "money trail", describing what the accused has done with the money he has made from either drug trafficking or "all crime" offences.

In order to follow the money trail, inquiries are made, usually on a number of occasions, with financial institutions, banks, building societies, hire purchase companies, car and boat showrooms, solicitors, accountants, benefits agencies and the Inland Revenue. The Crown is able to make these inquiries, having originally been given a new type of investigative power in relation to drug trafficking cases in the Criminal Justice (Scotland) Act 1987. This was extended by PCSA 1995 to cover "all crime" and then consolidated in relation to drug trafficking in CLCSA 1995. These Acts grant power to the Crown to apply to the sheriff for an order to make material available for the purpose of financial inquiries. The rules differ slightly depending on whether the Crown is following the financial trail of a drug trafficking or an "all crime" case, and will be dealt with separately below.

Drug Trafficking Cases

The relevant sections are sections 31 and 32 of CLCSA 1995. **2.02** Section 31 provides for the procurator fiscal to make application to the sheriff for an order to make material available. These orders have become known as production orders or inspection orders. The procurator fiscal applies to the sheriff for such an order in relation to particular material for the purpose of investigation into drug trafficking. Either the order is one which requires the holder of the material to produce the material in a form in which it can be taken away, or the order is one which requires the holder of the material to give access to the material, hence the names "production/ inspection orders". In drug trafficking investigations, the person who appears to be in possession of the material is obliged to produce it either to a constable or a person appointed by the Commissioners of Customs and Excise.

The definition of "drug trafficking" is in section 49(2) of PCSA 1995 and therefore includes trafficking other than in Scotland. In practice, a production order can be used to obtain accurate information where an English police force or an American or Spanish enforcement agency is investigating a case in its own country and in which it is believed that funds have ended up in Scotland.

When is a production order appropriate?

2.03   Once a drug trafficking investigation has commenced, the procurator fiscal may apply to the sheriff for an order. Usually, the investigation into the accused's financial affairs will take place after he has appeared before the court, but it is possible to obtain production orders before his appearance in court and before he is even aware that he is facing criminal charges. There are, however, three conditions in section 31(4) which the Crown must meet before a production order will be granted. There have to be reasonable grounds for suspecting that:

1. a specified person has carried on or has derived financial or other rewards from drug trafficking;

2. the material to which the production order relates is likely to be of substantial value to the investigation and does not include items subject to legal privilege;

3. it is in the public interest, having regard to the benefit likely to accrue to the investigation and to the circumstances under which a person in possession of material holds it, that the material should be produced.

Procedure for obtaining and enforcing a production order

2.04   In order to obtain a production order, the procurator fiscal applies to the sheriff in a written application which is similar to an application for a search warrant (see petition, Appendix 2, Style I). The application should contain details of the material requested, the name and address of the holder of the material, the reason the order is required and the names of the officers in gathering the material. It is presented to the sheriff *ex parte* in chambers and the suspected person, or the holder of the material, has no right to be present to oppose it.

Once the sheriff is satisfied that the application meets the conditions of section 31(4), he may make an order requiring the specified material to be produced within seven days, unless it appears to the sheriff that a longer or shorter period would be appropriate in the particular circumstances of the application.

Once the order is granted, the police constable or officer of Customs and Excise then attends at the premises of the holder of the material with the production order detailing the material to be produced within the seven-day period. Thereafter it is normally left to the holder of the material, be it bank, building society or similar, to ingather the material requested and have it available for the police or customs officer to uplift at the end of the seven-day period. Section 31(7) stipulates that if the material consists of information which is contained in a computer, then it has to be produced in a form in which it can be taken away and is visible and legible. At that stage, the officer uplifting the material should normally request the holder to complete the appropriate certificates in terms of Schedule 8 to the Criminal Procedure (Scotland) Act 1995[1] in relation to business records and copies.

Where the application is to allow access to the material, in terms of section 31(2)(b), as distinct to the requirement for the holder to produce it, the sheriff may make an order for any person who appears to him to be entitled to grant entry to the premises to allow a constable or customs officer entry and access to it within the period specified.

Premises, secrecy and privilege

The premises referred to in section 31 which can be the subject **2.05** of a production order are defined in section 33 and include "any place" and, in particular, a vehicle, a vessel, an aircraft or hovercraft, an offshore installation, and a tent or any moveable structure, which seems to cover most contingencies.

To ensure a complete investigation into drug trafficking, section 31(8) provides that the order shall have effect notwithstanding any obligation as to secrecy or other restriction upon the disclosure of information imposed by statute or otherwise, and may be made in relation to material in the possession of an authorised government department. The effect of that provision ensures that a production order can apply to material held, for example, by the Inland Revenue, an organisation normally bound by restricted disclosure of information rules. Section 31 also clarifies that a production order is now the recognised method of obtaining material in possession of a government department at that stage of the investigation.

[1] (c. 46).

There is also a civil power available to the Lord Advocate under section 35 of the Act whereby he can apply to the Court of Session to obtain material from a government department. However that section only applies where obtaining the material sought would facilitate the exercise of the powers of either the court or an administrator in relation to a restraint order made and not recalled. It is not available, therefore, as an investigative tool at the early stage of the criminal investigation.

Section 31(8)(a) does, however, state that a production order shall not confer any right to production of, or access to, items subject to legal privilege. "Items subject to legal privilege" are defined in section 33 of the Act as:

"(a) communications between a professional legal adviser and his client; or
(b) communications made in connection with or in contemplation of legal proceedings, and, for the purposes of these proceedings, being communications which would in legal proceedings be protected from disclosure by virtue of any rule of law relating to the confidentiality of communications".

In other words, such items are defined according to the existing case law. That does not mean, however, that anything in the hands of a solicitor is automatically protected, and this point is covered below (paragraph 2.10).

It can be seen, then, that a production or inspection order is almost like a polite version of a search warrant, allowing the holder of the material to be notified of what the Crown is looking for, and to be given a certain period of time in which to ingather that information from their own records and present it in the appropriate form to the police or customs officer to inspect or to take away. There are, of course, situations where the Crown does not wish to be so polite and those are dealt with by obtaining a search warrant, in terms of section 32 of the Act.

Search warrants

2.06 Section 32 of the Act narrates the circumstances in which a search warrant is more appropriate than a production or inspection order. It allows the procurator fiscal to apply to the sheriff for a warrant in relation to specified premises, for the purpose of an investigation into drug trafficking. The procedure for obtaining such a warrant is by means of an incidental application, as set out in section 134 of the Criminal Procedure

(Scotland) Act 1995. There are three situations in which a sheriff may grant a warrant authorising a police or customs officer to enter and search premises. These conditions are alternatives and the first relates to the situation where a production or inspection order made under section 31 has not been complied with. There are no other conditions imposed on the granting of such a search warrant and where the holder of the material, be it bank, building society or car showroom, has failed to provide it, then the Crown's remedy is to apply for the warrant on the basis that the section 31 order (the circumstances of which the sheriff has already considered) has not been complied with.

The two other "search warrant" situations under section 32 are similarly straightforward.

First, section 32(2)(b) requires that certain conditions be fulfilled. These include the same conditions required for a section 31 production order. To reiterate, there have to be reasonable grounds for suspecting that:

1. a specified person has carried on or has derived financial or other rewards from drug trafficking;

2. the material to which the production order relates is likely to be of substantial value to the investigation and does not include items subject to legal privilege;

3. it is in the public interest, having regard to the benefit likely to accrue to the investigation and to the circumstances under which a person in possession of material holds it, that the material should be produced.

Additionally, a production order would not be appropriate and a search warrant would be because:

(a) it is not practicable to communicate with any person entitled to produce the material; or

(b) it is not practicable to communicate with any person entitled to grant access either to the material or to the premises in which the material is situated; or

(c) the investigation might be seriously prejudiced unless the constable or customs officer could secure immediate access to the material.

In that situation, a search warrant is more appropriate than a production order because the Crown, although aware of the material it is seeking, is presumably fearful that it may be lost or destroyed if powers of search are not available.

Secondly, in terms of section 32(2)(c), an application for a search warrant contains not only the grounds expected for a section 31 production order, but in addition the material at the time of the application cannot be particularised; and

  (a) it is not practicable to communicate with any person entitled to grant entry to the premises; or

  (b) entry to the premises will not be granted unless a warrant is produced; or

  (c) the investigation might be seriously prejudiced unless immediate entry could be secured by a police or customs officer.

In that situation, a search warrant is more appropriate than a production order because the Crown is unable to particularise the material it is seeking, as well as being fearful that it may be lost or destroyed.

Finally, section 32(5) covers the seizure and retention of material under a section 32 search warrant. It is interesting to note, however, that once an officer is in the premises with the warrant, that subsection permits him to seize and retain *any* material (excluding items subject to legal privilege) which is likely to be of substantial value to the investigation.

"ALL CRIME"

Production orders

2.07 The rules relating to obtaining production orders in respect of all crimes other than drug trafficking offences are contained in section 18 of PCSA 1995. Again, it is for the procurator fiscal to apply by means of an incidental application to the sheriff for an order either to produce the material or to give access to it. The application is for the purpose of an investigation into whether a person has benefited from the commission of an offence to which the Act applies. Hence, a production order can be obtained in relation to any crime apart from drug trafficking (which is specifically excluded by section 8(11)) which falls into the category of a crime which would be subject to confiscation proceedings under the Act, namely a crime on indictment or a crime on a summary complaint, provided that the sentence can exceed the normal summary maximum.

One previous difference in "all crime" cases was that only police officers were entitled to execute production orders and not customs officers. However section 18 was amended by the Crime and Disorder Act 1998,[2] Sched. 8, para. 116 with effect from September 30, 1998, to include customs officers.

The sheriff requires to be satisfied that the conditions in section 18(4) are fulfilled when considering the application and these are similar to the drug trafficking situation. There have to be reasonable grounds for suspecting that:

1. a specified person has benefited from the commission of an offence;

2. the material is likely to be of substantial value to the investigation and does not consist of items subject to legal privilege;

3. it is in the public interest that the material should be produced or that access should be given to it.

The application is similarly made *ex parte* in chambers and, as in drug trafficking cases, if the sheriff makes an order giving access he may, on application by the fiscal, order that the constable or customs officer be given entry to the premises where the material is contained. The allowed period of seven days in which to ingather the information and produce it to the constable or customs officer is the same (section 18(3)). The same requirement, that computer-held materials should be provided in visible and legible form, also applies, as does the stipulation that a production order does not confer any right to items subject to legal privilege. As before, notwithstanding any obligations as to secrecy imposed by statute or otherwise, a production order may be made in relation to material in the possession of an authorised government department. The definitions of "legal privilege" and "premises" in section 18 are the same as in section 33 of CLCSA 1995.

When is a production order appropriate?
As stated above, a drug trafficking production order is for the   **2.08** purpose of an investigation into drug trafficking; an "all crime" production order is for the purpose of an investigation into

---

[2] (c. 37).

whether a person has benefited from the commission of an offence to which the Act applies and to the amount of that benefit. Unfortunately, section 18 is poorly drafted and when the "applicable offences" section, 1(2), is looked at, it states that it applies "to any offence which has been prosecuted". It could be argued, therefore, that a production order should not be granted until such time as the accused has been convicted. Such an interpretation, if accepted by the court, would defeat the purpose of section 18 as it would mean that a production order was not available until criminal proceedings had been concluded, thereby making the application for a production order pointless since the purpose is to obtain material at an early stage in order to commence confiscation proceedings, normally by restraint order. The observation that the Act is poorly drafted is assisted when considering that the same definition in section 1(2) applies to restraint orders under section 28 and section 29. Restraint orders are considered in detail in Chapter 3 but they are intended to be available at a very early stage of the investigation, and under section 29 as early as 28 days before proceedings commence. It would make no sense whatsoever to have such powers if they could not be used until an offence had been prosecuted.

The position must therefore be that the intention of the statute, to provide a system of investigation at an early stage, should prevail and that production orders in "all crime" cases are obtainable as soon as the fiscal has commenced an investigation into whether a person has benefited from the commission of an offence, provided that the sheriff is satisfied of the conditions in section 18(4). To date, there is no reported case on the point, but the definition contained in section 1(2) was considered by the Court of Session in an unreported opinion issued on January 21, 1999 in an appeal by the procurator fiscal at Greenock against William McKechnie. In that case, the Crown was seeking a restraint order over Mr McKechnie's realisable property following his appearance on petition on a single charge of fraud. The sheriff applied section 1(2) narrowly and rejected the Crown's summary application for a restraint order on the ground that the requirement in section 29(2)(a) of PCSA 1995 had not been satisfied in that the accused had not been prosecuted either on indictment or on summary complaint. It was argued by the Crown that the sheriff's interpretation of section 1(2) frustrated the plain intention of Parliament. The court held, in the circumstances of the case, that section 1(2) required to be read in a sense which "rendered the implement of the evident intention of Parliament practicable". In other words, the offence would, if prosecuted on a summary complaint, be punishable as set out in section 1(2) but without any requirement that the offence in question has actually been prosecuted. It went on to observe that the language of section 1(2), with the reference to "any offence which has been prosecuted", was an example of inept parliamentary draftsmanship!

A production order for "all crime" only extends furth of Scotland as a result of the definition in section 10(b) which states that the production and inspection order system is available for offences which, though not committed in Scotland, would have come under Part I of PCSA 1995 had they been committed in Scotland.

Search warrants

Section 19 of PCSA 1995 provides for the granting of search warrants in relation to "all crime" cases in the same way as for drug trafficking cases and under the same conditions (see above on section 32 of CLCSA 1995). **2.09**

Legal privilege

The one exception which runs through sections 31 and 32 of CLCSA 1995 and sections 18 and 19 of PCSA 1995 is that the Crown is not entitled to obtain material either by production or access which is subject to legal privilege. The definition of "legal privilege" in section 33 of CLCSA 1995 in effect allows matters to stand on the current law on legal privilege and the concept has not been revisited recently in the courts. However the existing law does not cover communications which are intended for the purpose of furthering a criminal act. The only case in point is *R. v. Central Criminal Court, ex parte Francis & Francis*.[3] Although an English decision, it sets out the views of the House of Lords and is expected to be followed in Scotland. The position would appear to be that if the production order in seeking information which shows the financial trail of drug trafficking or "all crime" proceeds, *e.g.* conveyancing files, ledger cards or other records of property ownership or payment methods, then legal privilege cannot be claimed. **2.10**

[3] [1989] A.C. 346.

INVESTIGATIVE TOOL?

2.11 The system of production and inspection orders can be very useful to the Crown, particularly at the start of an investigation in order to establish the financial position of the accused. The ingathering of information in this way is between the Crown and the financial institution involved and the subject of the inquiry should have no knowledge of it. The reason for this is easily understood, because should such inquiry come to light before the Crown has had an opportunity to determine if action requires to be taken, then the suspect or accused could merely move funds for the purpose of concealment.

Drug trafficking production orders and "all crime" production orders, obtainable before a suspect has been arrested, can show the financial trail and are a better indicator of where the proceeds of crime are coming from and going to than other traditional types of surveillance. Proper use of the production and inspection order system therefore permits the Crown to have a full financial picture of a suspect and where his finances are lodged and then to be in a position to restrain them at the time of arrest. (See Chapter 3 on restraint orders.)

CHAPTER 3

RESTRAINT ORDERS

Before looking at the procedure required to allow the court to **3.01** make a confiscation order it is necessary first of all to look at the powers available to the Crown for the purpose of securing the assets which would be covered by a confiscation order until such time as the court is in a position to make such an order. Frequently the securing of assets is the first priority, to ensure that there are funds left at a later stage in order to allow the court to exercise its discretion in relation to the making of a confiscation order. The method by which the Crown can secure assets at that early stage, therefore, is by a restraint order. The procedure for obtaining a restraint order is contained in sections 28 and 29 of PCSA 1995. A restraint order and any subsequent variation is a matter of civil law and can be obtained in both the Court of Session and the sheriff court in order to prevent the accused from dealing with his assets (although the sheriff court cannot grant warrant for inhibition).

A restraint order is simply a form of interdict which prevents any person dealing with assets suspected to be derived from either drug trafficking or "all crime" as defined by PCSA 1995. There is no doubt that the power to freeze assets in this way is draconian but the purpose is to prevent them being dissipated before the matter can be fully aired in court. The restraint order powers are viewed as draconian for a number of reasons, namely:

1. a restraint order can be made against someone who is not even an accused or even suspected of any crime, provided that he is the holder of drug trafficking proceeds or "all crime" benefits (such a person is known as an "implicative donee" in relation to drug trafficking and a "donee" in relation to "all crime"—see Chapter 4);

2. a restraint order can apply to all the assets of an accused person or an implicative donee or donee until the court can decide the exact position at a confiscation hearing; and

3. a restraint order can be made even before anyone has appeared in court or indeed has been charged with any crime.

The term "restraint order" is new to the law of Scotland and was directly imported in relation to drug trafficking cases under the Criminal Justice (Scotland) Act 1987 from English confiscation legislation. While it is a form of interdict it differs from the traditional interdict in that it is granted *ex parte* in chambers and the subject of the restraint order, whether it be an accused or merely the holder of funds, has no right to participate at that stage. The purpose of this is to ensure that the accused or any of his associates does not have an opportunity to dispose of assets as soon as he knows that he is the subject of investigation into his financial affairs.

ASSETS COVERED BY A RESTRAINT ORDER

3.02   Before considering exactly when a restraint order may be granted it is convenient at this point to look at another concept introduced by PCSA 1995 and mentioned earlier, that of "realisable property". A restraint order is intended to apply to the realisable property of a person who is either already an accused or within a fairly short period to become one.

"Realisable property" is defined in section 4 of PCSA 1995 as being:

"(a)   The whole estate wherever situated of a person—

(i)   against whom proceedings have been instituted for an offence to which this Part of this Act applies; or

(ii)   in respect of whom a restraint order has been made by virtue of section 29(3) of this Act;

(b)   the whole estate wherever situated of a person to whom any person whose whole estate is realisable by virtue of paragraph (a) above has (directly or indirectly and whether in one transaction or a series of transactions) made a gift caught by this Part of this Act or, as the case may be, an implicative gift;

(c)   any other property in the possession or under the control of a person mentioned in paragraph (a) or (b) above; and

(d)   any income or estate vesting in a person mentioned in paragraph (a) or (b) above."

The section goes on to say that property is not realisable if it is held in trust or if there is a suspended forfeiture order in force or if the property is subject to a restraint order in respect of other proceedings. The section then goes on to deal with the amount that might be realised at the time a confiscation order is made and how the value of realisable property is calculated taking into account any securities over the property (mortgages, etc.—this is dealt with in Chapter 5).

From the above definition the first thing that is clear is that the property does not have to be situated in Scotland and therefore the fact that the accused has decided to hold property in other countries is not a bar to a restraint order being obtained. There is a separate system for enforcement of an order covering foreign assets, and that is dealt with in Chapter 9. The second thing to note is that realisable property is the whole estate of a person, first, against whom proceedings have been instituted or, secondly, in respect of whom a section 29(3) restraint order has been made. A section 29(3) restraint order can be made up to 28 days *before* proceedings have been instituted. Section 49(6) of the Act defines "institution of proceedings" and, put simply, it is the earliest of:

1. arrest without warrant;
2. the accused being charged with the offence without being arrested;
3. warrant to arrest being granted;
4. warrant to cite being granted;
5. in summary cases, on the first calling of the case; or
6. when the petition is intimated to the accused; or
7. an indictment is served; or
8. a complaint is served.

It should be noted, therefore, that the institution of proceedings could take place at a very early stage and indeed could be well before the case itself is reported to the procurator fiscal.

Thirdly, the restraint order covers the whole estate of a person who has received either an implicative gift under section 6 of the Act (drug trafficking offence) or a gift under section 5 of the Act ("all crime" offence). That restraint order will apply to the whole estate of a third party to whom the accused has transferred assets, whether directly or indirectly.

There is no doubt that the definition of "realisable property" is very wide and indeed that was the intention of the Scottish

Law Commission when it made recommendations as to the approach to be adopted. The important thing to bear in mind is that when a restraint order is being obtained and the definition of "realisable property" applied, the exact amount of drug trafficking proceeds or "all crime" benefit will probably not be known. It is necessary therefore that the maximum amount of property available is frozen at that stage in order to ensure that when the court ultimately makes a decision the financial position remains as it was at the point the investigation commenced. In simple terms, the reason that the whole estate of an implicative donee or donee is included is to ensure that the accused cannot in this country transfer assets to such a person in order to prevent those assets becoming subject to either a restraint order or at a later stage a confiscation order.

When can a Restraint Order be Obtained?

Proceedings live

3.03 Section 28 of PCSA 1995 states that the court may, on the application of the prosecutor, make an order in the following circumstances either in terms of section 29(2) or (3) of the Act, interdicting either (a) any person from dealing with his own realisable property; or (b) any person, including one appearing to the court to have received an implicative gift or gift, from dealing with their own, or the other's, realisable property. "Realisable property" includes property no matter when it was acquired and also no matter whether it is described in the order or not. That may well seem rather a strange thing to do but it should be borne in mind that the purpose of the legislation is to deal with assets of the accused even where those assets are hidden. In practice, therefore, a restraint order will refer to and indeed specify the realisable property of which the Crown is aware, but will also include a general reference to realisable property, unspecified in detail. That means that the subject of the restraining order, the accused, would still be subject to sanctions imposed by the court should he dispose of any of that property (and indeed, of course, should the Crown find out about it). It also means that should any of that unspecified property come to light before the confiscation order is made then the restraint order can be intimated to the holder at that time, without the necessity of obtaining either another restraint order or a variation.

A restraint order is made on an *ex parte* application heard in chambers and is thereafter intimated to each person affected by it. In practice, this means it will be intimated to the accused, to any implicative donees or donees who are the subjects of the restraint order and to any other holders of funds, for example banks, building societies, etc., and also to any other persons who have an interest in the property whether as a holder of a security or having granted another type of loan; again, usually, these will be financial institutions.

As stated above, a restraint order in terms of section 28 can be made in two situations, by meeting the conditions in either section 29(2) or section 29(3). Section 29(2) is used when proceedings are "live".

The circumstances covered by section 29(2) and the first grounds for making a restraint order, are that proceedings have been instituted against an accused in Scotland and have not been concluded and, either a confiscation order has been made or it appears to the court that, in the event of conviction, there are reasonable grounds for thinking that a confiscation order may be made. Section 29(2) therefore covers the most usual situation, *i.e.* where an accused has been arrested and either is about to appear before the court (usually on petition) or indeed has already appeared on petition, has been committed for further examination and is in custody for the next eight days.

In practice, when proceedings are instituted against an accused, the Crown, on the basis of financial information then available to it about the accused's realisable property, details of any implicative gifts or gifts and the provisional extent of drug trafficking proceeds or "all crime" benefit, will decide whether or not to apply to the court for a restraint order.

As indicated earlier, restraint order proceedings are civil and the Crown will apply for a restraint order in the Court of Session if the criminal trial is likely to take place in the High Court or in the sheriff court if the criminal trial is likely to take place in the sheriff court (either as a sheriff and jury trial or as a summary trial).

Proceedings contemplated

The second type of situation where a restraint order is appropri- **3.04** ate is described in section 29(3). In that section the circumstances are that the court is satisfied that it is proposed to institute proceedings within 28 days and that in the event of conviction there are reasonable grounds for thinking that a confiscation order may be made; or the Crown has made or proposes within 28 days to make an application under section 11 or section 13 of the Act and there are reasonable grounds for thinking that the application may be granted. Section 11 is an application by the Crown to make a new confiscation order in the situation where there has been an increase in drug trafficking proceeds or "all crime" benefit or in the amount of property that might be realised; in other words, it now appears that one or other of the important amounts, whether proceeds or benefit or realisable property, was truly incorrect at the time the confiscation order was made (usually because new information is available). Frequently, this can be as simple as assets not reaching their expected value on realisation (commonly motor cars). Section 13 covers the situation where proceeds of drug trafficking or "all crime" are discovered at a later date and the Crown applies to the court to have a confiscation order made in that situation, where no confiscation order was made in the first place.

THE EFFECT OF A RESTRAINT ORDER

3.05   Once a restraint order has been made in terms of sections 28 and 29 of the Act it is an interdict against its subject(s), either the accused or a potential accused and his implicative donee or donees, *i.e.* those people who appear to have received gifts as defined by the Act, from dealing with their own realisable property. Once the restraint order has been granted it basically ensures that the accused's financial position is "freeze framed". It is an interdict which prevents the persons named in the order from dealing with the realisable property and implicative gifts or gifts until such time as the order is recalled, because either a confiscation order has been made and paid or the accused has been acquitted.

A simple example would be Mr A who appeared on petition in respect of section 4(3)(b) charges under the Misuse of Drugs Act 1971. If Mr A had £10,000 in the building society, a house with equity of £50,000, a girlfriend, Ms B, with no visible means of support but a flat and a sports car paid for by Mr A, valued in total at £50,000, and £5,000 in her own name in her own bank account, then a restraint order application by the Crown (either by petition to the Court of Session if the case is likely to be by High Court trial or by summary application to the sheriff court if the case is likely to be a sheriff and jury or summary trial) is likely to cover both the accused and his girlfriend and to refer to all their realisable property and implicative gifts and specifying in detail:

1. the £10,000 in the building society;

2. the house in Mr A's name;

3. the flat in Ms B's name;

4. the sports car in Ms B's name; and

5. the £5,000 in Ms B's bank account.

The restraint order would also be intimated to the creditor in any standard security over either the house or the flat. These assets then remain frozen until proceedings are concluded. In a bail case, to allow time for the criminal trial to take place, and in the confiscation proceedings thereafter for time for payment, that could be as long as 18 months to two years.

Dealing with realisable property, which is what the restraint order is intended to prevent, in terms of section 28(4) of the Act, includes making a payment to reduce debt, removing property from the jurisdiction of the court and transferring or disposing of property. As a restraint order is intimated in order to ensure that, practically, it has full effect, it will be intimated to the persons named in the order as being either subject to the order or holders of property.

Once a restraint order has been granted the intention is that the property remains in the same place and the accused can enjoy it to the extent of living in a house or driving a car but he cannot dissipate it by spending it. It is not the intention of the Act that property is all ingathered by the Crown or the court at that stage. There will, of course, be certain items of property which will be taken by the police at the time of arrest, etc., but these are items which will be necessary for evidence at the criminal trial. In general property remains where it is, subject to section 28(5) of the Act. That section gives power to a constable or Customs and Excise officer, for the purpose of preventing any property from being removed in drug trafficking cases from Great Britain and in "all crime" cases from the jurisdiction of the court, to seize that property. This type of situation would arise where there were indications that the accused or any of his associates intended to remove the property for the purposes of avoiding the restraint order and subsequent confiscation proceedings. Thereafter any property seized is to be dealt with in accordance with the directions of the court in terms of section 28(6).

As indicated above, a restraint order is an interdict and therefore if breached the remedy available is, as in any other interdict, proceedings for contempt of court. This is important to remember when one considers that the restraint order covers all the realisable property of an accused and is a complete prohibition, whether that property is specified in detail or not. In other words, once a restraint order is granted it covers the totality of the accused's assets, even those concealed and about which the Crown has no information at this stage. Practically, there is very little the Crown can do until it learns about these hidden assets but it does mean that the accused is subject to a general interdict and therefore subsequent sanction should he dispose of any of the hidden assets. In practice it is likely that the assets known about will be mentioned in the restraint order together with a general interdict preventing the accused from dealing with all his realisable property. In addition, as provided for in sections 32 and 33 of the Act, an interlocutor granting the restraint order will include, if requested by the Crown, a warrant for inhibition and arrestment, in effect a "belt and braces" exercise.

The court rules governing the obtaining of restraint orders and subsequent intimation are contained in the Act of Sederunt (Summary Applications, Statutory Applications and Appeals etc.) Rules 1999[1] in relation to sheriff court restraint orders, and in the Court of Session Rules 1994 (as amended by the Act of Sederunt (Rules of the Court of Session Amendment No. 3) (External Orders Affecting Proceeds of Crime) 1999[2]), in particular rule 76, in relation to Court of Session restraint orders. These rules lay down the procedure, *i.e.* by petition to the Court of Session and by summary application in the sheriff court, and also the requirements relating to intimation, which is by service of a certified copy interlocutor in the Court of Session and service of a copy interlocutor in the sheriff court.

RESTRAINT ORDER EXCEPTIONS

3.06   In terms of section 28 a restraint order may contain conditions and exceptions to which the interdict shall be subject and in particular section 28(2) details two such exceptions and states that the restraint order

[1] (S.I. 1999 No. 929).
[2] (S.I. 1999 No. 1220).

"(a) may provide for the release to the person named in
the order of such reasonable living expenses as the
court thinks fit; and

(b) shall provide for the release of property in so far as it
is required to meet reasonable legal expenses payable
or likely to be payable in relation to proceedings—

(i) as regards the offence by virtue of which the
restraint order has been made; or

(ii) as regards a confiscation order made on conviction of the offence."

It can be seen that one of these exceptions detailed is discretionary and the other one appears to be mandatory. The position in
England is that exceptions tend to be inserted when the restraint
order is obtained. In Scotland the practice is different and the
restraint order will not normally contain any exceptions. Certainly living expenses and whether or not funds are required for
legal expenses (depending on the legal aid position) are matters
within the knowledge of the defence rather than the Crown and
the defence therefore should be in a position to apply for a
variation of the restraint order to take these matters into
account if appropriate. In relation to living expenses the English
practice is to have a standard rate. That practice has not been
adopted here. Instead if the accused's position is that he
requires money for living expenses (if he is out on bail or has
financial commitments to meet) then a variation of the restraint
order should be sought for that amount. However as expenditure is the basis on which the Crown calculates drug trafficking
proceeds then the greater the living expenses which the accused
states, the higher will be the expenditure which the Crown can
then use at a later stage in the financial analysis (see Chapter 5).

VARIATION OF A RESTRAINT ORDER

Section 31 of the Act contains provisions for variation and recall **3.07**
of a restraint order. Recall of a restraint order occurs in those
situations where its purpose is over. Recall is discretionary except
in those circumstances where proceedings are finished, either
because the accused has been convicted and the confiscation
order paid, or at an earlier stage if the accused has been
acquitted. The right of recall is open to the Crown at any time or
to any other person having an interest. Obviously the accused will
always have an interest but it is highly unlikely that while

proceedings are ongoing and a financial investigation is being carried out into the accused's affairs in order to determine exactly the amount of drug trafficking proceeds or "all crime" benefit, the court would recall a restraint order, thereby allowing him, if he so wished, to dispose of his assets. What is probably more likely is that either the Crown or the accused, or any other holder of funds or person having an interest, may apply for a variation. If the application to vary is by an implicative donee or donee then the court requires to be satisfied on the balance of probabilities of three things before it will recall the restraint order in relation to that person. The three requirements are that:

1. the implicative donee or donee received the gift not knowing, not suspecting and indeed not having reasonable grounds to suspect, that the implicative gift or gift was linked to either drug trafficking or "all crime";

2. the implicative donee or donee was not associated with the giver in the commission of the offence (in other words, the civil court must be satisfied on the balance of probabilities that he was not involved in the crime); and

3. the implicative donee or donee would suffer hardship if the order were not recalled.

Bearing in mind that all three criteria require to be satisfied, this places the implicative donee or donee in a very difficult position and, especially in relation to the third requirement, it may well be very difficult to show such hardship when the restraint order is merely a temporary measure to "freeze frame" the financial picture until a later stage when the court can consider it fully.

In practice, therefore, applications for variation of a restraint order tend to be made after consultation with the Crown in order to determine what funds can be released and for what purpose between the making of the restraint order and either the conclusion of the trial or the confiscation hearing. Such variations could include release of funds for living expenses or to meet certain payments which it is in the interests of everyone to continue, for example mortgage payments, life insurance payments and variations to allow property or motor cars to be sold for the purposes of realising assets at the best market value available. Thereafter the proceeds would still be subject to the restraint order, usually held in a bank account intimated to the Crown.

Restraint Orders and Administrators

The intention of a restraint order, namely to prevent the **3.08**
accused from dealing with his realisable property together with
any implicative gifts or gifts, has, as already indicated, the basic
purpose of ensuring that all his assets are still available at the
point the court requires to make a decision about them at a
confiscation hearing. In most circumstances, therefore, it will be
sufficient to restrain funds in bank accounts and restrain houses,
cars, etc. The position changes somewhat when the property of
the accused is such that in order to maintain the status quo the
property requires to be managed in the meantime. This type of
situation would cover any businesses which the accused is
operating or indeed any business being operated by an implicative donee or donee.

Section 34 of the Act gives effect to Schedule 1 to the Act
which deals with administrators. Administrators can be
appointed in two situations: either to ingather and realise
property for enforcement of a confiscation order or to manage
property. (This is covered in Chapter 8.) This situation arises
where property has been affected by a restraint order and an
administrator is required to manage or otherwise deal with the
property. Paragraph 1 of Schedule 1 provides that, on the
application of the Crown, the court may appoint a person to
manage or otherwise deal with property affected by a restraint
order in accordance with the court's directions. The administrator will be supervised by the Accountant of Court in the
performance of the functions conferred under the Act, but his
expenses in the first instance, unless a confiscation is made and
there are sums available, will be paid by the Lord Advocate.
There have not yet been any Crown applications to appoint an
administrator for such property management purposes prior to
the making of a confiscation order.

Conclusion

Restraint orders are a formidable tool in the hands of the **3.09**
Crown at a very early stage in proceedings because they can be
used to prevent the accused and his associates from having
access to the putative proceeds of crime until such time as the
court has decided (1) the accused's guilt or otherwise of the
crime and (2) whether or not any of the money (or indeed all of
it) is to be subject to a confiscation order. It should be borne in

mind, therefore, that a restraint order can be enforced normally before the defence has been able to undertake any investigative work on the crime itself, never mind in relation to the accused's financial position. Notwithstanding that, however, the best person to know his own financial position is, of course, the accused. Criminal practitioners, therefore, should be aware of the need to act quickly, as soon as a restraint order has been obtained by the Crown, in order to ensure that their client's position is indeed truly preserved and that he still has access to funds for day-to-day living or, if he is in custody, at the very least his family does. That requires making proper use of the statutory provisions in relation to variation of restraint orders until such time as the accused is convicted of the relevant crime and it is clear that the court will move on to confiscation proceedings.

Chapter 4

IMPLICATIVE GIFTS AND THE CONFISCATION ASSUMPTIONS

Gifts and Implicative Gifts

The Criminal Justice (Scotland) Act 1987[1] introduced the **4.01** concept of an implicative gift. The term "implicative gift" was lifted from the English confiscation legislation and its purpose was to strike at the transfer of assets by the accused to other parties and to ensure that the accused did not avoid either restraint or confiscation procedures merely by transferring the proceeds of his drug trafficking activities in this way. The principle of implicative gifts was retained and re-enacted in PCSA 1995 in relation to drug trafficking offences and extended to "all crime" offences but termed "gifts" in "all crime".

Implicative gifts—Drug trafficking cases

Section 6 of PCSA 1995 relates to drug trafficking offences only **4.02** and lays down the rules surrounding implicative gifts. The section states that an implicative gift, whether made before or after the commencement of the Act, is a gift if

> "(a) made not more than six years before the date on which, in respect of a person suspected of, or charged with, a drug trafficking offence, the proceedings were commenced or a restraint order was made (whichever first occurs); or
>
> (b) made at any time if the gift was of property—
>
> > (i) received by the giver in connection with drug trafficking carried on by him or another, or
> >
> > (ii) which, in whole or in part, directly or indirectly represented in the giver's hands property received by him in that connection".

There are two situations covered here, the first relating to any transfer of property in the *six-year period* prior to commencement of proceedings and without the necessity of showing that that transfer was of drug trafficking property and the second

[1] s. 6.

situation covering the transfer of property made *at any time* if it was received by the giver in connection with drug trafficking (here the Crown would require to prove the drug trafficking aspect). Clearly, as the transfer of property of a drug trafficker is by its nature bound to be a secretive operation, it is unlikely that there will be clear evidence in most cases that the transfer of property was in connection with drug trafficking and therefore the most used part of this section is that in relation to the six-year period prior to commencement of proceedings.

It is helpful at this stage to consider the common types of transaction covered by section 6—implicative gifts. The most common assets covered will be those assets in the name of a wife or girlfriend, non-income earning and living off the accused, or properties paid for by the accused but put in the name of either another family member or an associate, or other assets such as cars, boats and businesses, in truth belonging to the accused but put in the names of others. In the case of *H.M. Advocate v. Donnelly*[2] Lord Bonomy held that the accused had made a number of implicative gifts in the following situations:

1. A house in the name of the accused's brother was held to be an implicative gift. In reaching that conclusion, Lord Bonomy relied on a number of matters:

    (a) the house title was in the brother's name but there were discrepancies over the amount paid to the accused as the purchase price (the house having originally been in the accused's name);

    (b) the purchase price was settled much later than the date of entry and no interest was paid;

    (c) the accused paid his brother's legal fees;

    (d) the accused handled the rental payments in respect of tenants living in the house and the accused's name appeared on council records relating to the tenants' housing benefits;

    (e) the accused's brother had a severe alcohol problem and had disappeared and the accused had paid the mortgage payments.

    Lord Bonomy's conclusion was that the transaction with the brother "was a sham".

---

[2] High Court, June 13, 1997, unreported; *Donnelly v. H.M. Advocate,* 1999 S.C.C.R. 508.

2. Two houses in the name of the accused's mother were also held to be implicative gifts and in this case Lord Bonomy relied on:

   (a) evidence that the purchase price was paid by a cheque drawn on the accused's building society account;

   (b) the fact that the accused was responsible for instructing and paying for renovation work to the houses;

   (c) the fact that the accused's mother had no satisfactory explanation of where she could have got the money to pay the purchase price; and

   (d) she had absolutely no idea of the sum realised when the houses were sold.

3. Lord Bonomy also held that an "office" property in the name of the accused's wife was an implicative gift from the accused. A claim by the accused's business associate that the property truly belonged to him and was only in the name of the accused's wife to conceal ownership for his purposes and not the accused's was rejected and Lord Bonomy stated: "There is no doubt in my mind that the only source of funds available for such a purpose was the accused."

4. A bank account in the name of the accused's wife was again held to be an implicative gift, rejecting the alternative position that at least part of the funds belonged to the wife's father and had been given to her by him in order to prevent him gambling.

From the above it is clear that in practice the court will regard assets as implicative gifts once it is established that the accused is at the root of the transactions and, being the only person who had available financial resources to fund such transactions, has been shown by a variety of methods to retain control over the assets despite the formal position on ownership. This clearly follows the principle of the legislation which was to prevent the accused from avoiding confiscation action by putting his assets in the names of others and using others as a front for his own financial activities.

REMOVAL OF AN IMPLICATIVE GIFT

4.03   There is a procedure in section 6(3) of PCSA 1995 whereby, if the court is satisfied of certain matters, it can, on the application of a person in receipt of an implicative gift, make an order declaring that it is not an implicative gift and removing it from the realisable property assessment. That application can be made either before or after a confiscation order has been made. It is an application which can be made either during a confiscation hearing by the recipient of an implicative gift who is represented (as part of the submissions) or by separate application to the sheriff court or to the High Court at any time.

A section 6(3) application is quite separate from one for variation of a restraint order in terms of section 31(2) and, notwithstanding that it relates to assets, it is made to the High Court (*i.e.* it is treated as a step in criminal proceedings). If the application is granted, it means that the property ceases to be realisable property for the purposes of Part I of the Act. To complete its removal from all proceedings, however, a section 31(2) variation would still be required to follow, on the basis that the restraint order proceedings are dealt with in Part III of the Act, although one would surely expect that following a successful section 6(3) application the Crown would seek to amend any restraint order in force.

Before a section 6(3) application can be successful there are certain fairly onerous conditions to discharge. The court must be satisfied in terms:

> "(a) that the person received the gift not knowing, not suspecting and not having reasonable grounds to suspect that the giver was in any way concerned in drug trafficking; and
>
> (b) that he is not, and has never been, associated with the giver in drug trafficking; and
>
> (c) that he would suffer hardship if the application were not granted."

It can be seen that all three conditions require to be satisfied and in particular it is difficult to see when the recipient of a gift would suffer hardship except perhaps where the implicative gift was the family home. There is nothing in this section indicating the standard of proof but the standard specifically mentioned in section 5 (which covers gifts in "all crime" cases) and in section 31(2) is the balance of probabilities and it is submitted that that would be the standard required by the applicant in section 6.

Section 6 then provides for an appeal to the High Court by either the applicant or the Crown, using the same procedure as an appeal against sentence.

It is worthy of comment that section 6 and section 31 deletions and variations of implicative gifts have to be considered together. The position could well be that although a restraint order had initially been made in the civil court, either the Court of Session or the sheriff court, the recipient of an implicative gift may decide that the best course of action is to apply under section 6(3) to delete the applicable gift from consideration in the criminal proceedings. That would then mean that the restraint order would require to be varied in the civil court to ensure that the property was completely excluded from both Parts I and III of the Act. It is not sufficient to have the order made in the criminal court alone and then rely on the definition of "realisable property" used for any restraint order made as now excluding a certain implicative gift when there is no procedure under the criminal rules to intimate that decision to the holder of any interest over the property. For example, if a section 6(3) application was successful in respect of a bank account which was subject to a restraint order the applicant would still require to seek to vary the restraint order under section 31(2) because the criminal court only has power to vary any order in criminal proceedings and none to intimate that order to the holder (*i.e.* not merely the holder of the account but the bank operating the account). Until a variation of the restraint order in terms of section 31(2) had been made the bank could continue to prevent the accused from dealing with funds in his bank account until such time as the original restraint order (intimated to the bank) was varied.

Valuation of Implicative Gifts

4.04 Section 6(2) of PCSA 1995 provides that the value of an implicative gift shall be assessed in accordance with section 7 of the Act. Section 7 deals with the valuation of implicative gifts in a variety of circumstances and in part refers to taking into account "subsequent changes in the value of money". However, it gives absolutely no indication as to how this might be done. The Scottish Law Commission Report dealing with this matter suggested indirectly that the Retail Price Index monthly tables could be used. Section 7 is particularly complicated. It rarely comes into effect as normally the implicative gift is still available to be valued at the market value (whether it be a house which has increased in value or a car which has depreciated) that the section is not worth any further explanation. Indeed while it may well be expected that the Crown will apply indexing to the valuation of an implicative gift there has not, as yet, been any judicial decision on the matter.

"ALL CRIME" GIFTS—SECTION 5

4.05   Section 5 of the 1995 Act is the equivalent section to section 6 but using the term "gift" rather than "implicative gift". The intention of the legislation was that gifts and implicative gifts are treated in the same fashion under the Act but the wording is slightly different. The first point to remember is that the rules are different for "single crime" and "double crime" cases and, for example, the six-year period does not apply in "single crime" cases. The rules in relation to section 5 are as follows:

A gift is caught by section 5 if:

"(a) it was made by the accused—

(i) in contemplation of, or after, the commission of the offence;

or if more than one,

(ii) in contemplation of any of the offences or after the commission of the earlier or earliest of the offences, to which the proceedings mentioned in section 4(1)(a)(i) of this Act for the time being relate, not being drug trafficking offences; or

(b) where subsection (4) of section 2 of this Act applies, it was made by the accused within the relevant period within the meaning of subsection (6) of that section."

In other words, there are two situations in relation to "all crime": either where the accused is facing a "single crime" offence and the gift was made in contemplation of, or after, the commission of the offence or, where he is facing a "double crime" offence, the gift was made within the six-year period preceding the commencement of proceedings.

Apart from that, the section is in similar terms to section 6 in that it links valuation back to section 7 of the Act. There is also a provision in section 5(3) intended to mirror section 6(3) for the removal of a gift. The comments earlier in relation to removal of implicative gifts and their valuation apply generally to gifts also. The wording differs in the two sections, however, in that the application under section 5 can be made at any time before the realisation of the gift or the property which represents benefit (there is no reference to the making of the confiscation order) and the standard of proof is clearly stated on this occasion as being on the balance of probabilities as stated in section 31. Similarly to section 6, however, the application is made to the sheriff court or the High Court and the appeal follows the same procedure as an appeal against sentence. It is difficult to see why the wording in the two sections should differ and there does not seem to be any different practical effect. One simple reason may well be that section 5 was in effect new drafting for PCSA 1995 and section 6 a re-enactment of the 1987 Act. Certainly Parliament's intention in both cases was to apply the same principle, *i.e.* to prevent the transfer of property in order to avoid the consequences of the confiscation legislation succeeding.

THE CONFISCATION ASSUMPTIONS

One of the most important matters to take into account in confiscation proceedings is that under the legislation certain assumptions apply in favour of the Crown. The proper use of these assumptions by the Crown goes to the core of the method of financial analysis used, as described in detail in Chapter 5. The assumptions under PCSA 1995 are relevant in three different situations as follows: **4.06**

Drug trafficking

Section 3(2) of PCSA 1995 contains the assumptions which operate in assessing the proceeds of drug trafficking. It is stated there that under the Act the court may, in making an assessment in relation to drug trafficking proceedings, make the undernoted assumptions except in so far as any of them may be shown to be incorrect in that accused's case. The assumptions are: **4.07**

"(a) that any property appearing to the court—

    (i) to have been held by him at any time since his conviction; or, as the case may be,

    (ii) to have been transferred to him at any time since a date six years before his being indicted, or being served with the complaint, was received by him, at the earliest time at which he appears to the court to have held it, as a payment or reward in connection with drug trafficking carried on by him;

(b) that any expenditure of his since the date mentioned in paragraph (a)(ii) above was met out of payments received by him in connection with drug trafficking carried on by him; and

(c) that, for the purpose of valuing any property received or assumed to have been received by him at any time as such a reward, he received the property free of any other interests in it".

The section goes on to state that these assumptions do not apply if the only offence is one under section 14 of the Criminal Justice (International Co-operation) Act 1990 or section 37 or 38 of the Criminal Law (Consolidation) (Scotland) Act 1995 (money laundering offences). Further, in relation to the assessment, there should be left out of account any proceeds of drug trafficking that have already been taken into account in a previous confiscation order made in Scotland under this Act or elsewhere in the U.K.

It should also be noted that the assumptions under section 3 are without prejudice to section 9 of PCSA 1995. Section 9 of the Act deals with the prosecutor's statement and is referred to in detail in Chapter 6. The point to note at this stage is that section 9 and section 3 are intended to operate hand-in-hand and are not alternatives.

"All crime"—"single" offences

4.08   Section 2 of PCSA 1995 deals with the assumptions in "all crime" cases as they are used to calculate benefits from the crime.

This is the simple situation mentioned in previous chapters where the application for a confiscation order is in respect of a single offence and the accused has no relevant previous convictions. In this case the prosecutor will use the assumptions in terms of section 2(2) of PCSA 1995 the assumptions relate to the date of the offence only. Put simply, in determining whether an accused has benefited from the commission of an offence and, if he has, the relevant amount derived therefrom, the court can assume:

"(a) that any property or other economic advantage which has been obtained by him since the relevant date has been obtained in connection with the commission of the offence; and

(b) that any expenditure by him since the relevant date was met out of property or other economic advantage obtained in connection with the commission of the offence."

The "relevant date" is the date of the offence.

The section also states that the court can make the assumptions unless the accused proves either of them to be incorrect on the balance of probabilities. It should be noted that this reference to the standard of proof is not contained in section 3 ("Assessing drug trafficking proceeds") although, as mentioned above, it is the standard expected to be used. Although the onus of the burden of proof to the criminal standard remains on the Crown. At a confiscation hearing the practical position is that there is a practical transfer of the burden to the accused that can be discharged on a balance of probabilities rather than beyond reasonable doubt. This arises provided the Crown makes proper use of the prosecutor's statement and the confiscation assumptions.

"All crime"—"double" offences

As indicated above, section 2 of PCSA 1995 deals separately **4.09** with "single crime" and "double crime" (the latter covering those situations where the Crown makes a confiscation order application either in respect of two or more offences or, during the relevant period (*i.e.* the previous six years from the date of institution of proceedings), the accused has been convicted of at least one other offence to which the Act applies). In these two situations only there are assumptions which the court may make except in so far as the accused proves either of the assumptions to be incorrect on the balance of probabilities. In terms of section 2(5) these assumptions are:

"(a) that any property or economic advantage which has been obtained by the accused during the relevant period has been obtained in connection with the commission of an offence to which this Part of this Act applies; and

(b) that any expenditure by him during the relevant period was met out of property or other economic advantage obtained in connection with the commission of such an offence."

The relevant period is the six years prior to the date on which proceedings were instituted against the accused. As a reminder, the institution of proceedings can be as early as the accused being arrested with a warrant, or his being charged.

The assumptions in relation to "double crime" are variations of the assumptions in drug trafficking cases but they require to be linked to the crimes rather than an overall analysis of the accused's financial position in the six year period. This is as a result of the decision in *Adamson v. H.M. Advocate*.[3] Prior to *Adamson v. H.M. Advocate*[4] it was thought that the assumptions in relation to "double crime" cases were variations of the assumptions in drug trafficking cases. That view was dependent on the meaning of "benefit" in section 1(6) being read with sections 2(4) and 2(5). In *Adamson* the Appeal Court rejected this wide approach when there was no clear statement of Parliament's intention to introduce "what would be fairly draconian legislation" and held that the only activities which were relevant for the purposes of a confiscation order were offences which had been prosecuted. The current position, therefore, is that the assumptions available for "double crime" cases in section 2(5) must be read as if the words "which has been prosecuted" were added after the word "offence" at the end of both paragraphs (a) and (b). This does mean that in "all crime" cases even "double crime" ones the benefit must be linked to the offences. The decision in *Adamson* is not particularly helpful in indicating how the six year period for "double crime" cases is meant to be applied, if not in general terms, but it does close the door on a general financial analysis over six years in relation to the accused's assets and expenditure as happens in drug trafficking cases.

There is specific mention of the standard of proof in respect of the accused being the balance of probabilities. (In practice the effect of this has been that at a confiscation hearing the accused normally leads evidence first, to show that matters contained in the prosecutor's statement are wrong and therefore the assumptions do not apply. This is covered further in Chapter 7.)

[3] High Court on appeal, October 20, 1999, unreported (Appeal No. C434/99).
[4] *ibid.*

Drug trafficking and the six year period

One difference which should be pointed out, as it may have a financial effect in certain cases, is that there is a difference between drug trafficking offences and "all crime" cases as to the end point for the six-year period. The position under PCSA 1995 seems to be as follows:

(1) in relation to drug trafficking the six-year period runs back from the date on which the indictment or complaint was served; and

(2) in relation to "all crime" the six-year period runs back from the date on which proceedings were instituted.

Obviously, (2) is going to be a much earlier date than the date on which the indictment or the complaint was served and logically a more sensible date if one remembers that in relation to a restraint order the six-year period runs back from the commencement of proceedings or the date on which the restraint order is made, whichever is the earlier. In practice these could all be different dates and there could be confusion if any of the realisable assets or implicative gifts falls within one six-year period but not another. As a simple example, if an accused appears on petition on drug trafficking charges on January 1, 1999 then the period relating to realisable assets that can be restrained will go back as far as January 1, 1993 but if the accused is not served with his indictment until June 1, 1999 (in a bail case) then the confiscation order can only be made in respect of realisable property covered by the period from June 1, 1993 to June 1, 1999 and of course during that period there will be a six-month interval, *i.e.* from January 1, 1999 to June 1, 1999, when the property has been restrained in any event. There appears to be no rhyme or reason within the Act as to why the dates are different. This should, of course, be borne in mind so that a check can be made when an accused is served with the prosecutor's statement containing a full financial analysis.

What do the assumptions mean?

The use of the assumptions in sections 2 and 3 of PCSA 1995 **4.10** determines the way the Crown sets about showing to the court the extent of proceeds made from drug trafficking or benefit from "all crime". In all crime cases following the *Adamson v.*

H.M. Advocate[5] decision the benefit must be linked to offences prosecuted. The assumptions are used to show that the accused's assets and expenditure have been made as a result of those crimes. (Normally a fairly straightforward financial sum). The position is different in drug trafficking cases the exact type of the financial analysis, is discussed in detail in Chapter 5. But, looking at it very simply, the Crown takes a six-year period (bearing in mind the different start dates) and looks at the assets obtained by the accused and the values of any implicative gifts during that period. It also looks at the expenditure made by the accused during the same period and thereafter presents a financial calculation to the court to show that any unaccounted for asset gains or expenditure ("unaccounted" is used here in the sense of coming from no known income source, whether legitimate or illegitimate) point to proceeds from criminal activity. The Crown does not require to prove that any other offences have been committed but by the use of the assumptions (together with the prosecutor's statement, described in Chapter 6) is able to present to the court a financial picture of the accused for the purposes of convincing it that the accused has unaccounted for assets and unaccounted for expenditure. The court, using section 3 assumptions assumes that the said unaccounted for assets and expenditure are drug trafficking monies unless the accused proves otherwise, on the balance of probabilities.

This method of financial calculation and the use of the assumptions have been approved by the court in *H.M. Advocate v. McLean*[6] and in *Donnelly v. H.M. Advocate.*[7] A guide to the financial analysis is contained in Chapter 5 and Appendix 2, Style III (the prosecutor's statement and model computation).

---

[5] High Court on appeal, October 20, 1999, unreported (Appeal No. C434/99).
[6] 1993 S.C.C.R. 917, *per* Lord Sutherland.
[7] 1999 S.C.C.R. 508.

CHAPTER 5

PROCEEDS—THE FINANCIAL ANALYSIS

INTRODUCTION

PCSA 1995 consolidates the provisions of the Criminal Justice **5.01**
(Scotland) Act 1987 in so far as drug trafficking proceeds are
concerned and introduces provisions to deal with the confiscation of the benefit from other crimes. The 1995 Act uses the
term "proceeds" in relation to drug trafficking and the term
"benefits" in relation to "all crime". From a financial accounting
point of view there is no difference in the result, no matter
which term is used, because the Act lays down one approach
only, *i.e.* a calculation which points to the two matters the judge
must know before he can reach his decision:

1. the value of drug trafficking proceeds or "all crime"
   benefits; and

2. the amount that might be realised at the time the
   confiscation order is made.

In reaching a result in 1. the Crown can make use of the rules in
relation to implicative gifts and the confiscation assumptions, all
referred to in Chapter 4.

When it comes to "all crime" cases, as a result of the decision
in *Adamson v. H.M. Advocate*,[1] there is likely to be very little
financial accounting work required as the "benefit" would
normally be clear from the crime. For example, a theft of £5,000
is going to mean £5,000 benefit to the accused and £5,000 loss to
the victim. There is no need to go into any further detail in
"crime" cases, therefore, where the benefit is self-evident and
frequently the only question will be: does the accused have
realisable property to meet the benefit from the crime?

Any reference will be to drug trafficking proceeds only in this
chapter, but the reader should bear in mind that it could apply
equally well to "all crime" (two or more offences) benefit cases
should the decision in *Adamson* be revised by legislation to
allow the Crown the same powers as in drug trafficking cases.

---

[1] High Court on appeal, October 20, 1999, unreported (Appeal No.
C434/99).

It will be helpful if, when reading this chapter, the model computation (Appendix 2, Style III) is continually referred to.

While symptoms of fear or boredom seem to affect non-accountants when first faced with accounting problems, there are no esoteric concepts involved in the assessment of drug trafficking proceeds and, provided that the logic underlying the format of the computation is understood, the rest is not difficult.

"Proceeds"—What does it Mean?

5.02   As described in Chapter 4, section 3 of the Act ("Assessing the proceeds of drug trafficking") states that any payments or other rewards received by a person in connection with drug trafficking carried on by him or another are his proceeds of trafficking and the value of his proceeds of drug trafficking is the aggregate of the value of the payments or other rewards.

That statement is not helpful. Accountants would generally agree that "proceeds", for example the proceeds of a sale, means the amount that was realised from a sale; it might be extended to include in the calculation costs that were necessarily incurred in making the sale (*e.g.* legal fees and expenses for the conveyance of a house). But "proceeds" certainly does not mean "profit" which, in the case of a house sale, would be the proceeds less the original cost of the house to the seller. The word "profit" is not used in section 3. However accounting conventions or jargon are certainly not binding on Parliament and "proceeds" in the gross sense might indeed be the intended measure.

If that is the intention then it presents virtually insoluble problems in the ascertainment of the "proceeds" figure. By its very nature, drug trafficking is a covert operation. Accounting records are not kept; in several years of confiscation cases there has yet to be one where they have been. But in order to compute a proceeds figure on the "gross" basis, details of every trafficking transaction would be needed over a period that could extend to up to six years. The "proceeds" route does not offer a practicable solution to the problem.

However, again as described in Chapter 4, section 3(2) of the Act allows certain assumptions to be made by the court in confiscation cases unless in the circumstances of the particular case they can be shown to be incorrect. These are powerful assumptions and are invariably used by the Crown in its computation for a confiscation petition.

Summarised, the assumptions amount to this:

(a) any property held by the trafficker or transferred to him within a period of six years before his indictment was received by him as a reward for drug trafficking; and

(b) any payments made by him within the six-year period were made out of drug trafficking receipts.

It is important that the use of these assumptions in the Crown's computations is properly understood. In many cases failure to do so has resulted in a considerable waste of time and money but it is possible to illustrate the logic, and by a very simple example.

Suppose that an honest, law-abiding citizen has an annual take-home pay of £20,000. Over the year his income will be spent first on the necessities of living (food, clothing, etc.) and anything that remains will go into savings.

(1) Take-home pay = Spend + Save

   £20,000   =   £18,000 + £2,000.

Now suppose that to supplement his legitimate income in the following year he starts to traffick in drugs and is then convicted of doing so but there is no direct evidence as to what his proceeds may have been. A financial investigation reveals that in this year the equivalent financial statement to that in (1) above is:

(2) Take-home pay = Spend + Save

   £20,000   =   £21,000 + £9,000
   plus £"x" drugs.

This equation is solved very simply by transferring the take-home pay to the right-hand side of the equation with the consequent change of sign from positive to negative.

(3) £x = Spend + Save − Take-home pay

   = £21,000 + £9,000 − £20,000

   = £10,000 = proceeds of drug trafficking.

Now turn to Appendix 2, Style III (the model computation referred to in the introduction to this chapter) and you will see that the model exactly parallels the logic in (3).

THE MODEL COMPUTATION

5.03

Equation (para. 5–2) (3)		Model computation	
Spend	£21,000	Other expenditure (Line B)	£185,534
Save	£9,000	Assets - Liabilities (Line A)	£447,531
	£30,000		£628,065
Take-home pay	£20,000	Income from known sources (Line D)	
			£255,239
Drug proceeds	£10,000	Proceeds of trafficking	£372,826

While the logic is clear it will be equally apparent that the accuracy of the computation is only as good as the accuracy of its component parts and in practice there can be many problems.

This approach to the computation of drug trafficking proceeds was first tested and accepted by the court in 1992, in *H.M. Advocate v. McLean*,[1a] which was followed in 1997 by *H.M. Advocate v. Donnelly*.[2] There, at least for the present, the matter rests.

THE MODEL EXAMPLE

5.04 In reading the following paragraphs it will be found helpful if the model computation in Appendix 2, Style III is considered along with the text. The model is a fiction but is based on the type of transactions expected in cases.

Schedule 1: Proceeds of drug trafficking

5.05 The computation itself is the final column on the right, headed 1993–97, covering in this case the five years ending November 20, 1997. The yearly columns are not essential but in practice it has been found to be convenient to assemble the information in this way. A six-year period is the maximum allowed in terms of section 2(6) of the Act but if the earlier years of the six were to

---

[1a] 1993 S.C.C.R. 917 at 1123.

[2] *per* Lord Bonomy High Court, June 13, 1997, unreported; *Donnelly v. H.M. Advocate*, 1999 S.C.C.R. 508.

show little in the way of proceeds they would normally be omitted.

Schedule 2: Assets less liabilities

Assets are those things owned by a person that have more than **5.06** a short-term value, for example houses, cars, investments and bank and building society accounts. Assets, by and large, will represent the individual's accumulated savings but there could be exceptions (*e.g.* there could be an asset that has come through an inheritance and, if received within the six years, it would be also included as income).

Liabilities are debts due by an individual which at some time in the future have to be repaid. A liability may be directly associated with a particular asset and may be secured over that asset (*e.g.* a mortgage) or may be no more than outstanding bills. For the purposes of a confiscation computation only liabilities that are legally secured over an asset that is included in the computation are taken into account.

The expression "net assets" means the total of the assets less the total of the liabilities.

Assets are recorded in the schedule at cost and no adjustment is made in the computation for any gain or loss of value that may occur. Valuations play no part in the computation but are taken care of when preparing the statement of the realisable value of the accused's assets.

For all assets that are identified or treated as the property of the accused it is necessary to ascertain:

(a) the date of acquisition;

(b) the cost of acquisition;

(c) how the cost was met (*e.g.* cheque or cash);

(d) if by cheque, on which bank account;

and if the asset has been sold within the six-year period:

(e) the date of sale;

(f) the proceeds of sale (net of the costs of sale);

(g) what has happened to the proceeds.

For secured loans the necessary information is:

(a) the source;

(b) the terms of the loan with regard to interest and repayment;

(c) how the interest and repayments have been paid (cheque or cash and, in respect of cheques, the bank on which they were drawn).

For all heritable assets the files of the solicitor who dealt with the transaction should be examined and a brief account of the transaction prepared (examples of such are to be found in Schedules 2.1–2.5).

Over the period covered by a confiscation computation assets may be disposed of and almost invariably there will be a gain or loss on the disposal. These gains and losses must be calculated (see Schedules 2.1, 2.13 and 2.14) and the gains included in the schedule of the person's income (Schedule 6). Losses are included in Schedule 4 (Other expenditure). While the asset will disappear from the schedule of assets the proceeds of the sale must be traced. In most cases the proceeds will have been lodged in a bank account. If that is the case no further adjustment is required. If the proceeds cannot be traced to a bank account then the implication is that they have been spent and must then be included in the computation as "Other expenditure".

A simplified example may assist in an understanding of this point. Suppose it is known that an accused has proceeds of £2,000 from trafficking and that was the total sum involved. Assume also that any other figures in the computation are entirely neutral and have no effect on the drugs proceeds figure. With the £2,000 he bought a car in Year 1. In the following year that car cannot be traced. At the end of Year 1 the car would appear in the assets schedule and the computation would reflect drug proceeds of £2,000. If, at the end of Year 2, the car is omitted from the assets and no other adjustment is made this would result in a negative figure of £2,000 appearing as proceeds and the effect over the two years would be to show a nil drugs proceeds figure—manifestly an incorrect result. If, however, in Year 2 £2,000 is included in "other expenditure" as a combination of a loss and assumed disposal cash proceeds spent, the misstatement is corrected and the £2,000 again emerges as the proceeds figure.

If the accused has received loans which are not secured over assets then the receipt of the loan is recognised in the ascertainable income (Schedule 6). Any repayments will be included as "Other expenditure", either as bank withdrawals (Schedule 3) or as cash spent (Schedule 4). So far as the schedule of realisable assets is concerned, such loans are ignored as the lender has no prior claim over any specific asset.

Bank accounts

The figures for bank and building society accounts included in 5.07 the assets statement are taken from detailed schedules for each bank or building society (Schedules 2.6–2.11). The details are obtained from bank statements and show the respective year-end balances, lodgments and withdrawals and interest earned, the latter being required for the "Ascertainable income" (Schedule 6).

Detailed examination of the bank statements may provide leads to additional bank accounts or other assets.

Business capital accounts

Where the accused has been involved in an unincorporated 5.08 business, accounts of the business should be sought. There is probably a more than even chance that they will be available, if only for the purposes of satisfying the Inland Revenue or a lending bank, and they may well have a professional accountant's report on them. Such a report is frequently referred to as an "audit" report but it is not. It will generally be in the following terms: "I have prepared the above accounts from the books of account and information given to me by Mr X." Such a report means nothing more than it says. It does not say anything about the books or the information and what reliability can be attached to them. However the usual approach is to accept the accounts so provided unless they appear to be manifestly at variance with other information that may be available. The accounts are likely to comprise a statement of the trading results and a balance sheet showing the assets and liabilities and a capital account which shows the owner's changing stake in the business from the start of one year to the end. Thus the capital account will show the opening and closing balances, any capital introduced, the profit or loss for the year and the owner's drawings from the business. The general approach to the business in a confiscation computation is to treat the various components of the capital account in the same way as the components of a bank account.

The parallel nomenclature is thus:

Capital account	Bank account
Opening balance	Opening balance
Closing balance	Closing balance
Capital introduced	Lodgments
Profit/loss	Interest received
Personal drawings	Withdrawals

The treatment of the capital account items is therefore as follows:

Opening and closing balances	Shown in "Assets and liabilities" (Schedule 2)
Capital introduced	No adjustment required; part of the difference between opening and closing balances.
Profit/loss	"Income" (Schedule 6)/"Losses" (Schedule 4)
Drawings	"Bank withdrawals" (Schedule 3)

There are two further steps that must be taken when dealing with the business accounts. If any personal drawings can be traced to lodgments into a bank account (see Schedule 3.1) these will be included in the adjustment line in Schedule 3. It is also important to ascertain the source of any capital that has been paid in. If that capital can be traced to one of the bank accounts then the amount must similarly be included in the adjustments line in Schedule 3 as it is equivalent to a transfer between bank accounts. If it is not found in any of the known bank accounts that may indicate an as yet undiscovered account or cash being laundered through the business. If not traced this figure will manifest itself as proceeds of drug trafficking.

If the accused has shares in a private limited company then the treatment of this asset for the purposes of the computation is as follows:

(a) the shares are treated as an investment;

(b) any salary or dividends paid to the accused is treated as income;

(c) any loan account between the accused and the company is treated as if it were a bank account.

Investments in stocks and shares (Schedule 2.13)

The model gives a comprehensive example of an extensive share **5.09** portfolio and the information that should be gathered. The rules for disposals, calculation of gains and losses and tracking of the disposal of the proceeds that have already been considered in respect of other assets apply equally well for investments. Dividends received on stocks and shares should be scheduled and included in Income (Schedule 6). (The model does not include such a schedule as it presents no particular difficulty.)

Motor vehicles

An example of a motor vehicle schedule is given in the model **5.10** (Schedule 2.14). There is no new principle involved in this class of asset and no commentary is necessary.

Cash seized at time of arrest

While the Crown may have successfully moved for forfeiture of **5.11** any cash at the conclusion of the accused's trial, the amount is still included in the computation as it was part of the accused's assets immediately prior to his arrest. The money, however, will not feature in the statement of realisable assets if forfeiture has been granted.

Wholesale value of drugs

The drugs seized at the time of the accused's arrest will have **5.12** been valued by the police, at the estimated cost to the accused. They are included in the computation in that they were part of the accused's assets at the time of his arrest but will not be included in the statement of realisable assets as they will have been forfeited.

The totals on Schedule 2 are transferred to Schedule 1 where the annual increases in the net assets are calculated.

Other expenditure

Schedule 3: Bank, building society and other withdrawals

One of the assumptions that section 3(2) of the Act permits the **5.13** court to make is that any payments made by the accused within the period under review are made out of the proceeds of drug trafficking and the inclusion of the total bank withdrawals in the computation is an application of that assumption.

Schedule 3 combines the total withdrawals from all the bank accounts and where appropriate the personal drawings in the business capital account (see above at paragraph 5.08) and strikes a subtotal from which a deduction is made before transferring the final total to Schedule 1. The deduction requires an explanation.

The adjustment is described as being for "Transfers between accounts and payments that have increased assets or reduced liabilities (deducted to avoid double counting)".

Transfers between accounts

5.14   Suppose that there are two bank accounts, A and B, with respective balances of £1,200 and £2,000. If Account A is closed and the balance transferred to Account B the total of the balances remains unchanged. In so far as the totality of the bank accounts is concerned there has been no withdrawal. Rather than break the pattern of including all the bank withdrawals in the schedule it is deemed sensible to include the withdrawal from account A as such and show an adjustment to eliminate the transfer.

Payments that have increased assets

5.15   Suppose now that a bank account shows withdrawals of £10,000 and that figure has been included in the withdrawals schedule. It is then discovered that a motor car has been bought for £8,500 and paid for by a cheque drawn on the bank account. The car is included in the assets schedule. The reality of these transactions is that one asset, the £8,500 part of the bank balance, has been converted into another, the car. If no adjustment was made the £8,500 would be counted twice: once as a new asset, the car, and again as a withdrawal from the bank.

Payments that have reduced liabilities

5.16   Payments that are made to reduce a liability have, in terms of accounting, exactly the same effect as payments to increase assets—an asset, the bank account, has been reduced, while a liability also has been reduced by the same amount, resulting in no change in the person's net assets. This and the preceding case can be illustrated by a simple example.

	Opening	Trans. 1	Result	Trans. 2	Result
Other assets	£20,000	+£2,000	£22,000		£22,000
Bank account	£5,000	−£2,000	£3,000	−£2,000	£1,000
	£25,000		£25,000		£23,000
Liabilities	£3,000		£3,000	£2,000	£1,000
Net assets	£22,000		£22,000		£22,000

The table above shows a person's assets less liabilities at the opening of a period. In Transaction 1 he buys a car and pays for it with a cheque. In Transaction 2 he reduces a loan he has received by withdrawing money from the bank account. In both cases the transactions have no effect on net assets.

Were the bank withdrawals to be taken into the computation with no adjustment for the two transactions, bank withdrawals of £4,000 would be shown as "Other expenditure" in the computation. There would be no movement in the net assets figure in the computation and a proceeds figure of £4,000 would emerge—clearly a wrong result. The adjustment made on the Bank withdrawals schedule for "payments that have increased assets or reduced liabilities" corrects the position.

Schedule 4: Other expenditure

During the course of the financial investigation into an accused's affairs it is not uncommon to find evidence clearly showing that he has spent relatively large sums of cash. There is nothing surprising in this in that his income from drug sales is likely to be in cash.   5.17

There may also be evidence showing his ownership of assets for which there can be found no evidence of how they were acquired and paid for. Clearly such assets fall within the terms of section 3(2)(ii) of the Act and the court is entitled to assume that the assets have been acquired from the proceeds of drug trafficking. Schedule 4 of the model computation gives several examples of the typical types of transactions that have been experienced.

In that some of the payments have resulted in the acquisition of assets which are included in the assets (Schedule 2) a deduction is required to avoid a double counting of the expenditure first in the Assets schedule and secondly in Other expenditure (Schedule 4) in the same way as discussed in paragraph 5.15 above.

Schedule 5: Household expenditure

5.18   At the beginning of this chapter, when discussing the logic of the confiscation computation, spending on the necessities of living (food clothing, etc.) was referred to. That part of the computation dealing with such expenditure is now considered. That such expenditure will have been incurred by the accused can not be gainsaid but to quantify it, in the absence of evidence, is impossible to do precisely.

On occasions it may be apparent from cheque stubs and credit card details that some household and family costs have been paid in that way but in the absence of such evidence it has to be assumed that the expenditure has been made in cash and no accurate quantification of the amount spent is going to be obtained.

In such cases it is normal to use the annual tables of family spending produced by the Office for National Statistics. Within these publications household expenditure is analysed in various ways and by various family categories, income groups, age bands, etc. and the table that best fits the accused's circumstances is used to give the average weekly expenditure per person in the household. It is extremely unlikely that the figure for household expenditure arrived at in the particular case of the accused will show precisely how, on average, he actually incurred these costs but it is believed that the resultant figure used in the computation is fair and it has been accepted by the courts.

Occasionally the statistical figures from the table may be adjusted to take account of an obvious difference between the circumstances of the accused and those of the average family. For example in Schedule 5 of the model, statistical expenditure on housing has been adjusted to exclude the accused's mortgage payments which have already been included in his bank withdrawals. Furthermore identified household costs (included in bank withdrawals) have been deducted from the statistics, leaving a balance assumed to have been made in cash. The adjustments made to the statistical figures in the model computation should be regarded purely as indicative of the kinds of adjustments made to suit the circumstances of specific cases only and are not routine.

Schedule 6: Ascertainable income

5.19   This figure is sometimes referred to as "legitimate" income but only in the sense that it does not include any income that is drug-related. It may include income to which the accused is not properly entitled, for example payments claimed from the Benefits Agency to which he was not entitled. Likewise it may include income that has not been declared for tax purposes. However these practices are not drug-related and money has been received that has had an effect on the financial affairs of the individual.

Where the person's income is subject to PAYE or tax deduction at source, in the case of dividends from shares, it is not the gross pay or dividend that is included in the schedule but the net. In both cases it is only the net that the individual can spend.

This schedule is also used to bring into the computation occasional and sometimes fortuitous receipts. The model schedule includes four examples (an insurance receipt, an inheritance, injury compensation and a bingo win) but the possibilities are unlimited.

In all probability if the Crown fails to find an income source the accused will declare it when he realises that to increase his income for the purposes of the computation will reduce the confiscation claim.

If such additional income is declared the Crown will want to satisfy itself that the new income has in fact been included in lodgments made to a bank account or in some other asset included in Schedule 2. If it has been included then the now disclosed income is properly dealt with if it is included in the income statement; if the income has not been included in bank lodgments or some other asset then to include it in the Income schedule would require the same amount to be included in "Other expenditure" as a cash spend. The overall result would then be neutral in so far as the quantum of drug proceeds is concerned.

Schedule 7: Realisable assets

Section 1(5) of the Act provides that the sum which a compensation order requires an accused to pay shall be the lesser of the value of the person's proceeds of drug trafficking or the realisable value of the assets. Accordingly Schedule 7 of the model shows the form of a realisable assets statement. **5.20**

It should be noted that all the assets of the accused are included even although some of them may have been acquired before the model computation period and even if it could be shown conclusively that an asset had been acquired from non-drug income (*e.g.* acquired through an inheritance). It is no more than a listing of the assets which the accused has available to meet the cost of the confiscation order.

The confiscation order is an order to pay a certain sum of money. In the first instance the accused has the opportunity to decide how he will discharge the order. If he fails to do this within the time granted by the court the Crown may return to court to seek the appointment of an administrator to realise the accused's assets and discharge the debt (see below, Chapter 8).

CHAPTER 6

THE PROSECUTOR'S STATEMENT AND ANSWERS

Chapter 5 considered the accountant's viewpoint of the financial **6.01**
analysis undertaken by the Crown and the method of its
presentation, as seen in the model computation in Appendix 2,
Style III. The format presented to the court is designed to allow
it to consider both the financial computation and the Crown's
explanation of it. The document, as seen in the style mentioned
above, is called the "prosecutor's statement".

This chapter seeks to explain the rules surrounding the
prosecutor's statement, its use in court and the requirements on
the defence once it has been served.

The concept of a prosecutor's statement was introduced in the
Criminal Justice (Scotland) Act 1987[1] for drug trafficking cases
and has been used by the Crown in every confiscation case
presented to court since then. The case of *H.M. Advocate v.
McLean*[2] indicates clearly the extent of information contained in
a prosecutor's statement and the types of response required by
the defence. It is probably fair to say that since that date there
have been a number of even more detailed and complicated
prosecutors' statements presented to the court in larger drug
trafficking cases, akin to the style in Appendix 2. Prosecutors'
statements were extended by section 9 of PCSA 1995 to include
both drug trafficking and "all crime" cases.

FORMAT OF THE PROSECUTOR'S STATEMENT

Section 9 provides a method to allow the court to consider fully **6.02**
the two figures being presented by the Crown and the computations in respect of each. The two figures which the court
requires to consider before the judge can decide whether or not
to exercise his discretion to make a confiscation order, and
indeed the amount of that order, are:

1. the amount of drug trafficking proceeds or benefit from
   "all crime" during the relevant period (six years in all
   cases except "single crime" cases); and

---

[1] (c. 41).
[2] 1993 S.C.C.R. 917.

2. the amount of assets available to be realised at the date of the proof (*i.e.* the accused's realisable property together with the value of all implicative gifts).

The court also needs to know, of course, the defence position in relation to both of these matters, whether they are accepted or challenged or if there is an alternative explanation for the accused's financial position of which the Crown has failed to take account. It may even be that the accused's financial position is truly legitimate and entirely separate from the crime of which he has been convicted. In order to allow the court to consider all these matters fully, the prosecutor's statement in effect starts the ball rolling.

Section 9 states that:

"Where the prosecutor applies for the making of a confiscation order [he] may lodge with the clerk of court a statement as to any matters relevant—

(a) in connection with a drug trafficking offence, to the assessment of the value of the accused's proceeds of drug trafficking; and

(b) in connection with any other offence—

(i) to determining whether the accused has benefited for the purposes of section 1(6)(a) of this Act; or

(ii) to an assessment of the value of the accused's benefit from the commission of the offence."

The first thing to be noted therefore is that the prosecutor's statement relates to providing information to the court about the assessment of the value of proceeds of drug trafficking or benefit from "all crime". The section does not require the statement to contain information about the extent of the accused's realisable property. However, the court *does* require information on both matters in order to determine whether the proceeds or benefits are greater or lesser than the accused's realisable property so that it can fix a figure should a confiscation order be made. To that end, then, the Crown normally includes information about the accused's realisable property as a matter of practice. It is in any event clearly arguable that a statement as to matters relevant in connection with the assessment of the value of the accused's proceeds of drug trafficking or benefit from "all crime" would include the extent of either proceeds or benefit still available in the hands of the accused or gifted to others.

Although there is no prescribed format for the prosecutor's statement, it has become fairly standard in recent cases and in general follows the style in Appendix 2, Style III. The extent of the prosecutor's statement depends on the complexity or otherwise of the accused's financial position, the length of time for which the Crown has been able to obtain accurate financial details and the extent of any realisable property, gifts or implicative gifts left. The statement can therefore range from a simple document of three or four pages to a complex 50– or 60–page document full of supporting schedules. Style III in Appendix 2 is one of the more detailed prosecutor's statement.

In brief, a prosecutor's statement should be a short verbal narration indicating clearly the total amount of proceeds or benefits the Crown states have been made from either drug trafficking or "all crime", and the total amount of realisable property (including gifts or implicative gifts) that the Crown says is available as at the date of proof These two figures will feature prominently in the narration at the start of the prosecutor's statement, drawing the attention of the court and the defence to them. There is a brief history of whether or not a restraint order has been obtained, a copy of which normally forms part of the prosecutor's statement too. Apart from that there will be a short verbal narration indicating what is contained in the supporting financial schedules and stating which assets the Crown considers to have been gifted by the accused to others. It has been observed that prosecutor's statements were originally akin to civil pleadings, but more recently they have become more like sets of financial accounts with a verbal explanation. It should be remembered that the prosecutor's statement in terms of section 9 is used in criminal and not civil proceedings and that, apart from specific statutory provisions in PCSA 1995, criminal rules of evidence apply.

From a defence point of view, the most important aspect of section 9 is that where a statement is lodged and served on an accused, an obligation can arise which is to the advantage of the Crown. That can be seen in section 9(3) which states:

"Where—

    (a) a statement is lodged under subsection (1) above; and

    (b) the court is satisfied that a copy of that statement has been served on the accused,

the court may require the accused to indicate within such period as it may specify, to what extent he accepts each allegation in the statement and, in so far as he does not accept any allegation, to indicate the basis of such non-acceptance."

Further, section 9(4) goes on to state that:

"If the accused fails in any respect to comply with a requirement under subsection (3) above, he may be treated for the purposes of this section as accepting every allegation in the statement apart from any allegation in respect of which he has complied with the requirement."

Therefore, once the Crown has lodged and served a prosecutor's statement and made the appropriate motion to the court to require the accused to indicate acceptance or otherwise in terms of subsection (3), the defence requires to answer each allegation in the prosecutor's statement, or fall foul of subsection (4). Moreover, as the proceedings are criminal and not civil, and because of the provision in subsection (3) that if any allegation is not accepted then the basis of the non-acceptance should be stated, it is insufficient to use terms such as "not known and not admitted". It could be argued that any such phrase is nothing other than a failure to comply with the requirement in subsection (3) and therefore a failure to indicate the basis for such non-acceptance. Given the terms of subsection (4), it could be open to the court then to hold that the accused is to be treated as having accepted the allegation where such a phrase alone is used. In other words, if the accused has an answer for the prosecutor's allegation, it is important for him to give that answer at this stage rather than have the court decide that bare denials amount to acceptance. Accordingly, if the accused attempts to "remain silent" at this stage of the proceedings, he may end up having a confiscation order made against him almost by default.

The Lodging of the Prosecutor's Statement

6.03 Section 9 indicates that the time to lodge the prosecutor's statement is when the prosecutor applies for the making of a confiscation order. In terms of section 1 this occurs when the accused is convicted. If convicted on indictment, this will be either when the prosecutor moves for sentence or, if the accused is remitted, before sentence is pronounced. If convicted in summary proceedings, it will be immediately following his conviction. In practice, that means that the prosecutor will move for sentence, move for a confiscation order and lodge a prosecutor's statement all at the same time. From a defence point of view, therefore, as soon as either the sheriff announces his decision or a jury verdict is recorded, the accused will be served with a copy prosecutor's statement as he is sitting in the dock, minutes or even seconds before the Crown moves for a confiscation order and lodges the original prosecutor's statement with the clerk of court. Prior to this, the only warning the accused will have been given that confiscation proceedings are being taken is if a restraint order has been obtained against him.

The procedure thereafter is that the Crown will move the court to order the accused to indicate the extent to which he accepts, or not, the allegations in the prosecutor's statement, and if not the basis of non-acceptance, all in terms of section 9(3). There is no set time period for the accused to do that under the Act and there is no set format. In practice the accused is normally given a period of between four and six weeks to indicate his position in terms of section 9(3) and the format is that he is normally required to lodge answers. Thereafter a hearing date is fixed, normally at the end of the period allowed to the accused. During that time the accused will require to formulate answers to all the allegations in the prosecutor's statement, lodge them in court and serve them on the Crown.

At the hearing, it is a matter for the Crown to indicate acceptance or not of the defence answers. If they are not all accepted, then a hearing in terms of section 9(6) will be fixed. While the Act refers to this as a hearing, in practice a hearing in terms of section 9(6) is called a confiscation proof, probably because it is only at that stage that evidence will be led. An indication of the less than satisfactory approach that has been taken in relation to this area of legislation can be seen in the fact that there are no statutory provisions or rules of court as to the procedure to be followed. With no set format for either the prosecutor's statement or the defence answers or, indeed, no provision for adjustments or any set time-limits, practice has led to a fairly standard procedure developing for all of these matters. It can be summarised as follows:

1. the prosecutor's statement will normally follow the format in Appendix 2, Style III;

2. the Crown will invariably lodge a prosecutor's statement. To date, there have been no cases where the Crown has moved for a confiscation order without one;

3. the Crown will move the court to require the accused to indicate acceptance or otherwise in terms of section 9(3) and such acceptance, or otherwise, must be lodged in the format of defence answers (see example in Appendix 2, Style IV);

4. at the instigation of the prosecutor, the court will normally give the defence a period of between four and six weeks to lodge answers and will fix a hearing at the end of that period;

5. at the hearing usually neither the prosecutor nor the accused is in a position to proceed. Time is sought to investigate either the prosecutor's statement or defence answers further. Accordingly, the court usually accedes to the request for further time to allow the Crown to adjust the prosecutor's statement in light of the information given by the defence and because of new financial information obtained by the Crown. On the other hand, the defence may need more time to consider the prosecutor's statement. In complicated financial computations, the defence usually needs more time since the first time the financial analysis in the prosecutor's statement is seen is at the point of conviction and, if the accused's financial position is complicated, the prosecutor's statement may well be a weighty document requiring some amount of time for proper consideration and analysis by an accountant acting for the defence;

6. once the prosecutor and the defence have provided written information to the court by means of an adjusted prosecutor's statement and defence answers and it is clear there are matters not accepted by either side, the court will fix a confiscation hearing (proof).

In practice, confiscation proofs in complex cases will be fixed some months after the date of the conviction, sometimes as much as six to 12 months after conviction. In simpler cases, there is no reason why a date for a hearing cannot be fixed fairly quickly. Certainly in sheriff court cases, it would be anticipated that the prosecutor's statement could be lodged, answered and adjusted and a hearing held within a six-month period.

Chapter 7

THE CONFISCATION HEARING OR PROOF

A confiscation hearing may take place in accordance with **7.01** section 9 of PCSA 1995. It is a criminal hearing and can be held in either the High Court or the sheriff court, according to where the trial was held. That section contains the rules for lodging a prosecutor's statement and defence answers, as discussed in Chapter 6. Section 9(6) provides that where the defence challenges an allegation in the prosecutor's statement or the prosecutor challenges the basis of non-acceptance by the accused in his defence answers of any allegation in the prosecutor's statement then the court shall consider the matters challenged at a hearing. There is no procedure laid down by the Act for the confiscation hearing and there are no rules in any Act of Adjournal. Court practice has followed the case of *H.M. Advocate v. McLean*,[1] a confiscation hearing held under the Criminal Justice (Scotland) Act 1987, and has continued the same practice under PCSA 1995. A confiscation hearing in terms of section 9(6) tends to be referred to by both the Crown and the defence as a confiscation proof, simply because it is a hearing at which evidence will be led by both sides. A confiscation hearing in terms of section 9(6) therefore will be referred to as a confiscation proof in the remainder of this chapter.

Before considering the expected procedure at a confiscation proof it is worth bearing in mind that its purpose is to allow the presiding judge to exercise his discretion as to whether or not he will make a confiscation order. In order to exercise that discretion he has to have information about two things:

1. In drug trafficking cases, evidence before him in relation to the proceeds of drug trafficking by the accused and the value of the accused's realisable property at the time the confiscation order is to be made (*i.e.* at the time of the confiscation proof).

2. In relation to all other crimes, the amount of benefit to the accused and the value of the accused's realisable property at the time the confiscation order is to be made (*i.e.* at the time of the confiscation proof).

[1] 1993 S.C.C.R. 917.

Quite simply, the judge cannot make a confiscation order unless he knows exactly which is the lesser of the above amounts, whether it is drug trafficking proceeds or benefit or the value of realisable property.

TIME-LIMITS

7.02   Section 10 of PCSA 1995 appears to provide a time-limit of six months in confiscation proceedings in two situations. If the court considers, first, that it has some, but not sufficient, relevant information to enable it to come to a decision as to whether to make a confiscation order or not or, secondly, that it does not have sufficient relevant information to enable it to decide the amount to be payable under a confiscation order, then it may postpone the decision for a period not exceeding six months after the date of conviction for the purpose of enabling further information to be obtained. Initially it appeared that section 10 provided a scheme whereby a confiscation proof required to be held and a confiscation order made within six months of the date of conviction. That interpretation appeared sensible in the light of section 10(6) which allowed the Crown, in a case where there was a supervening appeal against conviction, to extend the postponement until three months after the disposal of the appeal. However, section 10 has been interpreted by the appeal court in the case of *Donnelly v. H.M. Advocate*[2] as applying only to situations where it is *the court* which requires additional information and not where the Crown or defence requires time to prepare. For all practical purposes, therefore, there is no time-limit on confiscation proceedings and it is a matter for the court to ensure that matters progress quickly.

PROCEDURE AT A CONFISCATION PROOF

The parties

7.03   A confiscation proof is proceeding as the result of the Crown initially having made a motion for a confiscation order. Thereafter matters flow from the information put before the court by the Crown in the prosecutor's statement. Rarely, the accused may have no argument with the Crown's case, the analysis and

---

[2] 1999 S.C.C.R. 508.

the figures included in the prosecutor's statement and therefore there will be no need for a confiscation proof and a confiscation order will simply be made. This has happened in only two cases so far but is perhaps more likely to happen in "all crime", "single offence" cases where the immediate benefit to the accused can be seen from the crime itself and once the accused has been convicted there is no arguing with that. However, the more usual position is that the defence challenges the Crown's position in the prosecutor's statement, lodges answers and is represented at a proof.

There is always the possibility that other parties wish to be represented at the proof. Most frequently the recipients of implicative gifts or gifts have an interest in the making of a confiscation order and wish to have their position heard at a confiscation proof. These persons, whether they be the accused's wife, mother or other relatives or indeed business associates, are normally referred to as minuters and in practice the court has allowed minuters to be represented at the confiscation proof. There is unlikely ever to be any opposition by the Crown as it is in everyone's interest that all matters in relation to the assets are aired in one hearing. The normal procedure for a minuter to enter appearance is by means of a minute and oral representation at the first hearing of the case following conviction, *i.e.* the hearing when the defence is required to lodge answers in terms of section 9. At that point if the minuter is allowed to enter appearance it is usual to grant a further adjournment to allow him or her to be served with the prosecutor's statement and to lodge answers. This is merely a practice which has arisen for the convenience of the court and all parties in order to focus attention on the real issues at the proof. The minuter is not, however, bound by the procedure in terms of section 9. In practice the Crown does not object to such minuters becoming involved both in the proceedings and in any settlement discussions.

The documentation

At a confiscation proof there will always be certain documentation lodged with the clerk of court before proof: 7.04

1. the prosecutor's statement;

2. the defence answers to the prosecutor's statement, all in terms of section 9;

3. a joint minute between parties indicating matters of agreement; and recently and frequently

4. agreed schedules, referred to as "impact statements". Impact statements are merely schedules prepared by the Crown for the purposes of explaining easily to the court the effect of accepting certain pieces of evidence and the resulting effects on the prosecutor's statement. In other words, in order to assist the court the recent practice has been that the Crown and the defence have discussed the likely lines of evidence prior to proof and the effect that acceptance of either side's position may have on the overall financial analysis presented by the Crown in the prosecutor's statement. Those discussions are thereafter reduced to financial schedules made available to the court at the start of the proof.

An example of the type of thing to be included in an impact statement would be a house valued at £10,000 in the realisable property schedule and proceeds or benefit analysis schedule. The position may well be that it is argued by the Crown that the house truly belongs to the accused despite the fact that the title is in the name of another relative. The defence may well argue that the house has nothing to do with the accused and that title is correct. The impact statement would follow the financial trail relating to the house through the prosecutor's statement and show the effect of deleting reference to the house should the court take the view that it does truly belong to the other relative and is not part of the accused's realisable property. It should be emphasised that these impact statements are matters of agreement between the Crown and the defence and have been introduced recently in an effort to assist the court and focus the real issues at the proof. They can only work if parties are prepared to discuss matters prior to proof.

THE CROWN APPROACH

7.05 If the Crown uses the prosecutor's statement properly then the accused can only challenge the matters contained in it if he has a basis for non-acceptance, not merely to put the Crown to the test. It is not enough for the accused to deny that the Crown information is accurate without saying why. In practice at the proof, therefore, the Crown having listed accurate information which the defence cannot challenge without a basis means that information is accepted by the court without the necessity of further formal evidence. This is most easily seen in the case of bank or building society account information which the Crown usually lists as credits and withdrawals in schedule form. Non-challenge (and there are usually no grounds for any challenge) means that the bank or building society information is accepted without the need to call any witnesses or produce documents and it is only the interpretation of the information on which the Crown requires to lead evidence. Similarly if the Crown lists the accused's property and values in a realisable property schedule and it is unchallenged then no further evidence is required on the ownership or current values of the property.

At the proof by means of the prosecutor's statement and its explanation in evidence from a Crown expert witness, either a consultant accountant or police officer specialising in financial matters, the Crown approach is to rely on the build-up of assets by the accused and expenditure made by him to show that his monies, or at least most of his monies, are unaccounted for, thus seeking to persuade the court to apply the assumptions in section 2 or section 3 as appropriate. This is almost a back-to-front approach of:

1. look at the whole picture first;

2. decide that it makes financial sense only if the accused has made money from an illegitimate source, either drug trafficking or "all crime"; and then

3. apply the section 2 or section 3 assumptions to allow that to be done formally, in order to permit a confiscation order to be made, always bearing in mind that the total sum in an "all crime" case cannot exceed the actual benefit from the crimes prosecuted.

While it may appear that the Crown has an advantage there is nothing, of course, to prevent an accused who has made his money legitimately from indicating that in his answers, thus requiring the Crown to investigate the position further and if necessary amend the prosecutor's statement. So far, few accused have been in that position. This is perhaps one of the reasons why so many confiscation cases settle because both sides are dealing in true financial terms, both sides have accountants analysing the information available and the accountants are unlikely to disagree on the interpretation of a financial trail, thus meaning that only issues of true credibility will end up at a confiscation proof. Alternatively, if it appeared to the Crown initially that the accused had drug trafficking proceeds of a certain amount but the defence was able to show that part of that money had truly been made from the accused's genuine business but underdeclared to the Inland Revenue then the Crown would be obliged to amend the prosecutor's statement accordingly. It would not, of course, prevent the accused from having to pay up to the tax man!

CONDUCT OF THE PROOF

7.06 At the proof therefore there are likely to be represented:

1. the Crown, by either an advocate depute or procurator fiscal depute, depending on whether the proof is in the High Court or sheriff court;

2. the accused; and

3. any number of minuters.

There will be before the court the prosecutor's statement, defence answers and any adjustments, minuters' answers, a joint minute of agreement between parties (usually covering the proof of productions and other formal evidence to avoid witnesses from financial institutions requiring to attend) and impact statement schedules.

There is very little practical experience of procedure at confiscation proofs. In fact most confiscation cases settle by means of an agreed amount of the confiscation order between parties which is then imposed by the court. There have only been about half a dozen confiscation proofs and so far these have followed the format in *H.M. Advocate v. McLean*.[3] The practice so far is that the proof will usually open with brief submissions by each representative as to the matters truly in dispute and the order of leading evidence. Although a confiscation proof is part of the criminal proceedings and is part of the accused's sentencing procedure, it tends to have a civil feel about it and certainly the courts have been amenable to hearing opening submissions by each party, if for no reason other than to focus on the matters truly in dispute and to decide who will lead evidence first. PCSA 1995 is silent about the onus of proof

---

[3] 1993 S.C.C.R. 917.

at a confiscation hearing and the standard to be applied. The Crown's position has always been that proposed by the Scottish Law Commission, that the onus is on the Crown and the standard is proof beyond reasonable doubt, on the basis that the proceedings are part of the criminal sentencing process. However because of the practical effects of the assumptions in sections 2 and 3 of the Act and the use to which the prosecutor's statement in section 9 can be put, a practice has grown up of the accused leading evidence first. This allows the Crown's expert witness, usually the consultant accountant, to explain to the court (having heard all the evidence) the effect financially on the prosecutor's statement of accepting or rejecting the defence contentions, usually all as contained in the impact statements. Further, in practice both the Crown and the defence have accountancy experts in court throughout the proof, hearing all the evidence in order to allow both sides to comment constructively on the financial implications. Usually, therefore, the order of evidence will be:

1. the defence, *i.e.* the accused and any witnesses;
2. the minuter and any witnesses; and then
3. the Crown.

At the end of the oral evidence for all parties each side will make submissions. Despite the order it must be borne in mind that the onus of proof beyond reasonable doubt remains on the Crown throughout these criminal proceedings. It is then a matter for the judge to decide first if he is going to exercise his discretion to make a confiscation order and secondly for how much, taking into account the two figures presented to him (the extent of drug trafficking proceeds or "all crime" benefit and then the value of realisable property and implicative gifts or gifts at the date of the proof).

The format of a confiscation proof therefore bears no relation to any other criminal procedure but has evolved as a result of the advantages which the Crown does have under the Act in relation to the use to which it can put the prosecutor's statement and the assumptions in sections 2 and 3.

THE DECISION

Once a confiscation proof has been held, evidence led and submissions made it is a matter for the presiding judge to decide whether to make a confiscation order or not. Any such order 7.07

will refer to both the proceeds or benefit of the crime and the realisable property. The confiscation order must be for the lesser of the two. If the lesser of the two is the realisable property (which is usually the case) there will also be a finding in fact as to the extent of the proceeds or benefit. This is necessary should the Crown discover any further monies at a future date. A confiscation order having been made, the accused is usually given time to pay (as with a fine) and once the order is made it is remitted to the sheriff court for collection.

CHAPTER 8

ENFORCEMENT OF A CONFISCATION ORDER AND THE USE OF ADMINISTRATORS

Once a confiscation order has been made, and bearing in mind **8.01** that it is an order to pay a sum of money and not an order to realise assets, then it is enforced in a fashion similar to a fine unless the order remains unpaid in which case the Crown has powers to seek the appointment of an administrator (see below).

ENFORCEMENT

Section 14 of PCSA 1995 applies to the enforcement of confisca- **8.02** tion orders provisions relating to fines, but with some additional elements.

The usual practice is that if a confiscation order is made in the High Court it is remitted for payment to the sheriff clerk at the sheriff court in the area where the accused would normally reside. If the confiscation order is made in the sheriff court it is paid to the sheriff clerk in that court. As with a fine, therefore, it is the sheriff clerk who is responsible for ingathering the amount due under the confiscation order in the same way as he would ingather monies due by way of a fine. It is a matter for *the accused*, however, to realise his property in order to pay the confiscation order. Obviously he will require some time to do that. Frequently, therefore, when a confiscation order is made, there will be a fixed period of time for repayment. The periods of time for payment of a confiscation order can vary from around three months to 12 months, taking account of whether or not heritable property requires to be sold. Usually all the realisable property will be subject to a restraint order obtained at an earlier stage by the Crown and therefore the Crown requires to remain involved to ensure that the restraint order can be varied and recalled to allow property to be sold and sums paid over to the sheriff clerk. In practice, therefore, the Crown remains very much involved in the realisation of property by liaising with both the defence and the sheriff clerk in order to assist in the ingathering of the funds.

The duty on the accused at this stage (assuming that he wishes to pay the confiscation order) is to give authority to the holders of any realisable assets to realise them, either to be transferred direct to the sheriff clerk (if cash) or to be sold to raise funds to meet the confiscation order. The Crown usually assists by advising the holders of the funds that a confiscation order has been made and that the funds held are now part of the realised property which has been deemed by the court to be either drug trafficking proceeds or "all crime" benefit and if required the Crown will seek to vary the restraint order to allow property to be realised and monies paid to the sheriff clerk.

While it is to be hoped that all this realisation of property can be done within the original time period fixed by the court, frequently this is not the case and the procedure thereafter is that the case will call at the appropriate sheriff court means inquiry court to decide if additional time should be permitted. The sheriff clerk will fix the date and intimate it to both the accused and the Crown. At the means inquiry court both the Crown and the accused will be represented. Section 14(2)(c) gives the prosecutor an opportunity to be heard at any means inquiry court dealing with a confiscation order. In practice, the Crown tends to adopt the position that a confiscation order having been made and there being monies available to pay it, that should be pursued rather than allowing the accused to serve additional time and come out of jail to his illegally acquired funds. So, although section 14(4) provides that if a confiscation order has been made and the accused does not pay either the full amount or any part of it a period of imprisonment or detention can be imposed and that period of imprisonment can only be consecutive and not concurrent, the Crown usually oppose any defence motion to have the alternative imposed and instead seeks extra time to pay on behalf of the accused. This is rather a turnaround from the usual approach at a means inquiry court where the Crown has no role; it is the accused who is usually seeking extra time to pay. The reason is simple; the Act was introduced to ingather illegally acquired funds and if those funds are available then they should be pursued. The Crown seeks additional time to have the funds ingathered because if the accused does not voluntarily realise his property then the Act provides that the Crown can apply to the court to have an administrator appointed to do it for him. Section 16 of and Schedule 1 to the Act contain the rules in relation to administrators.

Therefore, the procedure for enforcing a confiscation order could follow the undernoted suggested timetable:

January 1, 1998: Confiscation order made for £100,000 at the High Court of Justiciary in Edinburgh and remitted to the sheriff court in Glasgow to be ingathered. The accused is given a period of three months to pay. The realisable property includes both moveable and heritable property.

January 1, 1998–March 1, 1998: Crown advises sheriff clerk of its interest and also where the realisable property is held and details of the restraint order. The defence takes steps to realise funds by (a) obtaining mandates from the accused to release funds from banks and building societies to the sheriff clerk and making arrangements for the sale of heritable property or non-cash items such as cars and boats; and (b) liaising with the Crown about the realisation of the property in order to ensure that as required the restraint order is varied.

March 1, 1998: (a) All sums ingathered and paid to the sheriff clerk. The sheriff clerk will then advise the Crown that the confiscation order has been paid and the Crown will recall the restraint order. Any monies restrained which were not deemed to be part of the confiscation order will then be returned to the accused.

(b) If the confiscation order has not been paid on time the sheriff clerk will fix a means inquiry hearing where one of three things may happen:

1. The accused will be given extra time to allow complete realisation of the property (this tends to be the most common outcome if the reason for non-payment is simply properties taking longer to realise than expected).

2. The alternative consecutive sentence is imposed (this is an extremely rare outcome).

3. The Crown requests extra time in order to petition the Court of Session for the appointment of an administrator. (This is only likely at a first means hearing if it is clear that the accused intends to take no steps voluntarily to realise his property.)

Usually if there is genuine difficulty in realising property then the means inquiry court will simply be continued until such time as the property is all realised and the confiscation order paid. If the sums realised fall short of the amount needed to pay the confiscation order then there is power under section 12 to have the confiscation order reduced (see Chapter 9).

ADMINISTRATORS

Section 16 of and Schedule 1 to PCSA 1995 deal with the **8.03** appointment of administrators and the administrator's powers.

The appointment of an administrator at the enforcement stage occurs when the accused is not willing (or perhaps is unable) voluntarily to realise the realisable property. The administrator is appointed to realise the realisable property held both by the accused and by any other person, in order to satisfy the confiscation order. Section 16 makes that purpose clear and further states in section 16(3) that in the case of realisable property held by another person because it has been received as a gift or an implicative gift then the administrator's powers can only be exercised in order to realise the value of that gift and no more. Section 16(6) states that when the administrator is exercising his powers he is to take no account of obligations to third parties by the accused or implicative donees or donees; in other words, confiscation order satisfaction takes precedence over all other debts. This is straightforward, to ensure that no one should be benefiting from crime money. It is severe from the point of view of ordinary creditors who have had no way of knowing that the accused or implicative donee or donee has been involved in either drug trafficking or other crime. In some cases before the stage of appointing an administrator is reached the Crown has been prepared to consider honouring debts due to ordinary creditors by releasing funds from realisable property restrained. That concession, however, depends very much on the circumstances in the individual case.

Appointment and powers

8.04   The Crown can apply to the court to have an administrator appointed in two situations:

1. in terms of Schedule 1(1)(a), in relation to property affected by a restraint order, to manage or otherwise deal with that property. This covers the type of situation where the Crown has restrained an ongoing business and until such time as the accused is convicted or acquitted requires that business to be kept running;

2. in relation to the enforcement in terms of Schedule 1(1)(b), once a confiscation order has been made, in order to realise the property in accordance with the court's directions.

The second situation is dealt with in this chapter. The court may, either on the making of the appointment or at later stages, require any person having possession of the property to give that possession to the administrator. The Crown requires to advise the court of the extent of the realisable property to be covered by the administrator's appointment.

The administrator's role in realising property is fairly similar to that of an insolvency practitioner and administrators appointed so far have been accountants specialising in that field. The functions of the administrator are clearly laid out in paragraph 2 of Schedule 1, all with the purpose of allowing the administrator properly to ingather the realisable property to satisfy the confiscation order. Once all monies have been ingathered then paragraph 4 of Schedule 1 applies. This details the order in which the administrator is to apply the proceeds of realisation:

1. expenses are to be paid to anyone entitled under paragraph 5(2) of Schedule 2 (this covers insolvency practitioners who have incurred expenses without knowing that there was a restraint order in force);

2. payments which the court may direct to be paid out of the proceeds; and

3. the balance goes towards the satisfaction of the confiscation order.

On receipt of that balance the sheriff clerk applies the money:

1. in payment of expenses, including expenses and remunerations due to the administrator, expenses incurred by the Lord Advocate under paragraph 8(2); and

2. in accordance with any directions of the court under section 8(4) or section 13(7) (applying any funds first towards satisfaction of a compensation order made along with a confiscation order and then the balance towards the confiscation order).

It is therefore not in the accused's interests, if he has realisable property which exceeds the confiscation order amount, to have an administrator appointed as he will end up paying these expenses as well as the sum due under the confiscation order.

The administrator's functions, supervision and discharge

The functions of an administrator are listed in paragraph 2 of **8.05** Schedule 1 and that paragraph indicates at the start that the administrator is entitled to take possession of the properties to which he has been appointed. That will be the realisable property of the accused together with all implicative gifts or gifts. In order to fulfil his duties, *i.e.* to realise that property and satisfy the confiscation order, the administrator is given the powers contained in paragraph 2, as follows:

(a) to have access to documents relating to the property or to the accused's assets, business or financial affairs;

(b) to bring, defend or continue any legal proceedings;

(c) to borrow money in order to safeguard the property;

(d) if the administrator considers that it would be beneficial for the realisation of the property, to carry on any business, exercise rights as holder of securities, grant a lease or enter into any contracts, all with regard to the property;

(e) where any right, option or other power forms part of the accused's estate, make payments or incur liabilities in order to obtain and maintain that right, option or power;

(f) effect or maintain insurance policies;

(g) complete title in any case where the accused has uncompleted title;

(h) sell, purchase or exchange property or discharge any securities;

(i) claim, vote or draw dividends in the sequestration of the estate of a debtor of the accused;

(j) discharge any of these functions through agents or employees;

(k) take professional advice;

(l) apply to the court for directions as to discharge of these functions;

(m) exercise any powers specifically conferred on him by the court;

(n) do anything incidental to the above powers and duties.

Under paragraph 5 of the Schedule the administrator is supervised in his duties by the Accountant of Court and if he proposes to exercise any of the functions listed at (b)–(n) above he must first obtain his consent. The accountant of court has a duty, if it appears to him that the administrator is failing to perform the duties imposed on him under the Act, to report the matter to court. Under paragraph (b) of Schedule 1 the administrator is required to keep accounts in relation to all his intromissions with the property and to lodge those accounts with the Accountant of Court at times as fixed by the court. It is thereafter a matter for the Accountant of Court to audit the accounts and issue a determination as to the amount of outlays and remuneration payable to the administrator. Once the administrator has lodged his final accounts he may apply to the Accountant of Court to be discharged from office and this, once granted, frees him from all liability in respect of acts and omissions in exercising his functions.

The administrator and sequestration

Section 44 of and Schedule 2 to the 1995 Act deal with the **8.06** sequestration of persons holding realisable property. The purpose of Schedule 2 is to make it clear when either sequestration or confiscation has priority. It is convenient to deal with it at this stage as it affects the administrator's powers. Basically confiscation and sequestration are not intended to run together and one should always have priority over the other, depending on the timing of events. The two crucial events are the making of a restraint order and the award of sequestration.

If the estate of a person who holds realisable property is sequestrated then his property, both moveable and heritable, already subject to a restraint order is excluded from the debtor's estate for the purposes of the Bankruptcy (Scotland) Act 1985. The sequestration date is given its usual meaning in terms of section 12(4) of the 1985 Act. As far as the restraint order dates are concerned, these differ. For moveable property the relevant date is the date the order was made and for heritable property the relevant date is the date the order was either recorded in the Register of Sasines or registered in the Land Register. The effective dates for moveable and heritable property therefore being excluded from the debtor's estate could differ. It could well happen that if an award of sequestration was made between those two dates moveable property could be excluded from the sequestration, *i.e.* excluded from the debtor's estate, but heritable property included. From a confiscation viewpoint, in order to avoid such an unsatisfactory situation the Crown should ensure that the restraint order is recorded or registered as appropriate as soon as possible after it is made (on the same day, in order to avoid problems).

If the confiscation proceedings are further advanced than the restraint order stage, and no matter whether or not there is even a restraint order in force, but if an administrator has realised any proceeds of property and it is held in his hands, that is excluded from the debtor's estate.

If, however, the position is that the award of sequestration takes place first then certain confiscation powers cannot be used. Restraint orders cannot be made, an administrator cannot be appointed and if an administrator is already appointed then that administrator cannot exercise his functions in relation to the property comprised in the whole estate of the debtor, or any income of the debtor which has been ordered to be paid to the permanent trustee or any estate vesting in the permanent trustee under section 31(10) or 32(6) of the Bankruptcy (Scotland) Act 1985. It is not competent to submit a claim in relation to the confiscation order to the permanent trustee.

If the stage reached in sequestration is only that of an interim trustee being appointed, then his powers do not apply to property subject to a restraint order.

Bearing in mind that the definition of "whole estate of the debtor" under the Bankruptcy (Scotland) Act 1985 and the definition of "realisable property" under PCSA 1995 are different, there may well be tricky questions in relation to whether or not confiscation is still appropriate. Paragraph 5 of Schedule 2 attempts to deal with the gift and implicative gift provisions in relation to sequestration. It provides, first, that where a person sequestrated has made a gift or implicative gift as understood by PCSA 1995, to another, then no decree shall be granted under section 34 or 36 of the Bankruptcy (Scotland) Act 1985 (covering gratuitous alienations and unfair preferences) at any time when proceedings in relation to either an "all crime" offence or drug trafficking offence have been instituted and, secondly, that where the estate of a person is sequestrated and he has made such a gift or implicative gift to another person and that person's property is subject to a restraint order, no decree shall be made in terms of sections 34 and 36 of the Act.

Once confiscation proceedings are concluded then any decree granted under sections 34 and 36 of the Bankruptcy (Scotland) Act 1985 shall take into account any realisation of property held by the donee or implicative donee for confiscation purposes.

Even taking into account the provisions in paragraph 5, it seems that there could still be situations where there could be ongoing prior sequestration proceedings over the debtor's whole estate, as understood by the 1985 Act, but the Crown will still have a right to restrain property which would not fall into the category of either the debtor's whole estate or a gratuitous alienation or unfair preference.

Schedule 2 goes on to deal with realisable property held by a bankrupt in England, held by a company or covered by a floating charge, in paragraphs 2, 3 and 4 respectively, along the same lines.

Perhaps in recognition that the confiscation and sequestration provisions may not sit tidily together, paragraph 5 of Schedule 2 provides insolvency practitioners with some measure of protection from actings in ignorance of a restraint order unless they have been acting negligently.

Chapter 9

MISCELLANEOUS

A New or Altered Confiscation Order

PCSA 1995 provides three situations where there is a right to **9.01**
return to court if there have been difficulties in getting the
confiscation order right first time:

1. where there is an increase in either of the two main
   figures required by the court to exercise its discretion,
   either the proceeds or benefit figure or the realisable
   property figure (section 11);
2. where the realisable property turns out to be less than
   anticipated (section 12); and
3. where the proceeds or benefit are only discovered at a
   later stage (section 13).

Section 11

This section applies where a confiscation order has already been **9.02**
made. It allows the Crown to apply to the court at a later stage
for the making of a new confiscation order:

1. in drug trafficking offence cases where the value of the
   proceeds or the amount that might be realised is greater
   than the amount of either which was taken into account
   when the order was made; and
2. in "all crime" cases where the benefit or the amount that
   might be realised is greater than was taken into account
   at the time the order was made.

Section 11(2) goes on to give examples of situations which may
satisfy the court and includes:

(a) If the drug trafficking proceeds or "all crime" benefit is
    greater than was taken into account originally or has
    increased in value (this can include previously
    undiscovered proceeds or benefits coming to light at a
    later stage).

(b) Further proceeds of drug trafficking or benefit have been
    obtained since the confiscation order was made (this can
    cover both new proceeds or benefit coming to light or

alternatively the accused receiving proceeds or benefit after the confiscation order has been made which were obviously not taken into account at the time).

(c) The value of the realisable property was greater than was taken into account at the time the order was made (*i.e.* hidden property coming to light).

(d) The realisable property which was taken into account at the time has increased in value (this is simply property realising more at sale than the valuation put on it when the confiscation order was made, such as increased property market values).

(e) The amount of a gift that was originally disregarded under section 7(6) can now be realised (*i.e.* property previously thought unlikely to be realised has now become realisable).

Basically this section allows the Crown to return to the court and by section 11(4) have a new confiscation order made if the relevant amounts have increased, the purpose being to prevent the accused from having access to funds that were not anticipated when the confiscation order was made. There are two important restrictions on the Crown in relation to increased confiscation orders. First subsection (3) provides a time-limit of six years. There is absolutely no logical reason for this other than that it accords with the time-limit under the English legislation. The six years run not from the date of the confiscation order but from the earlier date when the accused was convicted. Secondly, and perhaps more importantly, the assumptions applicable first time round in the making of the confiscation order, *i.e.* either under section 3(2) or 2(2) and 5 of PCSA 1995 do not apply to a section 11 application. From a practical point of view this will have more of an effect in relation to increased proceeds or benefit in that it is of course reliance on these assumptions which allows the Crown to point to funds being proceeds or benefit in the first place. There will not be such a difficulty with increased realisable property in the situation where the proceeds or benefit figure in the confiscation order has been greater than the realisable property figure (and that tends to be the more usual case).

Section 12

9.03 Section 12 covers the situation where realisable property turns out to be inadequate to meet the confiscation order, *i.e.* the accused doesn't receive as much for the sale of his assets as everyone has anticipated. This situation is fairly common in practice and tends to happen when the realisable property has included either heritable property which didn't reach the expected figure or, more commonly, moveables such as motor vehicles, jewellery or furniture where values decrease on a daily basis. Section 12 allows the court to recall the confiscation order and substitute an order for a lesser amount. An application can be made in terms of section 12(1) by either the accused or the Crown. It is obviously in the interests of the accused, if the realisable property fails to reach the expected sum, to apply for a reduced confiscation order in order to avoid serving an alternative custodial consecutive sentence in respect of sums of money which are no longer there. There are three points to note about this section:

1. the standard of proof is different from the criminal standard at the confiscation order and is the civil standard of the balance of probabilities;

2. the court is to take into account the extent to which the property is deemed to be part of the estate for the purposes of sequestration or bankruptcy under the Bankruptcy (Scotland) Act 1985 or the Insolvency Act 1986;

3. the court can disregard a reduction in the value of realisable property which is as a result of anything done by the accused for the purposes of protecting the property from realisation.

Section 13

The third situation is where no confiscation order was made at the appropriate time but proceeds or benefit are discovered later. Obviously this can cover a number of situations but the purpose of the section is really to ensure that an accused who has successfully concealed his proceeds or benefit does not escape confiscation proceedings completely. Section 13 provides that where no confiscation order was made under section 1 or section 10 of the Act the Crown can apply to the court to make such an order. Before it can make a confiscation order the court must be satisfied that the information necessary to enable one to be made at the appropriate time was not available to the prosecutor. There are, however, two important restrictions in relation to the making of a confiscation order at a later date under section 13. First, there is a time-limit of six years from the **9.04** date the person was convicted (as in section 11) and secondly, and perhaps more importantly, the assumptions do not apply. This means that the Crown has a fairly restricted period after conviction in which to look for proceeds or benefit and then will not be able to use the normal method of calculation of proceeds or benefit by use of the assumptions in order to convince the court that a confiscation order should be made. It surely follows that a section 13 confiscation order will only be made in those circumstances where the proceeds or benefit can be clearly linked to the crime for which the accused is convicted. That means that the purpose of the section, *i.e.* to ensure that the accused does not fully escape the consequences of the confiscation order by hiding his funds, fails miserably. Because of the restrictions under section 13, clearly if the accused can hide his funds until he can be convicted then it is unlikely that the Crown would be able to confiscate as high a sum as would have been available under a confiscation order made under section 1. If the accused can hide his funds for longer than six years he will escape the consequences of confiscation completely!

Section 46: Is death the end?

9.05   In confiscation cases, sadly not. The Crown and the defence can't just file their papers if an accused dies. Section 46 provides for the forfeiture of property if an accused dies after proceedings have been instituted. Although the term "forfeiture" is used, section 46 relates to those cases where, but for the accused's death, there would have been confiscation proceedings. The purpose of the section is easily understandable: it is to prevent the accused's family living off the proceeds of his crimes after his demise. Whether the section as currently drafted will achieve that purpose is another matter.

Section 46 provides that if criminal proceedings have been instituted, for either a drug trafficking or an "all crime" offence, and the accused dies before he has been sentenced (and remember that confiscation is part of the sentencing process) or otherwise dealt with, the Lord Advocate may apply to the Court of Session for an order to forfeit property. Before that property can be forfeited the Court of Session must be satisfied beyond reasonable doubt that it was property which the accused had obtained directly or indirectly in connection with the commission of either an "all crime" or drug trafficking offence or that the property is a gift or an implicative gift.

In practice this would mean that the Court of Session would require to decide first that the accused committed the offence in terms of section 46(2) (there is no procedure for using an extract conviction) and indeed if proceedings were at a very early stage the trial may not even have taken place, and secondly decide if there is property to be forfeited. If proceedings are at an early stage then the trial may not have taken place before the accused's death, so evidence will have to be led about the offence itself before property forfeiture is considered. The proceedings in terms of subsection (13) are deemed to be civil but the standard of proof is proof beyond reasonable doubt, *i.e.* the original matter is a criminal matter but since the proceedings are civil then the civil rules of evidence would apply. Under section 46(4) there is a time-limit of six years commencing with the date of death of the accused.

It is anticipated that such a section would be rarely used. Further, as section 46 does not provide for the use of either the prosecutor's statement or the assumptions, that deprives the Crown of the normal method of proof of proceeds or benefit and would surely restrict section 46 applications to those cases where any proceeds or benefit can be attributed directly to the crime in respect of which proceedings have been instituted against the accused. Therefore, despite the purpose of the section being to deprive the heirs of the proceeds of the accused's crimes, it is more likely that they will be able to enjoy those fruits if he dies rather than if he lives!

DISPOSAL OF THE FAMILY HOME

9.06 Section 45 is intended to provide a measure of protection where the accused's family is living in the family home. Previously there was no such protection under the Criminal Justice (Scotland) Act 1987.

Section 45(1) provides that where a confiscation order is made and the prosecutor has not satisfied the court that the interest in the family home was acquired either by drug trafficking proceeds or "all crime" benefit then before the Crown can dispose of any right or interest in that family home it must obtain the consent of the individual who lives there. If the family home is occupied by the spouse or former spouse then his or her consent must be obtained and if it is occupied by the accused and any child of the family then the accused's consent must be obtained.

If the Crown is unable to obtain this consent then before it can dispose of any right or interest in the family home it must apply to the court for authority either for an action for division and sale or an action to obtain vacant possession. In determining the application the court is to have regard to all the circumstances including both the needs and financial resources of the spouse and child, and the length of time the house has been used as the family home.

The definition of "family home" in section 45(5) includes property occupied by the spouse or former spouse and children but does not include unmarried partners.

DECISIONS—REPORTED AND UNREPORTED

9.07 There is not a great body of case law on confiscation. Legislation is still of course fairly recent and there have been very few confiscation cases which have proceeded to a confiscation proof. In practice most of the confiscation cases settle, the Crown having the upper hand once the accused has been convicted, provided that it has made proper use of the prosecutor's statement and assumptions. The undernoted cases indicate areas the court have considered to date:

H.M. Advocate v. McLean[1]

9.08 This was the first case to give full consideration to the confiscation provisions of the Criminal Justice (Scotland) Act 1987 and it gave practitioners an idea of how the courts viewed the legislation.

Ian McLean was convicted of a contravention of section 4(3)(b) of the Misuse of Drugs Act 1971 in respect of one date only, February 11, 1992 (the jury, on delivering its verdict, deleted earlier dates). He was sentenced to eight years' imprisonment. The case proceeded to a confiscation proof before Lord Sutherland. The Crown confiscation case was based on the method of financial analysis as described in Chapter 5. This approach, together with the appropriate use of the prosecutor's statement and assumptions, was considered correct by the court. The case can be read for its specific facts but, interestingly, certain matters arose which thereafter became commonplace in confiscation cases, namely:

[1] 1993 S.C.C.R. 917.

1. the inclusion of the accused's earnings not disclosed to the Inland Revenue but nonetheless regarded by the court as income, consequently reducing his drug trafficking proceeds (it was then a matter for the accused and the taxman to sort out what was due later);

2. the inclusion of monies relating to a charge on which the accused was acquitted but nonetheless deemed to be proceeds of drug trafficking in view of the statutory assumptions the court was entitled to make; and

3. the value of the drugs (which were forfeited at the end of the trial) included as the accused's assets (not, obviously, as realisable property) with the resultant increase in the drug trafficking proceeds figure.

H.M. Advocate v. Rowan[2]

This was a petition for an order to declare that property was not **9.09** an implicative gift under section 6(3) of PCSA 1995.

On May 22, 1996 Arthur Rowan pled guilty to a contravention of section 4(3)(b) of the Misuse of Drugs Act 1971. His wife, Victoria Rowan, who appeared on the same indictment, tendered a plea of not guilty which was accepted by the Crown. Arthur Rowan was sentenced to nine years' imprisonment and a forfeiture order was made for the sum of £137, 960. At a later hearing the Crown moved for a confiscation order for the sum of £165, 596 which was the total of Arthur Rowan's realisable assets less the forfeited sum. A confiscation order was made unopposed and without either Victoria Rowan or David Rowan (the accused's son) being party to the proceedings.

Thereafter both Victoria Rowan and David Rowan petitioned the court in terms of section 6(3) that among other things one of the items deemed to be realisable property, a house at 1 Cityford Crescent, Rutherglen, Glasgow, stated to be an implicative gift by Arthur Rowan to Victoria Rowan, was not such an implicative gift. In addition David Rowan's petition stated that he had an interest in the property as he was living there with his family. The circumstances surrounding the house at 1 Cityford Crescent appeared to be that during the relevant period (six years preceding service of the indictment) Arthur Rowan had given the sum of £56,000 to David Rowan in order to redeem the mortgage in David Rowan's name. Thereafter

[2] 1997 G.W.D. 12–512 (Lord Morison, February 26, 1997).

David Rowan transferred title to the property to his mother, Victoria Rowan, for love, favour and affection. According to the petition the understanding within the family had been that when he had repaid the £56,000 to Arthur Rowan the title would be transferred back to him. David Rowan's petition did not disclose the reason for the transfer of title to his mother except to say that he understood it would benefit Arthur Rowan. On the date of the hearing before Lord Morison the Crown and Victoria Rowan tendered a joint minute agreeing that £56,000 of the cost of acquiring 1 Cityford Crescent, Rutherglen came from Arthur Rowan and therefore since the title was now in Victoria Rowan's name she acknowledged that the value of that asset to the extent of £56,000 was recoverable from her as an implicative gift. The petitioner David Rowan maintained his position that he had an interest in the property as he lived there with his family and any sale would bring hardship to him. Lord Morison took the view that there was no legal basis on which Rowan was entitled to oppose the order, having conveyed it to his mother, and that he occupied it without title only so long as his mother permitted him to do so.

H.M. Advocate v. Adamson[3] and *Adamson v. H.M. Advocate*[4]

9.10   This case relates to a plea to the relevancy of the prosecutor's claim under section 9 of PCSA 1995.

The accused had pleaded guilty to the reset of 72 laptop computers on December 21, 1996 and to reset of one computer on December 9, 1996. According to the Crown he therefore fell into the category of an "all crime" "double offence" offender. The prosecutor's statement lodged in court applied the assumptions under section 2(4) and (5).

The defence plea to the relevancy was that in terms of section 1(4) of the Act the court was restricted as to when the assumptions could be used, that there was a distinction between drug trafficking and "all crime" cases and that in "all crime" cases, such as Adamson's, the court had to be satisfied that the accused had benefited from the commission of *the offence concerned*. If the defence position was accepted by the court it would have had the effect of restricting the confiscation order to

---

[3] 1999 G.W.D. 4–191 (Sheriff Forbes, Dunfermline, September 29, 1998).

[4] High Court on Appeal, October 20, 1999, unreported (Appeal No. C434/99).

the direct benefit in relation to the offences of which the accused was convicted. Indeed the defence position was that there should be before the court "prima facie evidence linking the accused's assets to the offences to which he had pleaded guilty in (the) indictment".

The Crown maintained that the accused fell into the category of a "double crime" offender and "confiscation fell to be calculated over a six-year period going back from the date of institution of the proceedings". The Crown went on to say that if the accused fell into that category where the assumptions were allowed, *i.e.* as in this case, then "it was not necessary to see if there was a link between his assets and the commission of the offences to which he has pleaded guilty on indictment".

The sheriff agreed with the Crown and stated that in his view "Parliament must have had it in mind that a criminal with convictions for two or more offences should be liable to confiscation procedures in relation to past activities which might no doubt be incapable of proof by the Crown". He further stated that he considered "that the proper interpretation to be placed upon section 2(4)(a) of the Act is that the court is entitled to consider factors such as the large quantity of money in the possession of the respondent which cannot reasonably be accounted for by the respondent and make assumptions in relation to it even in the absence of any proof that it accrued from criminal conduct".

This case proceeded to a confiscation proof and on July 1, 1999 Sheriff Forbes made a confiscation order for £89,614 (that being the "benefit of crime" figure and the lower in this case) and a finding in fact that the accused had realisable property valued at £296,792. In his opinion, issued on February 1, 1999, Sheriff Forbes accepted the Crown methodology in calculating benefit as described in Chapter 5.

Adamson appealed against the Sheriff Forbes' decision and his appeal was upheld on October 20, 1999 and the confiscation order was quashed. This is one of the most important decisions in relation to "all crime" confiscation because the Appeal Court, *per* Lord Sutherland, rejected the Crown's contention that in a "double crime" case the use of the confiscation assumptions was as wide as in drug trafficking cases and permitted the Crown to go back six years and analyse the accused's finances without linking his assets to the commission of the offences. Instead the Appeal Court criticised PCSA 1995 as being unclear and *per* Lord Sutherland stated: "Where the construction of legislation is in doubt, it is legitimate as an aid to construction to consider what was the clear intention of Parliament. It is not in our view at all clear that Parliament intended that the sort of regime which applies in drug trafficking cases should also be applied in non drug trafficking cases. Furthermore if Parliament intends to introduce what would be fairly draconian legislation it must do so in terms which make it clear what the legislation means."

These comments were made in relation to the proper construction to be placed on sections 2(4) and 2(5) in light of the definition of relevant offences in sections 1(2) and 1(6). The Court held that the correct approach was only to have regard to "an offence which has been prosecuted". This decision prevents the Crown from carrying out the same sort of financial exercise in "all crime" cases as in drug trafficking cases by looking at the accused's assets built up in the preceding six years. It restricts the financial calculation to the assets obtained and expenditure in relation to offences prosecuted. It follows, therefore, that in "double crime" cases the amount of benefit will need to be linked to the crimes of which the accused has been prosecuted. If any financial analysis turned up unexplained income then the Court could only regard it to the extent of actual benefit for the purpose of making a confiscation order.

Carnegie v. McKechnie[5]

9.11 This decision relates to an appeal by the procurator fiscal from a decision by the sheriff at Greenock to refuse to grant a restraint order in an "all crime" case.

William McKechnie appeared on petition at Greenock Sheriff Court on December 11, 1998. On the same date the Crown made a summary application for a restraint order. The importance of the case is that it allowed the appeal court to rule on the poor wording of section 1(2) in relation to the requirements for obtaining a restraint order in terms of section 29(2)(a) under PCSA 1995. A restraint order (as referred to in Chapter 3) can be obtained in relation to proceedings for an offence to which Part I of PCSA 1995 applies. Those offences are referred to in section 1(2) and that section states that "this part applies to any offence which *has been* prosecuted" (emphasis added). As the appeal court stated in its decision, this provision was unhappily worded in relation to its use to define the circumstances in which a restraint order might be made following the institution of proceedings but before conviction. In particular the words "any

<hr>

5 1999 S.L.T. 536.

offence which has been prosecuted (a) on indictment were difficult to reconcile with a situation in which proceedings had only just been instituted and where, at that stage, no indictment had been prepared or served. That was the principal difficulty which had prevented the sheriff from granting the application".

The court, however, took the view that it was necessary to look at section 1(2) in order to adopt a workable interpretation and that the provisions of section 29(2) in association with those of section 49(6) showed that it was "the intention of Parliament that restraint orders might be pronounced in appropriate circumstances immediately following the institution of proceedings against an individual which section 49(6) shows could occur at a time where no indictment was or could be in existence". The court stated that "In those circumstances we consider the provisions of section 1(2) require to be read in a sense which renders the implement of the evident intention of Parliament practicable". The court then went on to comment that section 1(2) in correlation to section 29 was "an inept example of parliamentary draftsmanship". The decision at the end of the day made it clear that restraint orders are permitted in "all crime" cases in the same circumstances as for drug trafficking, *i.e.* at the very earliest 28 days before the institution of proceedings.

H.M. Advocate v. Donnelly[6] and *Donnelly v. H.M. Advocate*[6a]

The accused was convicted of a contravention of section 4(3)(b) **9.12** of the Misuse of Drugs Act 1971 in relation to being concerned in the supply of heroin on an occasion between January 20, 1995 and April 25, 1995. After his conviction on April 19, 1996, the advocate depute moved for a confiscation order under section 1 of the Proceeds of Crime (Scotland) Act 1995. A prosecutor's statement was lodged and the realisable property included implicative gifts by the accused to his wife, his mother, his brother and a business associate.

A confiscation proof was held in May 1997 and there was representation from the Crown, the accused and the minuter, the accused's wife, Allison Donnelly. There were oral submissions, written submissions consisting of the prosecutor's statement, defence answers, minuter's answers, joint minute of agreement and an impact statement and there was evidence led from all three parties, including evidence from both Crown and

---

[6] Lord Bonomy, June 13, 1997, unreported.
[6a] 1999 S.C.C.R. 508.

defence accountants. There was no evidence to identify any particular sums of money as relating directly to either the drugs transaction of which the accused was convicted or any other drugs transaction during the relevant period (in Donnelly's case, five years), but it was accepted by all parties that the accused had handled large sums and purchased many assets during the relevant period. The Crown used the prosecutor's statement and the assumptions under the Act to show that the accused had drug trafficking proceeds. The Crown's position was that the standard of proof was proof beyond reasonable doubt in order to determine the transfer of property to the accused and his expenditure during the relevant period. The defence position was that Alexander Donnelly had not been engaged in drug trafficking, that some of the assets attributed to him were not his (the implicative gifts), that he had not spent any money on them and that he had a very substantial income from businesses in respect of which he had kept few records and no accounting had been made for tax.

Lord Bonomy accepted the Crown approach which was to rely on the considerable build-up in assets and substantial expenditure of the accused over the five-year period, demonstrating the absence of any satisfactory explanation that he had proceeds from drug trafficking, using the type of financial analysis in Chapter 5. Lord Bonomy made a confiscation order in the sum of £270,000.

His decision was appealed but was upheld by the appeal court in May 1999.[6b]

ARRANGEMENTS WITH FOREIGN STATES

9.13 The confiscation provisions under PCSA 1995 and CLCSA 1995 would be of very limited value if it were not recognised that criminals moved their assets around the globe and that rules designed to seize those assets must take account of that. Part IV of PCSA 1995 therefore contains rules for the enforcement of restraint and confiscation orders made in England, Wales, Northern Ireland and abroad. Briefly, the position is as follows:

England and Wales

9.14 Sections 35 and 38 cover orders made in England and Wales and provide for their recognition and enforcement by application to the Court of Session. Sections 37 and 38 provide for

---

[6b] *Donnelly v. H.M. Advocate*, 1999 S.C.C.R. 508.

the inhibition and arrestment of Scottish property covered by said English or Welsh orders, on the application of the Lord Advocate.

Perhaps of more interest to the Scottish practitioner is section 42 which provides for the making of Orders in Council in relation to enforcement of Scottish restraint and confiscation orders in England and Wales. The relevant statutory instrument is the Drug Trafficking Offences (Enforcement in England and Wales) Order 1988. It would appear that this only applies to drug trafficking and there is not yet an order in force for "all crime" cases.[7]

Northern Ireland

Section 39 refers to Northern Ireland and provides for the **9.15** enforcement of orders made in Northern Ireland in Scotland by means of Orders in Council. The relevant order is the Proceeds of Crime (Scotland) Act 1995 (Enforcement of Northern Ireland Orders) Order 1998[8] and relates to restraint and confiscation orders made after May 1, 1998.

Abroad

Outwith the United Kingdom sections 40 and 41 provide for **9.16** Orders in Council to be made for the registration of foreign restraint and confiscation orders. The relevant order is the Confiscation of the Proceeds of Crime (Designated Countries and Territories) (Scotland) Order 1999.[9] There are two lists of designated countries; one for drug trafficking (Part 1 of Schedule 1) which lists 152 countries, and one for "all crime" which only lists 27 countries.

The United Kingdom has confiscation arrangements with these countries and their legislation will include provisions to give effect to Scottish orders covering assets in their country.

In practice it frequently arises that the accused facing criminal charges in Scotland and subject to confiscation proceedings here has assets abroad in drug trafficking cases, commonly Spain or the USA. The procedure once a restraint order has been made is for the Crown to seek to have that order enforced by letter of request through normal diplomatic channels to the equivalent prosecuting authorities abroad. The incentive for countries to

---

[7] S.I. 1988 No. 593.
[8] S.I. 1998 No. 752.
[9] S.I. 1999 No. 673.

co-operate, apart from assistance in the fight against crime, is that once confiscation proceedings are concluded each country can retain what has been found there. In the case of *H.M. Advocate v. Donnelly*[10] property in Florida bought as a family holiday home was seized by the United States enforcement authorities as drug trafficking proceeds in their country.

---

[10] Lord Bonomy, July 1997, unreported; *Donnelly v. H.M. Advocate*, 1999 S.C.C.R. 508.

APPENDIX 1

THE CONFISCATION TIMETABLE

MODEL FICTITIOUS EXAMPLE

Charles Owen Caine is 41 years of age. He resides in Glasgow with his wife, Anne Caine, and two dependent children.

He was arrested on November 20, 1997 after a drug squad surveillance operation. He appeared at Glasgow Sheriff Court on November 21, 1997 on a petition containing contraventions of the Misuse of Drugs Act 1971 and including a contravention of section 4(3)(b) in respect of Class A drugs having a street value of £100,000 found during a search of his home. During that search drugs squad officers also seized cash and documentation relating to his financial assets. Information obtained during the search and the surveillance operation shows that he has considerable assets in Scotland and abroad.

Typically, proceedings against Charles Owen Caine could proceed according to the timetable attached and the styles in Appendix 2.

CONFISCATION TIMETABLE

Date	Procedure
November 20, 1997	Charles Owen Caine arrested and charged with contravention of section 4(3)(b) of the Misuse of Drugs Act 1971 (street value of drugs £100,000; wholesale value £10,000).
November 21, 1997	Petition appearance at Glasgow Sheriff Court. Petition contains the contravention of section 4(3)(b) of the Misuse of Drugs Act 1971 in relation to the £100,000 worth of drugs found at Charles Caine's home. Accused committed for further examination.
November 21, 1997	Restraint order granted at Court of Session (as trial potentially a High Court trial). Restraint order served on accused and his wife, Anne Caine, and intimated to all holders of the funds. (See Appendix 2, Style II.)
November 21, 1997	Charles Caine discusses the implications of the restraint order with his agents and if appropriate a variation of restraint order is obtained at the Court of Session (normally to release funds for living expenses and essential costs until date of trial).
November 27, 1997	Charles Caine reappears at Glasgow Sheriff Court and is fully committed and granted bail.
November 27, 1997— March 18, 1998	Crown and defence prepare for trial. Information is ingathered by means of production orders. (See Appendix 2, Style I.) During this period the Crown will also prepare a financial analysis of the accused to be used as a prosecutor's statement in the event of conviction. It would be in the accused's interests during this period to instruct an accountant. During this period the Crown will also by the usual diplomatic channels send a letter of request to any appropriate foreign authorities (in Caine's case, Spain) in order to have the restraint order registered and enforced in that country.

March 18, 1998	Trial at Glasgow High Court. Accused convicted of a contravention of section 4(3)(b) in respect of the drugs found in his house. Immediately following the jury verdict Mr Caine is served with the prosecutor's statement. (See Appendix 2, Style III.) The prosecutor's statement is lodged with the clerk of court at that stage. While moving for sentence the advocate depute seeks a confiscation order against Mr Caine in terms of section 1 of PCSA 1995.
	The accused is sentenced to six years' imprisonment. In respect of the confiscation proceedings the judge allows the defence four weeks to consider the prosecutor's statement and lodge answers in terms of section 9 of PCSA 1995. A hearing in respect of the statement and answers is fixed for six weeks ahead.
By April 15, 1998	The defence lodges answers with the clerk of court (Justiciary) and sends a copy of the answers to the Crown. (See Appendix 2, Style IV.)
April 22, 1998	Confiscation hearing at High Court, Edinburgh. The Crown indicates that the answers submitted by the defence require proof and are not acceptable in full. The accused's wife, Mrs Anne Caine, enters appearance as a minuter. She is given four weeks to consider the prosecutor's statement and defence answers and if she so wishes to lodge answers. Further hearing fixed five weeks ahead to consider Mrs Caine's answers.
May 20, 1998	Answers lodged on behalf of minuter, Mrs Anne Caine, and copies sent to the Crown and to the accused, Mr Charles Caine.
May 27, 1998	Confiscation hearing at High Court, Edinburgh. At this hearing the Crown indicates that proof is required and a hearing in terms of section 9 of PCSA 1995 requires to be held in respect of the prosecutor's statement and the answers lodged by Charles Caine and Anne Caine. The court fixes a hearing in terms of section 9, three months ahead.
August 18, 1998	Confiscation hearing at High Court, Edinburgh in terms of section 9 of PCSA 1995, usually referred to as a proof. At the proof there will be written submissions as follows:
	1. prosecutor's statement;
	2. defence answers;
	3. minuter's answers;
	4. joint minute containing matters agreed between the parties (normally in relation to all productions lodged by both sides to prevent financial representatives requiring to appear at court);
	5. impact statement—this is a document which has in practice been agreed between Crown and defence prior to the confiscation hearing to illustrate to the court the effect of the presiding judge accepting certain pieces of evidence. It is a voluntary matter between parties and is normally prepared by the Crown with a view to cutting down the length of the confiscation proof.

	There will also of course be appropriate evidence from witnesses on both sides. After hearing the evidence and considering submissions at the proof the presiding judge makes a confiscation order in the sum of £300,000 against Charles Owen Caine and he is given three months to pay. The order is remitted to the sheriff clerk at Glasgow to ingather.
From July 18, 1998 onwards	Mr Caine's agents should obtain the appropriate mandates from him in order to commence realisation of the assets. Liaison with the Crown is necessary to ensure that the restraint order can be varied if required to allow assets to be sold, etc. If the assets are realised quickly and the sum sent in full to the sheriff clerk at Glasgow there will be no further procedure. If the assets are not realised quickly then at the end of the three-month period the sheriff clerk at Glasgow will convene a means inquiry court with a view to enforcing payment. (See Chapter 8.) During this period the Crown will also intimate to the foreign authorities holding funds that a confiscation order has been made, thus allowing them to take steps to retain those funds.
October 18, 1998	The confiscation order has been paid in full. The sheriff clerk advises the Crown of this and the restraint order is recalled.

APPENDIX 2

STYLES

STYLE I

PETITION FOR PRODUCTION ORDER (SHERIFF COURT)

UNDER THE CRIMINAL LAW (CONSOLIDATION) (SCOTLAND)
ACT 1995
IN THE SHERIFF COURT OF GLASGOW AND STRATHKELVIN
AT GLASGOW
THE PETITION OF THE REGIONAL PROCURATOR FISCAL,
GLASGOW AND STRATHKELVIN

Glasgow: December 20, 1997

HUMBLY SHEWETH:

That there are reasonable grounds for suspecting that CHARLES OWEN CAINE, Rose Cottage, Leafy Lane, Anytown has carried out or has benefited from drug trafficking and the Petitioner has a duty to investigate same. That the Bank of Caledonia, Downtown Branch, Glasgow appears to be in possession of material relevant to said investigation, viz. all documentation of whatever nature relative to the opening and operation of account numbers 00777515 and 00189470 in the name of Charles Owen Caine.

That there are reasonable grounds for suspecting that said material:

   (i)   is likely to be of substantial value (by itself or together with other material) to said investigation; and

  (ii)   does not consist of or include items subject to legal privilege.

That there are reasonable grounds for believing that it is in the public interest, having regard:

   (i)   to the benefit likely to accrue to said investigation if said material is obtained; and

  (ii)   to the circumstances under which said Bank of Caledonia, Downtown Branch, Glasgow in possession of said material holds it;

that said material should be produced.

> The petitioner therefore craves the court to order in terms of section 31(2)(a) of the Criminal Law (Consolidation) (Scotland) Act 1995, said Bank of Caledonia, Downtown Branch, Glasgow to produce said material for Detective Constable John Smith of Strathclyde Police to take away within seven days of the date of this order.
> And further in respect that said material may consist of information contained in a computer to order in terms of section 31(7)(a) of

such Act that said material be produced in a form in which it can be taken away and in which it is visible and legible or to do further or otherwise as to your Lordship may deem appropriate.

ACCORDING TO JUSTICE

Principal Procurator Fiscal Depute

At GLASGOW the   day of   [year].

The Sheriff having considered the foregoing Petition grants Warrant as craved.

SHERIFF

STYLE II

Petition for restraint order (Court of Session)

This style application for a restraint order is based on the Charles Caine example. It does not specifically state all Charles Caine's assets but only those known to the Crown at the time the order is sought. In the example stocks and shares, life insurance policies and pension policies are excluded as, typically, these items could have come to light later. That does not mean that the restraint order is not effective against these assets as far as Charles Caine is concerned because obviously he knows what he owns and the restraint order is framed in general terms. In practice once these items come to light during the financial investigation the Crown will intimate the restraint order to the holders of the funds, thus making it fully effective against them too.

IN THE COURT OF SESSION

PETITION
of
THE RIGHT HONOURABLE
THE LORD HARDIE

against

CHARLES OWEN CAINE, presently
a prisoner in HMP Barlinnie

FIRST RESPONDENT

ANNE CAINE, Rose Cottage, Leafy Lane, Anytown

SECOND RESPONDENT

MARGARET CAINE, Flat 1/1, 1742 Argyll Road, Anytown

THIRD RESPONDENT

for

A restraint order in terms of
section 28 of the Proceeds of
Crime (Scotland) Act 1995

HUMBLY SHEWETH:

1. That the Proceeds of Crime (Scotland) Act 1995 (herein referred to as "the Act") makes provision by section 28 in the circumstances described in said section and in section 29 of the Act interdicting (a) a person in respect of whom it is made and (b) any persons named in the order as appearing to the court to have received an implicative gift as defined by section 6 from dealing with their own or the other's realisable property as defined by section 4 *inter alia* in cases where the circumstances mentioned in section 29(2) apply, namely where proceedings have been instituted against an accused in Scotland for an offence to which Part I of the Act applies, proceedings have not concluded and either a confiscation order has been made or it appears to the court that in the event of conviction of the accused of the

offence there are reasonable grounds for thinking that a confiscation order may be made in those proceedings. Section 32 of the Act empowers the court to grant warrant for inhibition against any property interdicted by a restraint order in respect of heritable realisable property in Scotland affected by the restraint order and section 33 of the Act empowers the court to grant warrant for arrestment of moveable realisable property affected by a restraint order.

2. On November 21, 1997 Charles Owen Caine appeared on petition at Glasgow Sheriff Court and was committed for further examination. He was remanded in custody. The said Charles Owen Caine has been charged with a contravention of section 4(3)(b) of the Misuse of Drugs Act 1971. A copy of said petition in respect of said offences is produced and referred to for its terms which are held as repeated herein *brevitatis causa.*

3. The second-named respondent, Anne Caine, is the wife of the first-named respondent, Charles Owen Caine.

4. The third-named respondent, Margaret Caine, is the sister of the first-named repondent, Charles Owen Caine.

5. The heritable estate of the said Charles Owen Caine held by him includes:

  (a) the dwelling-house at Rose Cottage, Leafy Lane, Anytown;
  (b) Flat 2/1, 1742 Argyll Road, Anytown;
  (c) the dwelling-house at Acacia Villa, San Toro, Spain.

The moveable estate of said Charles Owen Caine held by him includes:

  (a) the sum at credit of bank account numbers 00777515 and 00189470 at the Bank of Caledonia, Downtown Branch, Glasgow;
  (b) the sum at credit of account number 18–242–7194 at Anytown Building Society, Glasgow;
  (c) the sum at credit of account number BST81296CAI at the Bank of San Toro, Spain;
  (d) motor vehicles C41 NEC (Audi Cabriolet) and H10 WEN (Mitsubishi Shogun);
  (e) the sum of £4,064 in cash seized by the police from the possession of said Charles Owen Caine ;
  (f) a jet ski;
  (g) two boats and a trailer;
  (h) a Rolex watch;
  (i) personal jewellery valued at £5,000;
  (j) a TV and video within the premises of Rose Cottage, valued at £1,250.

6. The heritable estate of the said Anne Caine held by her includes:

  (a) the dwelling-house at Rose Cottage, Leafy Lane, Anytown.

The moveable estate of the said Anne Caine held by her includes:

  (a) the sum at credit of account number 00101202 at the Bank of Caledonia;
  (b) the sum at credit of account numbers 18–242–7194 and 72–196–8003 at the Anytown Building Society.

7. The heritable estate of the said Margaret Caine held by her includes:

(a) the dwelling-house at Flat 1/1, 1742 Argyll Road, Anytown.

8. The said Anne Caine has insufficient sources of income known to the prosecutor which account for the acquisition of her interest in the said items of heritable and moveable estate as above mentioned and thus said items represent implicative gifts by the said Charles Caine to the said Anne Caine within the meaning of section 6 of the Act.

9. The said Margaret Caine has insufficient sources of income known to the prosecutor which account for the acquisition of her interest in the said items of heritable estate as above mentioned and thus said item represents an implicative gift by the said Charles Caine to the said Margaret Caine within the meaning of section 6 of the Act.

10. The petitioner is desirous is in the foregoing circumstances to obtain (a) a restraint order in respect of the realisable property of the said Charles Caine and (b) a restraint order in respect of any dealing by the said Anne Caine and Margaret Caine with the realisable property of the said Charles Caine and without prejudice to that generality his interest in the said items of heritable and moveable estate above mentioned and their interest in any implicative gifts received by them from him and without prejudice to that generality the said Anne Caine's interests in the said items of heritable and moveable estate above mentioned and the said Margaret Caine's interests in the said items of heritable estate above mentioned.

May it therefore please your Lordships to make a restraint order against the said CHARLES CAINE in terms of section 28 of the Act interdicting him from dealing with his realisable property and in particular and without prejudice to that generality with:

(a) the dwelling-house at Rose Cottage, Leafy Lane, Anytown;

(b) the dwelling-house at Flat 2/1, 1742 Argyll Road, Anytown;

(c) the dwelling-house at Acacia Villa, San Toro, Spain;

(d) the sums at credit of account numbers 00777515 and 00189470 at the Bank of Caledonia and account number 18–242–7194 at Anytown Building Society;

(e) the sum at credit of account number BST18296CAI at the Bank of San Toro, Spain;

(f) motor vehicles C41 NEC and H10 WEN;

(g) the sum of £4,064 in cash;

(h) a jet ski, two boats and a trailer;

(i) a Rolex watch, personal jewellery to the value of £5,000 and a TV and video;

to make a restraint order against the said Anne Caine by virtue of section 28 of the Act interdicting her from dealing with the realisable property of the said Charles Caine and her interest in any implicative gifts received from him and in particular and without prejudice to that generality with:

(a) the dwelling-house at Rose Cottage, Leafy Lane, Anytown;

(b) the sum at credit of account number 00101202, Bank of Caledonia;

(c) the sums at credit of account numbers 18–242–7194 and 72–196–8003 at Anytown Building Society;

to make a restraint order against the said Margaret Caine by virtue of section 28 of the Act interdicting her from dealing with the realisable property of the said Charles Owen Caine and her interests in any implicative gift received from him and in particular and without prejudice to that generality with:

(a)   the dwelling-house at Flat 1/1, 1742 Argyll Road, Anytown;

to appoint the petitioner to give notice of the said order upon the persons named and designed in the schedule appended hereto; to grant warrant for inhibition and arrestment or to do further or otherwise in the premises as to your Lordships shall seem proper.

According to Justice.

Interlocutor

A typical interlocutor then issued would therefore read:

"The Lord Ordinary [etc.] . . . makes a restraint order against Charles Owen Caine and by virtue of section 28 of the Act interdicts him from dealing with his realisable property and in particular and without prejudice to that generality with the dwelling-house at Rose Cottage, Leafy Lane, Anytown, the house at Flat 2/1, 1742 Argyll Road, Anytown, the dwelling-house at Acacia Villa, San Toro, Spain, the sums at credit of account numbers 00777515 and 00189470 at the Bank of Caledonia, the sum at credit of account number 18–242–7194 at Anytown Building Society, the sum at credit of account number BST18296CAI at the Bank of San Toro, Spain, motor vehicles registration numbers C41 NEC and H10 WEN, the sum of £4,064 in cash, a jet ski, two boats, a trailer, a Rolex watch, personal jewellery to the value of £5,000 and a TV and video recorder; and makes a restraint order against Anne Caine by virtue of section 28 of the Act and interdicts her from dealing with the realisable property of the said Charles Caine and her interest in any implicative gifts received from him and in particular and without prejudice to that generality with the dwelling-house at Rose Cottage, Leafy Lane, Anytown, the sum at credit of account number 00101202 at the Bank of Caledonia and the sums at credit of account numbers 18–242–7194 and 72–196–8003 at Anytown Building Society; and makes a restraint order against Margaret Caine by virtue of section 28 of the Act and interdicts her from dealing with the realisable property of the said Charles Caine and her interest in any implicative gifts received from him and in particular and without prejudice to that generality with the dwelling-house at Flat 1/1, 1742 Argyll Road, Anytown; appoints the petitioner to give notice of the said orders upon the persons named and designed in the schedule appended hereto; grants warrant for inhibition and arrestment."

[Judge]

STYLE III

Prosecutor's statement

It should be remembered that the six year period is calculated from the date of service of the indictment in drug trafficking cases. It is common practice therefore for the financial analysis to use only that five year period preceding the date of arrest in bail cases provided the accused's assets were restrained around the same time.

IN THE HIGH COURT OF JUSTICIARY

Under section 9 of the Proceeds of Crime (Scotland) Act 1995

Statement by the Prosecutor

in causa

Her Majesty's Advocate

against

Charles Owen Caine

1. The statement by the prosecutor contains seven schedules all as attached hereto. Said schedules contain financial information in respect of Charles Owen Caine and are referred to in detail for their terms.

2. Schedule 1 is a calculation of the proceeds of drug trafficking of Charles Owen Caine and shows his total expenditure as the sum of:

A	the increase or decrease of assets over liabilities from the start to the end of the years there specified; and
B	his total other expenditure as detailed in said schedule including bank withdrawals, other expenditure and living expenses:

from which total sum (C) is then deducted:

D	his income so far as ascertained by the prosecutor, bringing out expenditure funded other than from known sources in respect of the years 1993–97.
C	Such expenditure, amounting *in cumulo* to £372,826, represents the proceeds of drug trafficking of Charles Owen Caine.

3. Schedule 2 specifies at cost the assets and liabilities of Charles Owen Caine and the balance of assets and liabilities at the dates there mentioned. Said accompanying Schedules 2.1 to 2.15 explain said calculations in detail. All said schedules are referred to for their terms.

4. Schedule 3 and accompanying Schedule 3.1 explain the balances, lodgments, withdrawals and interest credited in the bank and building society accounts detailed in said schedules. Said schedules are referred to for their terms. Said schedules have been adjusted, taking account of inter-account transfers, to avoid double counting.

5. Schedule 4 and accompanying Schedule 4.1 detail expenditure including payments made in cash or from an unknown source. Said schedules are referred to for their terms.

6. Schedule 5 details the household expenditure of Charles Owen Caine and Anne Caine, his wife, based on government statistics for the years there specified. The weekly expenditure figures from the government statistics have been reduced to take account of items paid through bank accounts, in order to avoid double counting.

7. Schedule 6 details the known income so far as can be ascertained by the prosecutor of Charles Caine and Anne Caine.

8. Schedule 7 details the realisable property together with the value of all implicative gifts of Charles Caine and includes implicative gifts made to Anne Caine and Margaret Caine so far as can be ascertained by the prosecutor and amounting in total to £663,475.

9. On November 21, 1997 the Lord Ordinary in the Court of Session made an order in terms of sections 28 and 29 of the Proceeds of Crime (Scotland) Act 1995 interdicting Charles Owen Caine, Anne Caine and Margaret Caine from dealing with his realisable property and implicative gifts and granted warrant for inhibition and arrestment in terms of the Act. A copy of the relevant petition and interlocutors are annexed to this statement and referred to for their terms *brevitatis causa*.

Advocate Depute

CHARLES OWEN CAINE *SUMMARY*

Summary of the Crown Position

Value of Proceeds of Drug Trafficking

As detailed in Schedule 1 £372,826

Value of Realisable Property

As detailed in Schedule 7 £663,475

SCHEDULE 1

CHARLES OWEN CAINE

PROCEEDS OF DRUG TRAFFICKING

Year Ended 20 November	Schedule	1993	1994	1995	1996	1997	1993–97
ASSETS less LIABILITIES							
Net assets at start of period	2	114,151	175,741	262,411	354,377	463,855	114,151
Net assets at end of period	2	175,741	262,411	354,377	463,855	556,682	556,682
Increase (Decrease) in net assets	(A)	61,590	86,670	91,966	109,478	92,827	442,531
OTHER EXPENDITURE							
Bank, building society and other withdrawals	3	14,764	14,783	24,889	21,925	24,703	101,064
Other payments made	4	1,359	2,356	217,932	14,080	2,260	47,987
Household expenditure per government statistics	5	6,767	7,444	7,297	7,038	7,937	36,483
Total of Other Expenditure	(B)	22,890	24,583	60,118	43,043	34,900	185,534
TOTAL KNOWN EXPENDITURE (A+B)	(C)	84,480	111,252	152,084	152,521	127,727	628,065
ASCERTAINABLE INCOME FROM KNOWN SOURCES	6 (D)	49,354	44,993	56,475	59,662	44,755	255,239
	(D)						
PROCEEDS OF DRUG TRAFFICKING (C − D)		35,126	66,260	95,609	92,859	82,972	372,826

CHARLES OWEN CAINE

SCHEDULE 2

ASSETS LESS LIABILITIES

As at 20 November	Schedule	1991	1992	1993	1994	1995	1996	1997
ASSETS								
Property								
17 Mosspark Drive, Westend, Anytown	2.1	60,000	60,000	60,000	60,000	—	—	—
Rose Cottage, Leafy Lane, Anytown	2.2	—	—	—	—	121,980	121,980	121,980
Flat 2/1, 1742 Argyll Road, Anytown	2.3	—	—	—	20,760	20,760	20,760	20,760
Flat 1/1, 1742 Argyll Road, Anytown	2.4	—	—	—	—	—	22,830	22,830
Acacia Villa, San Toro, Spain	2.5	—	—	—	—	87,500	87,500	87,500
Bank and Building Society Accounts								
Bank of Caledonia—Account no. 00189470	2.6	3,942	2,745	—	1,577	(1,612)	2,032	—
—Account no. 00777515	2.7	—	—	3,121	211	2,824	6,590	915
—Account no. 00101202	2.8	852	2,458	2,652	—	—	—	821
Anytown Building Society—Account no. 18–242–7194	2.9	27,614	28,257	30,065	25,216	34,744	27,699	39,066
—Account no. 72–196–8003	2.10	—	—	—	3,394	5,736	8,083	10,550
Banco San Toro—Account no. BST 81296 CAI	2.11	—	—	15,000	51,750	9,116	12,405	55,190
Capital Accounts								
Anne's Pot Shop	2.12	32,706	34,353	37,572	42,030	51,222	46,906	53,484
Investments								
Stocks and shares as scheduled	2.13	17,179	40,871	71,498	86,548	107,407	126,467	142,740

SCHEDULE 2 (Cont.)

CHARLES OWEN CAINE

ASSETS LESS LIABILITIES (Cont.)

As at 20 November	Schedule	1991	1992	1993	1994	1995	1996	1997
ASSETS								
Motor Vehicles								
Motor vehicles as scheduled	2.14	3,000	3,000	13,000	27,000	27,000	40,000	40,000
Other Assets								
Jetski		—	—	—	—	—	3,000	3,000
Boat and trailer		—	—	—	—	—	9,000	9,000
Boat (Spain)		—	—	—	—	—	26,000	26,000
Rolex watch		—	—	—	—	—	9,842	9,842
Jewellery		—	—	—	—	—	3,169	5,881
TV and video		—	—	—	—	—	—	1,575
Cash seized at time of arrest		—	—	—	—	—	—	4,064
Wholesale Value of Drugs		—	—	—	—	—	—	10,000
TOTAL ASSETS		145,293	171,684	232,908	318,486	466,677	574,263	665,198
LIABILITIES								
Mortgage								
Anytown Building Society								
17 Mosspark Drive, Westend, Anytown	2.1	55,000	55,000	55,000	55,000	—	—	—
Rose Cottage, Leafy Lane, Anytown	2.2	—	—	—	—	108,000	108,000	108,000

CHARLES OWEN CAINE SCHEDULE 2 (*Cont.*)

ASSETS LESS LIABILITIES (*Cont.*)

As at 20 November	Schedule	1991	1992	1993	1994	1995	1996	1997
LIABILITIES								
Other Loans Secured on Assets								
Bank of Caledonia—Home Improvement Loans								
Secured over:								
17 Mosspark Drive, Westend, Anytown	2.15	—	2,533	2,167	1,075	—	—	—
Rose Cottage, Leafy Lane, Anytown	2.15	—	—	—	—	4,300	2,408	516
TOTAL LIABILITIES		55,000	57,533	57,167	56,075	112,300	110,408	108,516
ASSETS LESS LIABILITIES (Transferred to Schedule 1)		90,293	114,151	175,741	262,411	354,377	463,855	556,682

CHARLES OWEN CAINE   *SCHEDULE 2.1*

17 MOSSPARK DRIVE, WESTEND, ANYTOWN

This house was purchased for £60,000 with date of entry on July 18, 1988 in the names of Mr and Mrs Caine.

An endowment mortgage of £55,000 was obtained from Anytown Building Society.

The house was sold on April 2, 1995. The details were as follows:

Sale price		£78,000
Outlays	£ 447	
Solicitors fees	763	
		1,210
Leaving net proceeds of		£76,790
which was used to:		
repay the mortgage	£55,000	
repay the outstanding balance on the		
Home Improvement Loan	248	
meet deposit on Rose Cottage, Leafy Lane,		
Anytown	12,000	
remit on 3 May 1991 to Mr & Mrs Caine	9,542	
		£76,790

The gain on sale is shown in Schedule 6 and calculated as follows:

Net proceeds of sale (above)	£76,790
Less: cost	£60,000
	£16,790

The treatment of the above figures that has been adopted in the Statement is as follows:

1. The cost and mortgage have been included in the appropriate years in Schedule 2.

2. The gain on sale is included as Income in Schedule 6.

ROSE COTTAGE, LEAFY LANE, ANYTOWN

This house was purchased for £120,000 with date of entry June 15, 1995 in the names of Mr and Mrs Caine.

An endowment mortgage of £108,000 was obtained from Anytown Building Society.

The cost was as follows:

Purchase price		£120,000
Survey fee, outlays and costs	£1,216	
Solicitors' fees	764	
		1,980
		£121,980

The purchase price was settled as follows:

Mortgage from Anytown Building Society	£108,000
From proceeds of 17 Mosspark Drive, Westend,	
Anytown	12,000
From Mr Caine in cash on July 7, 1995	1,980
	£121,980

The treatment of the above figures that has been adopted in the Statement is as follows:

1. The cost and mortgage have been included in the appropriate years in Schedule 2.

CHARLES OWEN CAINE   SCHEDULE 2.3

FLAT 2/1, 1742 ARGYLL ROAD, ANYTOWN

This property was purchased for £20,000 with date of entry September 9, 1994 in the name of Owen Caine.

The cost was as follows:

Purchase price		£20,000
Outlays	£360	
Solicitors' fees	400	
		760
		£20,760

The purchase price was settled in cash on September 8, 1994.

The treatment of the above figures that has been adopted in the Statement is as follows:

1. The cost has been included in the appropriate years in Schedule 2.

CHARLES OWEN CAINE   *SCHEDULE 2.4*

FLAT 1/1, 1742 ARGYLL ROAD, ANYTOWN

This property was purchased for £22,000 with date of entry June 26, 1996 in the name of Miss Margaret Caine, the sister of Charles Owen Caine.

The cost was as follows:

Purchase price		£22,000
Outlays	£390	
Solicitors' fees	440	
		830
		22,830

The purchase price was settled by bank draft on June 24, 1996.

The banks records show that the £22,830 bank draft was requested by Charles Owen Caine who deposited cash in respect of the draft.
The Crown considers this to be an implicative gift to Miss Margaret Caine and has therefore included this as an asset of Charles Owen Caine.

The treatment of the above figures that has been adopted in the Statement is as follows:

1. The cost has been included in the appropriate years in Schedule 2.

Acacia Villa, San Toro, Spain

This property was purchased for 21,000,000 spanish pesetas in August 1995 in the name of Owen Caine.

The purchase price was settled by a draft drawn on Charles Owen Caine's account with Banco San Toro.

An exchange rate of 240 pesetas to £1 sterling has been used in this Statement giving a starting equivalent cost of £87,500.

The treatment of the above figures that has been adopted in the Statement is as follows:

1. The cost has been included in the appropriate years in Schedule 2.

CHARLES OWEN CAINE   *SCHEDULE 2.6*

BANK OF CALEDONIA

ACCOUNT NUMBER—00189470

This account is a current account held at the Downtown branch in the name of Charles Owen Caine.

The account was opened prior to the period covered by the Prosecutor's Statement and was closed on March 20, 1993 and the balance transferred to account no. 00777515.

The transactions on the account can be summarised as follows:

Year Ending November 20	Opening Balance	Lodged	Withdrawn	Interest Earned	Closing Balance
1992	3,942	34,863	36,060	—	2,745
1993	2,745	39,196	41,941	—	—

The treatment of the above figures that has been adopted in the Statement is as follows:

1. The opening and closing balances have been included in the appropriate year in Schedule 2.
2. The interest earned has been included as Income in Schedule 6.
3. The withdrawals have been included in Schedule 3.
4. Interest charged (as distinct from interest earned) is included in the withdrawn figure.

CHARLES OWEN CAINE   SCHEDULE 2.7

BANK OF CALEDONIA

ACCOUNT NUMBER—00777515

This account is an interest earning current account held at the Downtown branch in the name of Charles Owen Caine.

The account was opened on March 20, 1993 with a transfer from account no. 00189470.

The transactions on the account can be summarised as follows:

Year Ending November 20	Opening Balance	Lodged	Withdrawn	Interest Earned	Closing Balance
1993	—	38,561	35,458	18	3,121
1994	3,121	35,584	37,139	11	1,577
1995	1,577	63,401	66,604	14	(1,612)
1996	(1,612)	76,688	73,065	21	2,032
1997	2,032	41,425	42,558	16	915

The treatment of the above figures that has been adopted in the Statement is as follows:

1. The opening and closing balances have been included in the appropriate year in Schedule 2.
2. The interest earned has been included as Income in Schedule 6.
3. The withdrawals have been included in Schedule 3.
4. Interest charged (as distinct from interest earned) is included in the withdrawn figure.

CHARLES OWEN CAINE   SCHEDULE 2.8

BANK OF CALEDONIA

ACCOUNT NUMBER—00101202

This account is an interest earning account held at the Downtown branch in the name of Mrs Anne Caine.

The account was opened prior to the period covered by the Prosecutor's Statement.

The transactions on the account can be summarised as follows:

Year Ending November 20	Opening Balance	Lodged	Withdrawn	Interest Earned	Closing Balance
1992	852	10,777	9,187	16	2,458
1993	2,458	11,602	11,426	18	2,652
1994	2,652	12,828	15,282	13	211
1995	211	13,397	10,801	17	2,824
1996	2,824	14,616	10,877	27	6,590
1997	6,590	15,031	20,815	15	821

The treatment of the above figures that has been adopted in the Statement is as follows:

1. The opening and closing balances have been included in the appropriate year in Schedule 2.
2. The interest earned has been included as Income in Schedule 6.
3. The withdrawals have been included in Schedule 3.
4. Interest charged (as distinct from interest earned) is included in the withdrawn figure.

CHARLES OWEN CAINE   SCHEDULE 2.9

ANYTOWN BUILDING SOCIETY

ACCOUNT NUMBER 18–242–7194

This account is an instant access investment account held at the Downtown branch in the name of Mr and Mrs Owen Caine.

The account was opened prior to the period covered by the Prosecutor's Statement.

The transactions on the account can be summarised as follows:

Year Ending November 20	Opening Balance	Lodged	Withdrawn	Interest Earned	Closing Balance
1992	27,614	3,000	4,152	1,795	28,257
1993	28,257	4,000	4,012	1,820	30,065
1994	30,065	—	6,744	1,895	25,216
1995	25,216	14,542	6,908	1,894	34,744
1996	34,744	19,000	28,247	2,202	27,699
1997	27,699	16,500	8,182	3,049	39,066

The treatment of the above figures that has been adopted in the Statement is as follows:

1. The opening and closing balances have been included in the appropriate year in Schedule 2.
2. The interest earned has been included as Income in Schedule 6.
3. The withdrawals have been included in Schedule 3.
4. Interest charged (as distinct from interest earned) is included in the withdrawn figure.

CHARLES OWEN CAINE   SCHEDULE 2.10

ANYTOWN BUILDING SOCIETY

ACCOUNT NUMBER 72–196–8003

This account is a TESSA account held at the Downtown branch in the name of Mrs Anne Caine.

The account was opened on February 1, 1994.

The transactions on the account can be summarised as follows:

Year Ending November 20	Opening Balance	Lodged	Withdrawn	Interest Earned	Closing Balance
1994	—	3,000		394	3,394
1995	3,394	1,800		542	5,736
1996	5,736	1,800		547	8,083
1997	8,083	1,800		667	10,550

The treatment of the above figures that has been adopted in the Statement is as follows:

1. The opening and closing balances have been included in the appropriate year in Schedule 2.
2. The interest earned has been included as Income in Schedule 6.
3. The withdrawals have been included in Schedule 3.
4. Interest charged (as distinct from interest earned) is included in the withdrawn figure.

CHARLES OWEN CAINE   SCHEDULE 2.11

BANCO SAN TORO

ACCOUNT NUMBER—BST 81296 CAI

This account is a deposit account held at the San Toro branch in the name of Owen Caine.

The account was opened on August 18, 1993.

The transactions on the account can be summarised as follows:

Year Ending November 20	Opening Balance	Lodged	Withdrawn	Interest Earned	Closing Balance
1993	—	15,000	—	—	15,000
1994	15,000	36,000	—	750	51,750
1995	51,750	44,000	89,222	2,588	9,116
1996	9,116	32,000	29,918	1,207	12,405
1997	12,405	48,000	5,823	608	55,190

The treatment of the above figures that has been adopted in the Statement is as follows:

1. The opening and closing balances have been included in the appropriate year in Schedule 2.
2. The interest earned has been included as Income in Schedule 6.
3. The withdrawals have been included in Schedule 3.
4. Interest charged (as distinct from interest earned) is included in the withdrawn figure.
5. Remittances from the U.K. are included in bank lodged at the actual sterling amounts remitted. Other amounts have been converted from pesetas to sterling at average rates for each year. Any exchange differences arising on conversion have been adjusted in the bank withdrawn figure.

ANNE'S POT SHOP

Background to the business

This is a kitchen equipment business run by Mrs Anne Caine in partnership with her sister-in-law Miss Margaret Caine. It also provides employment for Mr Caine's mother. Mr Charles Owen Caine writes up the cash book for his wife.

Accounts are prepared by Cookham & Co., Accountants, Anytown to November 25 each year and who report as follows:

"Prepared by us from the books and from information provided by Mr and Mrs Caine and certified to be in accordance therewith."

The capital account of Mrs Anne Caine in the business can be summarised as follows:

Year Ending November 20	Opening Capital	Capital Introduced	Profits (Losses)	Personal Drawings	Closing Capital
1992	32,706		6,847	5,200	34,353
1993	34,353		8,419	5,200	37,572
1994	37,572	5,000	5,178	5,720	42,030
1995	42,030	20,000	4,912	15,720	51,222
1996	51,222	10,000	6,924	21,240	46,906
1997	46,906	5,000	7,818	6,240	53,484

The results to November 25 have been taken for the purposes of this Statement to represent the equivalent period to November 20 in the same year.

The treatment of the above figures that has been adopted in the Statement is as follows:

1. The opening and closing balances on the capital account have been included in the appropriate year in Schedule 2.
2. The profits (losses) have been included as Income in Schedule 6.
3. The personal drawings have been included as other withdrawals in Schedule 3.
4. In so far as any part of the personal drawings have been paid into bank accounts or included in assets in Schedule 2 or those bank accounts contain debits in respect of monies paid into the business, then both classes of transaction have been adjusted in Schedule 3 to avoid double counting.

CHARLES OWEN CAINE

STOCKS AND SHARES (AT COST)

Year ending November 20	1992	1993	1994	1995	1996	1997
Opening balance	17,179	40,871	71,498	86,548	107,407	126,467
Investments made— Bank of Caledonia						
account no. 00189470	23,692	12,527	—	—	—	—
account no. 00777515	—	18,100	15,050	20,859	20,060	19,673
At cost	23,692	30,627	15,050	20,859	20,060	19,673
Investments sold etc.						
Proceeds banked in Bank of Caledonia						
account no. 00777515	—	—	—	—	3,160	3,274
Gains on sales	—	—	—	—	(2,160)	—
Losses on sales	—	—	—	—	—	126
At cost	—	—	—	—	1,000	3,400
Closing balance	40,871	71,498	86,548	107,407	126,467	142,740

The treatment of the above figures that has been adopted in the Statement is as follows:

1. The opening and closing balances have been included in the appropriate year in Schedule 2.
2. Gains on sale are included as Income in Schedule 6 and losses on sale as Expenditure in Schedule 4.
3. Where investments have been paid for out of the identified bank accounts, these have been eliminated in Schedule 3.1 to avoid double counting.

The following pages give detailed information on individual investment transactions.

SCHEDULE 2.13 (Cont.)
(Page 2 of 5)

CHARLES OWEN CAINE

STOCKS AND SHARES—HOLDINGS

As at November 20	No.	1991	1992	1993	1994	1995	1996	1997
ABC plc								
20/11/91 Held	800	3,300	3,300	3,300	3,300	3,300	3,300	3,300
18/07/94 Bonus issue (1:1)	800	—	—	—	—	—	—	—
BCD plc								
20/11/91 Held	2000	1,879	1,879	1,879	1,879	1,879	1,879	1,879
CDE plc								
31/03/92 Bought	1230	—	8,892	8,892	8,892	8,892	8,892	8,892
31/12/92 Bought	1620	—	—	11,927	11,927	11,927	11,927	11,927
DEF plc								
30/06/92 Bought	1200	—	1,000	1,000	1,000	1,000	1,000	1,000
30/06/93 Rights issue (1:3)	400	—	—	500	500	500	500	500
30/06/94 Rights issue (1:4)	400	—	—	—	600	600	600	600
EFG plc								
27/04/93 Bought	10,000	—	—	2,000	2,000	2,000	2,000	—
18/07/96 Sold	(5,000)	—	—	—	—	—	(1,000)	—
Balance	5,000	—	—	—	—	—	—	1,000
FGH plc								
14/08/93 Bought	1,000	—	—	2,400	2,400	2,400	2,400	2,400
06/03/97 Bought	250	—	—	—	—	—	—	971

CHARLES OWEN CAINE

STOCKS AND SHARES—HOLDINGS (Cont.)

As at November 20	No.	1991	1992	1993	1994	1995	1996	1997
GHI plc								
30/11/93 Bought	200	—	—	—	650	650	650	650
16/02/95 Bought	430	—	—	—	—	2750	2750	2750
06/03/97 Sold	(630)	—	—	—	—	—	—	(3400)
HIJ plc								
16/02/95 Bought	1500	—	—	—	—	1309	1309	1309
06/03/95 Bought	1500	—	—	—	—	—	—	1702
IJK plc								
18/07/96 Bought	650	—	—	—	—	—	3,260	3,260
XYZ Investment Trust plc								
20/11/92 Bought (by monthly savings scheme payments)	1011		1,800	1,800	1,800	1,800	1,800	1,800
20/11/93	844			1,800	1,800	1,800	1,800	1,800
20/11/94	955				1,800	1,800	1,800	1,800
20/11/95	741					1,800	1,800	1,800
20/11/96	670						1,800	1,800
20/11/97	646							2,000

CHARLES OWEN CAINE

STOCKS AND SHARES—HOLDINGS (*Cont.*)

As at November 20	No.	1991	1992	1993	1994	1995	1996	1997
Personal Equity Plans—								
Charles Owen Caine								
Highland Brokers Managed PEP								
20/11/91 Held		6,000	6,000	6,000	6,000	6,000	6,000	6,000
12/4/92 Invested		—	6,000	6,000	6,000	6,000	6,000	6,000
8/4/93 Invested		—	—	6,000	6,000	6,000	6,000	6,000
10/4/94 Invested		—	—	—	6,000	6,000	6,000	6,000
15/4/95 Invested		—	—	—	—	9,000	9,000	9,000
18/4/96 Invested		—	—	—	—	—	9,000	9,000
9/4/97 Invested		—	—	—	—	—	—	9,000
		17,179	40,871	71,498	86,548	107,407	126,467	142,740
Anne Caine								
Lowlands Investment Managers								
Select PEP								
20/11/91 Held		6,000	6,000	6,000	6,000	6,000	6,000	6,000
12/4/92 Invested		—	6,000	6,000	6,000	6,000	6,000	6,000
8/4/93 Invested		—	—	6,000	6,000	6,000	6,000	6,000
10/4/94 Invested		—	—	—	6,000	6,000	6,000	6,000
15/4/95 Invested		—	—	—	—	6,000	6,000	6,000
8/4/96 Invested		—	—	—	—	—	6,000	6,000
9/4/97 Invested		—	—	—	—	—	—	6,000

SCHEDULE 2.13 (Cont.)
(Page 5 of 5)

CHARLES OWEN CAINE

STOCKS AND SHARES—GAINS (LOSSES) ON SALE

Year ended November 20	No.	£	1992	1993	1994	1995	1996	1997
EFG plc								
18/07/96 Proceeds of sale	(5,000)	3,160						
Cost	5,000	1,000					2,160	
GHI plc								
06/03/97 Proceeds of sale	(630)	3,274						
Cost	630	3,400						(126)
							2,160	(126)

CHARLES OWEN CAINE   *SCHEDULE 2.14*
                                              (Page 1 of 3)

MOTOR VEHICLES (AT COST)

Year ending November 20	1992	1993	1994	1995	1996	1997
Opening balance	3,000	3,000	13,000	27,000	27,000	40,000
Cars bought Bank of Caledonia account no.						
00777515	—	10,000	14,000	—	17,000	—
Cash	—	—	2,000	—	8,000	—
Contra-trade-ins	—	—	1,000	—	15,000	—
At cost	—	10,000	17,000		40,000	—
Cars sold						
Contra-trade-ins	—	—	1,000	—	15,000	—
Losses on sales	—	—	2,000	—	12,000	—
At cost	—	—	3,000	—	27,000	—
Closing balance	3,000	13,000	27,000	27,000	40,000	40,000

The treatment of the above figures that has been adopted in the Statement is as follows:

1. The opening and closing balances have been included in the appropriate year in Schedule 2.
2. Gains on sale are included as Income in Schedule 6 and losses on sale as Expenditure on Schedule 4.
3. When costs of purchase have been paid for out of identified bank accounts, these have been eliminated in Schedule 3.1 to avoid double counting.
4. Cash costs of purchases are shown in Schedule 4 and will be eliminated in Schedule 4.1 to avoid double counting.

The following pages give detailed information about the individual cars.

CHARLES OWEN CAINE

MOTOR VEHICLES (AT COST) (Cont.)

As at November 20		1991	1992	1993	1994	1995	1996	1997
Ford Escort	D 821 EOE	3,000	3,000	3,000				
Mercedes	H 444 JWK			10,000	10,000	10,000		
Porsche	H 878 FDS				17,000	17,000		
Audi Cabriolet	C 41 NES						15,000	15,000
Mitsubishi Shogun	H 10 WEN						25,000	25,000
		<u>3,000</u>	<u>3,000</u>	<u>13,000</u>	<u>27,000</u>	<u>27,000</u>	<u>40,000</u>	<u>40,000</u>

Notes:

Ford Escort
Held at November 20, 1991—original cost was £3000.
Traded in against Porsche (H 878 FDS) on March 23, 1994 at a value of £1000.
Loss on sale £2000 (Schedule 4).

Mercedes
Purchased by cheque drawn on account no. 00777515 with Bank of Caledonia for £10,000 on August 16, 1993.
Traded in against Audi Cabriolet (C 41 NES) on February 15, 1996 at a value of £3,500.
Loss on sale £6,500 (Schedule 4).

Porsche
Purchased on March 23, 1994 for £17,000 settled as follows:
Trade in value of Ford Escort (D 821 EOE)   £1,000
Cash deposit (Schedule 4)   £2,000
Cheque drawn on account no. 00777515 with Bank of Caledonia   £14,000
Traded in against Mitsubishi Shogun (H 10 WEN) on February 15, 1996 at a value of £11,500.

CHARLES OWEN CAINE

SCHEDULE 2.14 (Cont.)
(page 3 of 3)

MOTOR VEHICLES (AT COST) (Cont.)

Audi Cabriolet

Purchased on February 15, 1996 for £15,000 settled as follows:

Trade in value of Mercedes (H 444 JWK)	£3,500
Cash deposit (Schedule 4)	£3,000
Cheque drawn on account 00777515 with Bank of Caledonia	£8,500

Mitsubishi Shogun

Purchased in February 15, 1996 for £25,000 settled as follows:

Trade in value of Porsche (H 878 FDS)	£11,500
Cash deposit (Schedule 4)	£5,000
Cheque drawn on account no. 00777515 with Bank of Caledonia	£8,500

HOME IMPROVEMENT LOANS

During the period covered by this Statement two home improvement loans were taken out.

1. In respect of 17 Mosspark Drive, Westend, Anytown (secured by a second charge)—advanced on December 1, 1991.

Year ending November 20	Opening Loan	Repaid	Interest Element	Closing Loan
1992	3100	960	393	2533
1993	2533	619	253	2167
1994	2167	1849	757	1075
1995 (to 24/4/95)	1075	1210	383	248
(24/4/95)	248	248	—	—

Note: The final balance was settled out of the proceeds of sale of the house (Schedule 2.1)

2. In respect of Rose Cottage, Leafy Lane, Anytown (secured by a second charge)—advanced on July 1, 1995.

Year ending November 20	Opening Loan	Repaid	Interest Element	Closing Loan
1995	6200	2575	675	4300
1996	4300	2575	683	2408
1997	2408	2575	683	516

The treatment of the above figures that has been adopted in the Statement is as follows:

1. The opening and closing balances have been included in the appropriate year in Schedule 2.
2. The monthly repayments are included in bank withdrawals in Schedule 3.
3. The capital element of the repayments which has reduced the outstanding liability has been included in Schedule 3.1 to avoid double counting.

CHARLES OWEN CAINE

SCHEDULE 3

BANK, BUILDING SOCIETY AND OTHER WITHDRAWALS

Year ended November 20	Schedule	1992	1993	1994	1995	1996	1997
Bank, Building Society and Account Number							
Bank of Caledonia—Account no. 00189470	2.6	36,060	41,941	—	—	—	—
—Account no. 00777515	2.7	—	35,458	37,139	66,604	73,065	42,558
—Account no. 00101202	2.8	9,187	11,426	15,282	10,801	10,877	20,815
Anytown Building Society—Account no. 18–242–7194	2.9	4,152	4,012	6,744	6,908	28,247	8,182
—Account no. 72–196–8003	2.10	—	—	—	—	—	—
Banco San Toro—Account no. BST 81296 CAI	2.11	—	—	—	89,222	29,918	5,823
Business Drawings							
Anne's Pot Shop	2.12	5,200	5,200	5,720	15,720	21,240	6,240
		54,599	98,037	64,885	189,255	163,347	83,618
LESS: Transfers between accounts and payments that have increased assets or reduced liabilities (deducted to avoid double counting)	3.1	37,659	83,273	50,102	164,366	141,422	58,915
TOTALS TRANSFERRED TO SCHEDULE 1.		16,940	14,764	14,783	24,889	21,925	24,703

CHARLES OWEN CAINE   *SCHEDULE 3.1*

TRANSFERS BETWEEN ACCOUNTS AND PAYMENTS THAT HAVE INCREASED ASSETS OR REDUCED LIABILITIES

Year ended November 20

Transfers Between Accounts

Detail	Schedule	1992	1993	1994	1995	1996	1997
Date							
*							
From B of C account no. 00189470 to B of C account no. 00777515	2.6	—	12,360	—	—	—	—
From B of C account no. 00189470 to B of C account no. 00101202		5,200	1,870	—	—	—	—
From B of C account no. 00189470 to ABS account no. 18–242–7194		3,000	—	—	—	—	—
From B of C account no. 00189470 to B of C account no. BST 81296 CAI		—	15,000	—	—	—	—
From B of C account no. 00777515 to B of C account no. 00101202	2.7	—	3,850	6,240	6,760	7,430	7,810
From B of C account no. 00777515 to ABS account no. 18–242–7194		—	3,000	—	5,000	4,000	12,500
From B of C account no. 00777515 to B of C account no. BST 81296 CAI		—	—	—	24,000	—	—
From B of C account no. 00777515 to Anne's Pot Shop account		—	—	—	—	10,000	—
From B of C account no. 00101202 to ABS account no. 18–242–7194	2.8	—	1,000	—	—	—	4,000
From B of C account no. 00101202 to Anne's Pot Shop account		—	—	5,000	—	—	5,000
From ABS account no. 18–242–7194 to B of C account no. 00777515	2.9	—	—	—	—	20,000	—
From ABS account no. 18–242–7194 to ABS account no. 72–196–8003		—	—	3,000	1,800	1,800	1,800
From Anne's Pot Shop account to B of C account no. 00777515	2.12	—	—	—	10,000	—	—
From Anne's Pot Shop account to B of C account no. 00101202		5,200	5,200	5,720	5,720	6,240	6,240
From Anne's Pot Shop account to ABS account no. 18–242–7194		—	—	—	15,000	15,000	—

[* Normally each individual transfer or payment would be shown with the date of the transaction.]

CHARLES OWEN CAINE   *SCHEDULE 3.1 (Cont.)*

TRANSFERS BETWEEN ACCOUNTS AND PAYMENTS THAT HAVE INCREASED ASSETS OR REDUCED LIABILITIES (*Cont.*)

Year ended November 20

Payments that have increased assets or reduced liabilities

Date Detail	Schedule	1992	1993	1994	1995	1996	1997
*							
From B of C account no. 00189470—stocks and shares	2.13	23,692	12,527	—	—	—	—
From B of C account no. 00777515—stocks and shares	2.13	—	18,100	15,050	20,859	20,060	19,673
—motor vehicles	2.14	—	10,000	14,000	—	17,000	—
—jetski		—	—	—	—	3,000	—
—boat and trailer		—	—	—	—	9,000	—
From BST account no. BST 81296 CAI—Acacia villa	2.5	—	—	—	87,500	—	—
—boat		—	—	—	—	26,000	—
Capital element of Home Improvement Loan repayments	2.15	567	366	1,092	2,727	1,892	1,892
TOTALS TRANSFERRED TO SCHEDULE 3		37,659	83,273	50,102	164,366	141,422	58,915

[*Normally each individual transfer would be shown with the date of the transaction]

CHARLES OWEN CAINE

SCHEDULE 4

OTHER EXPENDITURE (INCLUDING PAYMENTS MADE IN CASH OR FROM AN UNKNOWN SOURCE)

Year Ended November 20		Schedule	1992	1993	1994	1995	1996	1997
Date	Detail							
	Property transaction							
7/7/95	Balance of cost of Rose Cottage, Leafy Lane, Anytown	2.2	—	—	—	1,980	—	—
9/9/95	Purchase of Flat 2/1, 1742 Argyll Road, Anytown	2.3	—	—	20,760	—	—	—
26/6/96	Purchase of Flat 1/1, 1742 Argyll Road, Anytown	2.4	—	—	—	—	22,830	—
	Motor vehicles							
23/4/94	Deposit on Porsche H 878 FDS	2.14	—	—	2,000	—	—	—
15/2/96	Deposit on Audi Cabriolet C 41 NES	2.14	—	—	—	—	3,000	—
15/2/96	Deposit on Mitsubishi Shogun H 10 WEN	2.14	—	—	—	—	5,000	—
	Other cash payments							
	Visa card payments	4.2	943	1,359	356	503	235	—
15/8/95	New driveway at Rose Cottage		—	—	—	4,124	—	—
8/9/95	Kitchen refurbishment at Rose Cottage		—	—	—	9,718	—	—
11/10/95	Double glazing at Rose Cottage		—	—	—	11,413	—	—
9/2/96	Rolex watch		—	—	—	—	9,842	—
9/2/96	Jewellery		—	—	—	—	3,169	—
6/2/97	Jewellery		—	—	—	—	—	2,712
14/8/97	TV and video		—	—	—	—	—	1,575
26/4/95	Designer clothing		—	—	—	2,174	—	—
15/12/95	Designer clothing		—	—	—	—	1,845	—
31/3/97	Designer clothing		—	—	—	—	—	2,134

CHARLES OWEN CAINE SCHEDULE 4 (Cont.)

OTHER EXPENDITURE (INCLUDING PAYMENTS MADE IN CASH OR FROM AN UNKNOWN SOURCE) (*Cont.*)

Year Ended November 20

Date	Detail	Schedule	1992	1993	1994	1995	1996	1997
	Losses on sales							
	Stocks and shares	2.13	—	—	—	—	—	126
	Motor vehicles	2.14	—	—	2,000	—	12,000	—
			943	1,359	25,116	29,912	57,921	6,547
	LESS: other payments made that have increased assets or reduced liabilities (deducted to avoid double counting)	4.1	—	—	22,760	1,980	43,841	4,287
	TOTALS TRANSFERRED TO SCHEDULE 1.		943	1,359	2,356	27,932	14,080	2,260

CHARLES OWEN CAINE

SCHEDULE 4.1

OTHER EXPENDITURE THAT HAS INCREASED ASSETS OR REDUCED LIABILITIES

Year ended November 20	1992	1993	1994	1995	1996	1997
Property expenditure						
Rose Cottage, Leafy Lane, Anytown	—	—	—	1,980	—	—
Flat 2/1, 1742 Argyll Road, Anytown	—	—	20,760	—	—	—
Flat 1/1, 1742 Argyll Road, Anytown	—	—	—	—	22,830	—
Motor vehicle expenditure						
Porsche H 878 FDS	—	—	2,000	—	—	—
Audi Cabriolet C 41 NES	—	—	—	—	3,000	—
Mitsubishi Shogun H 10 WEN	—	—	—	—	5,000	—
Other asset expenditure						
Rolex watch	—	—	—	—	9,842	—
Jewellery	—	—	—	—	3,169	2,712
TV and video	—	—	—	—	—	1,575
TOTALS TRANSFERRED TO SCHEDULE 4	—	—	22,760	1,980	43,841	4,287

CHARLES OWEN CAINE *SCHEDULE 4.2*

VISA CARD PAYMENTS

All payments made *in cash* except where indicated otherwise.

1991–92

14/1/92	100	
20/2/92	250	
13/4/92	108	Cheque from Bank of Caledonia account no. 00189470
6/8/92	393	
9/10/92	200	
	1,051	

1992–93

7/12/92	250	
8/2/93	350	
14/4/93	350	
18/6/93	300	
26/8/93	73	Cheque from Bank of Caledonia account no. 00777515
16/10/93	109	
	1,432	

1993–94

18/5/94	356

1994–95

12/12/94	300
16/4/95	203
	503

1995–96

6/9/96	235

The treatment of the above figures that has been adopted in the Statement is as follows:

1. The cheque payments are included within bank withdrawals on Schedule 3.
2. The cash payments are shown in Schedule 4.

CHARLES OWEN CAINE

SCHEDULE 5

HOUSEHOLD EXPENDITURE PER GOVERNMENT STATISTICS

Year ended November 20

	1992	1993	1994	1995	1996	1997
CSO Family Spending Survey—1991 Table "*" Page "*" [Expenditure by household composition—two adults, two children] £78.07 × 4 × 52	16,239					
CSO Family Spending Survey—1992 Table "*" Page "*" [Expenditure by household composition—two adults, two children] £82.66 × 4 × 52		17,193				
CSO Family Spending Survey—1993 Table "*" Page "*" [Expenditure by household composition—two adults, two children] £85.22 × 4 × 52			17,726			
CSO Family Spending Survey—1994/95 Table "*" Page "*" [Expenditure by household composition—two adults, two children] £87.01 × 4 × 52				18,098		
ONS Family Spending Survey—1995/96 Table 4.1 Page 65 [Expenditure by household composition—two adults, two children] £86.13 × 4 × 52					17,915	
ONS Family Spending Survey—1996/97 Table 4.1 Page 65						

CHARLES OWEN CAINE   SCHEDULE 5 (*Cont.*)

HOUSEHOLD EXPENDITURE PER GOVERNMENT STATISTICS (*Cont.*)

Year ended November 20	1992	1993	1994	1995	1996	1997
[Expenditure by household composition—two adults, two children] £94.96 × 4 × 52						19,752
	16,239	17,193	17,726	18,098	17,915	19,752
Less: Household costs paid out of Bank of Caledonia Account no. 000101202 (via cash machine withdrawals, direct debits, standing orders etc)	9,187	10,426	10,282	10,801	10,877	11,815
TOTALS TRANSFERRED TO SCHEDULE 1	7,052	6,767	7,444	7,297	7,038	7,937
As mortgage payments are included in bank withdrawals an adjustment has been made to the statistics to eliminate the mortgage content and so avoid a double count as follows:						
As per Spending Survey (weekly amount per person)	86,81	91,91	94,96	96,75	97,09	105,59
Less: mortgage element estimated at 60% of net housing element	8,74	9,25	9,47	9,74	10,96	10,63
As used above	78,07	82,66	85,22	87,01	86,13	94,96

Notes

1. The survey is that ending within the periods covered by the Statement. The surveys were for calendar years to 1993 and for a year to 31 March thereafter.

2. On occasion it is appropriate to prorate the statistics over the Statement period where the family circumstances change and justify using different statistical tables. In this case the family has remained static and so no such adjustments have been made.

[For this example the figures for the first four years 1992–1995 have been estimated as the appropriate tables are not readily available.]

CHARLES OWEN CAINE

SCHEDULE 6

ASCERTAINABLE INCOME FROM KNOWN SOURCES

Year ended November 20

Date	Detail	Schedule	1992	1993	1994	1995	1996	1997
	Interest received							
	Bank of Caledonia—Account no. 00777515	2.7	—	18	11	14	21	16
	—Account no. 00101202	2.8	16	18	13	17	27	15
	Anytown Building Society—Account no. 18–242–7194	2.9	1,795	1,820	1,895	1,894	2,202	3,049
	—Account no. 72–186–8003	2.10	—	—	394	542	547	667
	Banco San Toro—Account no. BST 81296 CAI	2.11	—	—	750	2,588	1,207	608
	Dividends on stocks and shares		237	748	1,179	1,280	1,312	1,791
	Salary—National Coke Works plc		23,526	24,073	24,782	25,921	26,738	26,360
	Profits—Anne's Pot Shop	2.12	6,847	8,419	5,178	4,912	6,924	7,818
	Property Letting Income		—	—	300	1,600	2,100	3,450
	Child Benefit		377	682	868	917	946	981
18/9/93	Insurance policy following mother's death		—	13,576	—	—	—	—
14/3/94	Balance of mother's estate		—	—	9,623	—	—	—
5/5/95	Injury compensation		—	—	—	—	1,750	—
1/11/96	National Bingo win		—	—	—	—	13,728	—
	Gains on sales							
24/4/95	17 Mosspark Drive, Westend, Anytown	2.1	—	—	—	16,790	—	—
	Stocks and shares	2.13	—	—	—	—	2,160	—
	TOTALS TRANSFERRED TO SCHEDULE 1		32,798	49,354	44,993	56,475	59,662	44,755

CHARLES OWEN CAINE   SCHEDULE 7

REALISABLE ASSETS

Property (as valued)
Rose Cottage, Leafy Lane, Anytown	160,000	
Less outstanding mortgage	108,000	
	52,000	
Flat 2/1, 1742 Argyll Road, Anytown	22,000	
Flat 1/1, 1742 Argyll Road, Anytown	27,000	
Acacia Villa, San Toro, Spain	85,000	
		186,000

Bank and Building Society Accounts
Bank of Caledonia—Account no. 00777515	841	
—Account no. 00101202	319	
Anytown Building Society—Account no. 18–242–7194	40,612	
—Account no. 72–196–8003	10,550	
Banco San Toro—Account no. BST 81296 CAI	52,608	
		104,930

Business Capital
Anne's Pot Shop—capital account	53,484

Investments
Stocks and shares (Schedule 7)	208,154

Motor vehicles
Audi Cabriolet C 41 NES	11,000	
Mitsubishi Shogun H 10 WEN	18,500	
		29,500

Cash
Seized on arrest	4,064

Other Assets
Jet ski	3,000	
Boat & Trailer	9,000	
Boat (Spain)	22,000	
Rolex watch	9,500	
Personal jewellery	5,000	
TV and video	1,250	
		49,750

Life Assurance and Pension Policies
Mainstream Life Assurance:
Endowment Policy no. P 19887412 (Surrender Value)	6,872	
Policy no. M 19958146 (Surrender Value)	2,166	
Long Life Pension Fund:		
Policy no. 474 ABC 612 (Open Market Option Value)	14,813	
Policy no. 770 RPX 847 (Open Market Option Value)	3,742	
		27,593
		663,475

The above values as at March 18, 1998 may require to be updated to the date
fixed for the confiscation proof.

CHARLES OWEN CAINE   SCHEDULE 7.1

STOCKS AND SHARES VALUATION

	No.	Value	
ABC plc	1600	424p	6,784
BCD plc	2000	189p	3,780
CDE plc	2850	375p	10,688
DEF plc	2000	39p	780
EFG plc	5000	28p	1400
FGH plc	1250	458p	5,725
HIJ plc	3000	192p	5,760
IJK plc	650	596p	3,874
XYZ Investment Trust plc	4867	320p	15,574

Personal Equity Plans:	
Charles Owen Caine	83,208
Anne Caine	70,581
	208,154

The above values were taken from the *Financial Times* on March 18, 1998.
The Personal Equity Plan values were provided by Highland Brokers for the
Charles Owen Caine Plan and by Lowlands Investment Managers for that of
Mrs Anne Caine.

Style IV

Answers

IN THE HIGH COURT OF JUSTICIARY

UNDER SECTION 9 OF THE PROCEEDS OF CRIME
(SCOTLAND) ACT 1995

ANSWERS

For the Accused Charles Owen Caine

to

Statement by the Prosecutor

in causa

Her Majesty's Advocate

against

Charles Owen Caine

1. Accepted that the prosecutor's statement contains seven schedules. *Quoad ultra* denied. The accused does not accept the accuracy of the schedules and, while they contain certain financial information in respect of him, that information is incomplete and inaccurate. Reference is made to the answers below.

2. Denied that Schedule 1 is a calculation of the proceeds of drug trafficking of the accused. Explained and averred that the accused, notwithstanding the fact of his conviction, has never obtained any sums from dealing in drugs.

3. Denied that Schedule 2 specifies the costs, the assets and the liabilities of the accused and the balance of assets and liabilities at the dates mentioned. Explained and averred that the true position is as follows:

Schedule 2.1: This schedule is referred to for its terms beyond which no admission is made.

Schedule 2.2: The property at Rose Cottage, Leafy Lane, Anytown was purchased by the accused from the proceeds of sale of property previously owned by him together with a mortgage from Anytown Building Society. The sum of £1,980 in cash referred to in said schedule was also proceeds from the sale of the previous property.

Schedule 2.3 is referred to for its terms beyond which no admission is made but explained that the cash sum of £20,000 was not proceeds of drug trafficking but sums received by the accused as a result of genuine business activities referred to below.

Schedule 2.4: Denied that the property at Flat 1/1, 1742 Argyll Road, Anytown is an implicative gift. Explained that the sum of £22,830 referred to in said schedule belonged to the accused's sister, Miss Margaret Caine, and was deposited in cash by the accused merely to assist his sister with her banking arrangements. Said cash always truly belonged to Miss Margaret Caine who had saved it up over a period of years. Said Charles Owen Caine has no connection whatsoever with the flat at 1/1, 1742 Argyll Road, Anytown and said flat truly belongs to Miss Margaret Caine.

Schedule 2.5: Accepted that the accused owns Acacia Villa, San Toro, Spain. Explained that said property was purchased by funds received by the accused during his business activities explained below.

Schedules 2.6 and 2.7: Accepted.

Schedule 2.8: Denied. The accused has no information as to the accuracy of the schedules. Denied that the accused made any contribution to this account. Explained that this account is held by the accused's wife, Mrs Anne Caine, alone.

Schedule 2.9: Accepted.

Schedule 2.10: Denied. Explained that the accused made no contribution to this account which is an account held by his wife, Mrs Anne Caine, alone.

Schedule 2.11: Accepted that the schedule bears to detail certain matters but explained that any monies lodged to said account were lawfully acquired by the accused during his business activities explained below.

Schedule 2.12: Denied. The accused is unable to accept the accuracy of this schedule as he has no detailed knowledge of the business "Anne's Pot Shop", it being a business run by his wife, Mrs Anne Caine, and his sister, Miss Margaret Caine.

Schedule 2.13: Accepted.

Schedule 2.14: Accepted that the schedule bears to detail certain matters, the accuracy of which is not accepted by the accused. Explained that said motor vehicles referred to in said schedules all truly belong to Mrs Anne Caine and were purchased from the proceeds of her own business. Said Anne Caine allowed the accused the use of the motor vehicles only.

Schedule 2.15: Accepted.

4. Schedules 3 and 3.1 are referred to for their terms beyond which no admission is made.

5. Schedule 4: Denied, under explanation that the balance of the cost of Rose Cottage came from the proceeds of the previous house sale. The purchase price of Flat 1/1, 1742 Argyll Road, Anytown was paid by Miss Margaret Caine from her own funds. The motor vehicles' deposits were paid by Mrs Anne Caine from her own funds and the kitchen refurbishment at Rose Cottage was paid for by the accused's mother as a birthday present.

6. Schedule 5: Accepted.

7. Schedule 6: Denied. Explained that said schedule is inaccurate and incomplete. Said schedule fails to take account of the accused's income from his activities as a disc jockey and rave organiser. Explained that since 1990 the accused has regularly travelled between Scotland and Spain for the purposes of appearing as a celebrity D.J. in night clubs in Spain and organising raves in both countries. Since 1990 said activities have provided an income to the accused of at least £35,000 per year. Said income for the years 1993–97 is estimated at £210,000.

8. Schedule 7: Denied. Explained that:

   (a) Rose Cottage is valued at only £140,000;
   (b) Flat 1/1, 1742 Argyll Road, Anytown truly belongs to Margaret Caine;
   (c) Acacia Villa, San Toro, Spain is valued at £75,000;
   (d) Bank of Caledonia account number 00101202 relates to funds belonging only to Anne Caine;
   (e) the business capital of "Anne's Pot Shop" belongs only to Anne Caine and Margaret Caine;
   (f) motor vehicles Audi Cabriolet and Mitsubishi Shogun belong only to Anne Caine.

   Schedule 7.1: Accepted.

9. Accepted that certain orders were pronounced in the Court of Session and the petition and interlocutors are referred to for their terms.

10. The accused does not accept the accuracy of the prosecutor's statement nor the accuracy of the figures for realisable property of £663,475 and drug trafficking proceeds of £372,826. The basis for such non-acceptance is that during the relevant period the accused obtained large quantities of cash from his business activities as a D.J. and rave organiser as explained above. The business was not registered for VAT, the accused did not declare his income for the purposes of income tax and the proceeds of said business were received in cash. As stated above this amounted to approximately £210,000 during the relevant period. In these circumstances the accused has had considerable sums of money available in cash which accounts for the assets he has.

According to Justice

Solicitor for the Accused, Glasgow

APPENDIX 3

STATUTES

CRIMINAL LAW (CONSOLIDATION) (SCOTLAND) ACT 1995

(1995 c. 39)

ARRANGEMENT OF SECTIONS

. . .

. . .

An Act to consolidate for Scotland certain enactments creating offences and relating to criminal law there.   [November 8, 1995]

. . .

PART V

DRUG TRAFFICKING

Investigations and disclosure of information

Order to make material available

31.—(1) The procurator fiscal may, for the purpose of an investigation into drug trafficking, apply to the sheriff for an order under subsection (2) below in relation to particular material or material of a particular description.

(2) If on such an application the sheriff is satisfied that the conditions in subsection (4) below are fulfilled, he may, subject to section 35(11) of this Act, make an order that the person who appears to him to be in possession of the material to which the application relates shall—

   (a)   produce it to a constable or person commissioned by the Commissioners of Customs and Excise for him to take away; or

   (b)   give a constable or person so commissioned access to it, within such period as the order may specify.

(3) The period to be specified in an order under subsection (2) above shall be seven days unless it appears to the sheriff that a longer or shorter period would be appropriate in the particular circumstances of the application.

(4) The conditions referred to in subsection (2) above are—

   (a)   that there are reasonable grounds for suspecting that a specified person has carried on, or has derived financial or other rewards from, drug trafficking;

   (b)   that there are reasonable grounds for suspecting that the material to which the application relates—

      (i)   is likely to be of substantial value (whether by itself or together with other material) to the investigation for the purpose of which the application is made; and

      (ii)   does not consist of or include items subject to legal privilege; and

   (c)   that there are reasonable grounds for believing that it is in the public interest, having regard—

      (i)   to the benefit likely to accrue to the investigation if the material is obtained; and

      (ii)   to the circumstances under which the person in possession of the material holds it,

that the material should be produced or that access to it should be given.

(5) Where the sheriff makes an order under subsection (2)(b) above in relation to material on any premises he may, on the application of the procurator fiscal, order any person who appears to him to be entitled to grant entry to the premises to allow a constable or person commissioned as aforesaid to enter the premises to obtain access to the material.

(6) Provision may be made by rules of court as to—

   (a)   the discharge and variation of orders under this section, and

   (b)   proceedings relating to such orders.

(7) Where the material to which an application under this section relates consists of information contained in a computer—

   (a)   an order under subsection (2)(a) above shall have effect as an order to produce the material in a form in which it can be taken away and in which it is visible and legible; and

   (b)   an order under subsection (2)(b) above shall have effect as an order to give access to the material in a form in which it is visible and legible.

(8) An order under subsection (2) above—

   (a)   shall not confer any right to production of, or access to, items subject to legal privilege;

(b) shall have effect notwithstanding any obligation as to secrecy or other restriction upon the disclosure of information imposed by statute or otherwise; and

(c) may be made in relation to material in the possession of an authorised government department.

Authority for search

32.—(1) The procurator fiscal may, for the purpose of an investigation into drug trafficking, apply to the sheriff for a warrant under this section in relation to specified premises.

(2) On such application the sheriff may issue a warrant authorising a constable, or person commissioned by the Commissioners of Customs and Excise, to enter and search the premises if the sheriff is satisfied—

(a) that an order made under section 31 of this Act in relation to material on the premises has not been complied with; or

(b) that the conditions in subsection (3) below are fulfilled; or

(c) that the conditions in subsection (4) below are fulfilled.

(3) The conditions referred to in subsection (2)(b) above are—

(a) that there are reasonable grounds for suspecting that a specified person has carried on, or has derived financial or other rewards from, drug trafficking; and

(b) that the conditions in subsection (4)(b) and (c) of section 31 of this Act are fulfilled in relation to any material on the premises; and

(c) that it would not be appropriate to make an order under that section in relation to the material because—

   (i) it is not practicable to communicate with any person entitled to produce the material; or

  (ii) it is not practicable to communicate with any person entitled to grant access to the material or entitled to grant entry to the premises on which the material is situated; or

 (iii) the investigation for the purposes of which the application is made might be seriously prejudiced unless a constable or person commissioned as aforesaid could secure immediate access to the material.

(4) The conditions referred to in subsection (2)(c) above are—

(a) that there are reasonable grounds for suspecting that a specified person has carried on, or has derived financial or other rewards from, drug trafficking; and

(b) that there are reasonable grounds for suspecting that there is on the premises material relating to the specified person or to drug trafficking which is likely to be of substantial value (whether by itself or together with other material) to the investigation for the purpose of which the application is made, but that the material cannot at the time of the application be particularised; and

(c) that—

   (i) it is not practicable to communicate with any person entitled to grant entry to the premises; or

(ii) entry to the premises will not be granted unless a warrant is produced; or

(iii) the investigation for the purpose of which the application is made might be seriously prejudiced unless a constable or person commissioned as aforesaid arriving at the premises could secure immediate entry to them.

(5) Where a constable or person commissioned as aforesaid has entered premises in the execution of a warrant issued under this section, he may seize and retain any material, other than items subject to legal privilege, which is likely to be of substantial value (whether by itself or together with other material) to the investigation for the purpose of which the warrant was issued.

Interpretation of sections 31 and 32

33. In sections 31 and 32 of this Act—

"items subject to legal privilege" means—

(a) communications between a professional legal adviser and his client; or

(b) communications made in connection with or in contemplation of legal proceedings and for the purposes of these proceedings, being communications which would in legal proceedings be protected from disclosure by virtue of any rule of law relating to the confidentiality of communications; and

"premises" includes any place and, in particular, includes—

(a) any vehicle, vessel, aircraft or hovercraft;

(b) any offshore installation within the meaning of section 1 of the Mineral Workings (Offshore Installations) Act 1971; and

(c) any tent or moveable structure.

Prosecution by order of the Commissioners of Customs and Excise

34.—(1) Summary proceedings for a specified offence may be instituted by order of the Commissioners and shall, if so instituted, be commenced in the name of an officer.

(2) In the case of the death, removal, discharge or absence of the officer in whose name any proceedings for a specified offence were commenced, those proceedings may be continued by another officer.

(3) Where the Commissioners investigate, or propose to investigate, any matter with a view to determining—

(a) whether there are grounds for believing that a specified offence has been committed; or

(b) whether a person should be prosecuted for a specified offence,

that matter shall be treated as an assigned matter within the meaning of the Customs and Excise Management Act 1979.

(4) Nothing in this section shall be taken—

(a) to prevent any person (including any officer) who has power to arrest, detain or prosecute any person for a specified offence from doing so, or

(b) to prevent a court from proceeding to deal with a person brought before it following his arrest by an officer for a specified offence, even though the proceedings have not been instituted by an order made under subsection (1) above.

(5) In this section—

"the Commissioners" means the Commissioners of Customs and Excise;

"officer" means a person commissioned by the Commissioners; and

"specified offence" means—

(a) an offence under section 36, 37, 38, 39 or 40 of this Act or section 14 of the Criminal Justice (International Cooperation) Act 1990 (concealing or transferring proceeds of drug trafficking);

(b) attempting to commit, conspiracy to commit or incitement to commit, any such offence; or

(c) any other offence of a kind prescribed in regulations made by the Secretary of State for the purposes of this section.

(6) Regulations under subsection (5) above shall be made by statutory instrument subject to annulment in pursuance of a resolution of either House of Parliament.

Disclosure or information held by government departments

35.—(1) Subject to subsection (4) below, the Court of Session may on an application by the Lord Advocate order any material mentioned in subsection (3) below which is in the possession of an authorised government department to be produced to the Court within such period as the Court may specify.

(2) The power to make an order under subsection (1) above is exercisable if—

(a) the powers conferred on the Court by subsection (1) of section 28 of the Proceeds of Crime (Scotland) Act 1995 are exercisable by virtue of subsection (2) of section 29 of that Act; or

(b) those powers are exercisable by virtue of subsection (3) of the said section 29 and the Court has made a restraint order (within the meaning of section 28 of that Act) which has not been recalled.

(3) The material referred to in subsection (1) above is any material which—

(a) has been submitted to an officer of an authorised government department by a person who holds, or has at any time held, realisable property (within the meaning of section 4 of the said Act of 1995);

(b) has been made by an officer of an authorised government department in relation to such a person; or

(c) is correspondence which passed between an officer of an authorised government department and such a person,

and an order under that subsection may require the production of all such material or of a particular description of such material, being material in the possession of the department concerned.

(4) An order under subsection (1) above shall not require the production of any material unless it appears to the Court of Session that the material is likely to contain information that would facilitate the exercise of the powers conferred on the Court by section 28 of the said Act of 1995 or paragraph 1 or 12 of Schedule 1 to that Act or on an administrator appointed under sub-paragraph (1) of the said paragraph 1.

(5) The Court may by order authorise the disclosure to such an administrator of any material produced under subsection (1) above or any part of such

material; but the Court shall not make an order under this subsection unless a reasonable opportunity has been given for an officer of the department to make representations to the Court.

(6) Material disclosed in pursuance of an order under subsection (5) above may, subject to any conditions contained in the order, be further disclosed for the purposes of the functions under the said Act of 1995 of the administrator or the High Court.

(7) The Court of Session may by order authorise the disclosure to a person mentioned in subsection (8) below of any material produced under subsection (1) above or any part of such material but the Court shall not make an order under this subsection unless—

(a) a reasonable opportunity has been given for an officer of the department to make representations to the Court; and

(b) it appears to the Court that the material is likely to be of substantial value in exercising functions relating to drug trafficking—

(8) The persons referred to in subsection (7) above are—

(a) a constable;

(b) the Lord Advocate or any procurator fiscal; and

(c) a person commissioned by the Commissioners of Customs and Excise.

(9) Material disclosed in pursuance of an order under subsection (7) above may, subject to any conditions contained in the order, be further disclosed for the purposes of functions relating to drug trafficking.

(10) Material may be produced or disclosed in pursuance of this section notwithstanding any obligation as to secrecy or other restriction upon the disclosure of information imposed by statute or otherwise.

(11) An order under subsection (1) above and, in the case of material in the possession of an authorised government department, an order under section 31(2) of this Act may require any officer of the department (whether named in the order or not) who may for the time being be in possession of the material concerned to comply with such order; and any such order shall be served as if the proceedings were civil proceedings against the department.

(12) The person on whom an order under subsection (1) above is served—

(a) shall take all reasonable steps to bring it to the attention of the officer concerned; and

(b) if the order is not brought to that officer's attention within the period referred to in subsection (1) above, shall report the reasons for the failure to the Court of Session,

and it shall also be the duty of any other officer of the department in receipt of the order to take such steps as are mentioned in paragraph (a) above.

Offences

Offence of prejudicing investigation

36.—(1) A person who, knowing or suspecting that an investigation into drug trafficking is taking place, does anything which is likely to prejudice the investigation is guilty of an offence.

(2) In proceedings against a person for an offence under subsection (1) above, it is a defence to prove—

(a) that he did not know or suspect, or have reasonable grounds to suspect, that by acting as he did he was likely to prejudice the investigation; or

   (b)   that he had lawful authority or reasonable excuse for acting as he did.

(3) Nothing in subsection (1) above makes it an offence for a professional legal adviser to disclose any information or other matter—

   (a)   to, or to a representative of, a client of his in connection with the giving by the adviser of legal advice to the client; or

   (b)   to any person—

        (i)   in contemplation of, or in connection with, legal proceedings; and

       (ii)   for the purpose of those proceedings.

(4) Subsection (3) above does not apply in relation to any information or other matter which is disclosed with a view to furthering any criminal purpose.

(5) A person guilty of an offence under subsection (1) above shall be liable—

   (a)   on conviction on indictment, to imprisonment for a term not exceeding five years or to a fine or both; and

   (b)   on summary conviction, to imprisonment for a term not exceeding six months or to a fine not exceeding the statutory maximum or to both.

Acquisition, possession or use of proceeds of drug trafficking

37.—(1) A person is guilty of an offence if, knowing that any property is, or in whole or in part directly or indirectly represents, another person's proceeds of drug trafficking, he acquires or uses that property or has possession of it.

(2) It is a defence to a charge of committing an offence under this section that the person charged acquired or used the property or had possession of it for adequate consideration.

(3) For the purposes of subsection (2) above—

   (a)   a person acquires property for inadequate consideration if the value of the consideration is significantly less than the value of the property; and

   (b)   a person uses or has possession of property for inadequate consideration if the value of the consideration is significantly less than the value of his use or possession of the property.

(4) The provision for any person of services or goods which are of assistance to him in drug trafficking shall not be treated as consideration for the purposes of subsection (2) above.

(5) Where a person discloses to a constable or to a person commissioned by the Commissioners of Customs and Excise a suspicion or belief that any property is, or in whole or in part directly or indirectly represents, another person's proceeds of drug trafficking, or discloses to a constable or a person so commissioned any matter on which such a suspicion or belief is based—

   (a)   the disclosure shall not be treated as a breach of any restriction upon the disclosure of information imposed by statute or otherwise; and

   (b)   if he does any act in relation to the property in contravention of subsection (1) above, he does not commit an offence under this section if—

        (i)   the disclosure is made before he does the act concerned and the act is done with the consent of the constable or person so commissioned, or

(ii) the disclosure is made after he does the act, but on his initiative and as soon as it is reasonable for him to make it.

(6) For the purposes of this section having possession of any property shall be taken to be doing an act in relation to it.

(7) In proceedings against a person for an offence under this section, it is a defence to prove that—

(a) he intended to disclose to a constable or a person so commissioned such a suspicion, belief or matter as is mentioned in subsection (5) above; but

(b) there is reasonable excuse for his failure to make the disclosure in accordance with paragraph (b) of that subsection.

(8) In the case of a person who was in employment at the relevant time, subsections (5) and (7) above shall have effect in relation to disclosures, and intended disclosures, to the appropriate person in accordance with the procedure established by his employer for the making of such disclosures as they have effect in relation to disclosures, and intended disclosures, to a constable or a person so commissioned.

(9) A person guilty of an offence under this section is liable—

(a) on summary conviction, to imprisonment for a term not exceeding six months or to a fine not exceeding the statutory maximum or to both; or

(b) on conviction on indictment, to imprisonment for a term not exceeding fourteen years or to a fine or to both.

(10) No constable, person so commissioned or other person shall be guilty of an offence under this section in respect of anything done by him in the course of acting in connection with the enforcement, or intended enforcement, of any provision of this Act or of any other enactment relating to drug trafficking or the proceeds of such trafficking.

Offence of assisting another to retain the proceeds of drug trafficking

38.—(1) Subject to subsection (3)(b) below, a person shall be guilty of an offence if, knowing or suspecting that another person (in this section referred to as "A") is a person who carries on, or has carried on, or has derived financial or other rewards from, drug trafficking, he enters into, or is otherwise concerned in, an arrangement whereby—

(a) the retention or control, by or on behalf of A, of A's proceeds of drug trafficking is facilitated (whether by concealment, removal from the jurisdiction, transfer to nominees or otherwise); or

(b) A's proceeds of drug trafficking—

(i)   are used to secure that funds are placed at A's disposal; or
(ii) are used for A's benefit to acquire property by way of investment.

(2) In this section, references to proceeds of drug trafficking shall be construed as including any property which, whether in whole or in part, directly or indirectly constitutes such proceeds.

(3) Where a person discloses to a constable or to a person commissioned by the Commissioners of Customs and Excise a suspicion or belief that any funds or investments are derived from or used in connection with drug trafficking or

discloses to a constable or a person so commissioned any matter on which such a suspicion or belief is based—

(a) the disclosure shall not be treated as a breach of any restriction imposed by statute or otherwise on the disclosure of information; and

(b) if the disclosure relates to an arrangement entry into which, or concern in which, by the person would (but for this paragraph) contravene subsection (1) above, he does not commit an offence under that subsection if—

    (i) the disclosure is made before, with the consent of the constable or as the case may be of the person so commissioned, he enters into, or becomes concerned in, that arrangement; or

    (ii) though made after he enters into, or becomes concerned in, that arrangement, it is made on his own initiative and as soon as it is reasonable for him to do so.

(4) In proceedings against a person for an offence under subsection (1) above, it shall be a defence to prove—

(a) that he did not know or suspect that the arrangement related to any person's proceeds of drug trafficking; or

(b) that he did not know or suspect that by the arrangement the retention or control by or on behalf of A of any property was facilitated or, as the case may be, that by the arrangement any property was used as mentioned in subsection (1) above; or

(c) that—

    (i) he intended to disclose to a constable or to a person commissioned as aforesaid such a suspicion, belief or matter as is mentioned in subsection (3) above in relation to the arrangement; but

    (ii) there is reasonable excuse for his failure to make disclosure in accordance with paragraph (b) of that subsection.

(5) In the case of a person who was in employment at the relevant time, subsections (3) and (4) above shall have effect in relation to disclosures, and intended disclosures, to the appropriate person in accordance with the procedure established by his employer for the making of such disclosures as they have effect in relation to disclosures, and intended disclosures, to a constable or a person commissioned as aforesaid.

(6) A person guilty of an offence under subsection (1) above shall be liable—

(a) on conviction on indictment, to imprisonment for a term not exceeding fourteen years or to a fine or to both; and

(b) on summary conviction, to imprisonment for a term not exceeding six months or to a fine not exceeding the statutory maximum or to both.

Failure to disclose knowledge or suspicion of money laundering

39.—(1) A person is guilty of an offence if—

(a) he knows, or suspects, that another person is engaged in drug money laundering;

(b) the information, or other matter, on which that knowledge or suspicion is based came to his attention in the course of his trade, profession, business or employment; and

(c) he does not disclose the information or other matter to a constable or to a person commissioned by the Commissioners of Customs and Excise as soon as is reasonably practicable after it comes to his attention.

(2) Subsection (1) above does not make it an offence for a professional legal adviser to fail to disclose any information or other matter which has come to him in privileged circumstances.

(3) It is a defence to a charge of committing an offence under this section that the person charged had a reasonable excuse for not disclosing the information or other matter in question.

(4) Where a person discloses to a constable or a person so commissioned—

(a) his suspicion or belief that another person is engaged in drug money laundering; or

(b) any information or other matter on which that suspicion or belief is based,

the disclosure shall not be treated as a breach of any restriction imposed by statute or otherwise.

(5) Without prejudice to subsection (3) or (4) above, in the case of a person who was in employment at the relevant time, it is a defence to a charge of committing an offence under this section that he disclosed the information or other matter in question to the appropriate person in accordance with the procedure established by his employer for the making of such disclosures.

(6) A disclosure to which subsection (5) above applies shall not be treated as a breach of any restriction imposed by statute or otherwise.

(7) In this section "drug money laundering" means doing any act which constitutes an offence under—

(a) section 37 or 38 of this Act; or

(b) section 14 of the Criminal Justice (International Co-operation) Act 1990 (concealing or transferring proceeds of drug trafficking),

or, in the case of an act done otherwise than in Scotland, would constitute such an offence if done in Scotland.

(8) For the purposes of subsection (7) above, having possession of any property shall be taken to be doing an act in relation to it.

(9) For the purposes of this section, any information or other matter comes to a professional legal adviser in privileged circumstances if it is communicated, or given, to him—

(a) by, or by a representative of, a client of his in connection with the giving by the adviser of legal advice to the client;

(b) by, or by a representative of, a person seeking legal advice from the adviser; or

(c) by any person—

(i) in contemplation of, or in connection with, legal proceedings; and
(ii) for the purpose of those proceedings.

(10) No information or other matter shall be treated as coming to a professional legal adviser in privileged circumstances if it is communicated or given with a view to furthering any criminal purpose.

(11) A person guilty of an offence under this section shall be liable—

   (a) on summary conviction, to imprisonment for a term not exceeding six months or a fine not exceeding the statutory maximum or to both, or

   (b) on conviction on indictment, to imprisonment for a term not exceeding five years or a fine, or to both.

Tipping-off

40.—(1) A person is guilty of an offence if—

   (a) he knows or suspects that a constable or a person commissioned by the Commissioners of Customs and Excise is acting, or is proposing to act, in connection with an investigation which is being, or is about to be, conducted into drug money laundering within the meaning of subsections (7) and (8) of section 39 of this Act; and

   (b) he discloses to any other person information or any other matter which is likely to prejudice that investigation, or proposed investigation.

(2) A person is guilty of an offence if—

   (a) he knows or suspects that a disclosure has been made to a constable, or a person so commissioned, under section 37, 38 or 39 of this Act; and

   (b) he discloses to any other person information or any other matter which is likely to prejudice any investigation which might be conducted following the disclosure.

(3) A person is guilty of an offence if—

   (a) he knows or suspects that a disclosure of a kind mentioned in section 37(8), 38(5) or 39(5) of this Act has been made; and

   (b) he discloses to any person information or any other matter which is likely to prejudice any investigation which might be conducted following the disclosure.

(4) Nothing in subsections (1) to (3) above makes it an offence for a professional legal adviser to disclose any information or other matter—

   (a) to, or to a representative of, a client of his in connection with the giving by the adviser of legal advice to the client; or

   (b) to any person—

      (i) In contemplation of, or in connection with, legal proceedings; and
      (ii) for the purpose of those proceedings.

(5) Subsection (4) above does not apply in relation to any information or other matter which is disclosed with a view to furthering any criminal purpose.

(6) In proceedings against a person for an offence under subsection (1), (2) or (3) above, it is a defence to prove that he did not know or suspect that the disclosure was likely to be prejudicial in the way mentioned in that subsection.

(7) A person guilty of an offence under this section shall be liable—

   (a) on summary conviction, to imprisonment for a term not exceeding six months or a fine not exceeding the statutory maximum or to both, or

(b)   on conviction on indictment, to imprisonment for a term not exceeding five years or a fine, or to both.

(8) No constable, person so commissioned or other shall be guilty of an offence under this section in respect of anything done by him in the course of acting in connection with the enforcement, or intended enforcement, of any provision of this Act or of any other enactment relating to drug trafficking or the proceeds of such trafficking.

Offences relating to controlled drugs: fines

41.—(1) Without prejudice to section 211(7) of the Criminal Procedure (Scotland) Act 1995 (fines) but subject to section 10(3)(a) of the Proceeds of Crime (Scotland) Act 1995, where a person is convicted on indictment of an offence to which this section relates and sentenced in respect of that offence to a period of imprisonment or detention, the Court where—

(a)   paragraph (b) below does not apply shall, unless it is satisfied that for any reason it would be inappropriate to do so, also impose a fine;

(b)   it makes a confiscation order under section 1(1) of the Proceeds of Crime (Scotland) Act 1995 as regards the person, may also impose a fine.

(2) In determining the amount of a fine imposed under paragraph (a) of subsection (1) above, the Court shall have regard to any profits likely to have been made by the person from the crime in respect of which he has been convicted.

(3) This section relates to an offence which is a drug trafficking offence within the meaning of the said last mentioned Act of 1995.

(4) Where in any proceedings a fine has been imposed by virtue of subsection (1) above as regards a person and a period of imprisonment or detention is imposed on him in default of payment of its amount (or as the case may be of an instalment thereof), that period shall run from the expiry of any other period of imprisonment or detention (not being one of life imprisonment or detention for life) imposed on him in the proceedings.

(5) The reference in subsection (4) above to "any other period of imprisonment or detention imposed" includes (without prejudice to the generality of the expression) a reference to such a period imposed on default of payment of a fine (or instalment thereof) or of a confiscation order (or instalment thereof); but only where that default has occurred before the warrant for imprisonment is issued for the default in relation to the fine imposed by virtue of subsection (1) of this section.

Extension of certain offences to Crown servants and exemptions for regulators etc.

42.—(1) The Secretary of State may by regulations provide that, in such circumstances as may be prescribed, sections 36 to 40 of this Act shall apply to such persons in the public service of the Crown, or such categories of person in that service, as may be prescribed.

(2) Section 39 of this Act shall not apply to—

(a)   any person designated by regulations made by the Secretary of State for the purpose of this paragraph; or

(b)   in such circumstances as may be prescribed, any person who falls within such category of person as may be prescribed for the purpose of this paragraph.

(3) The Secretary of State may designate for the purpose of paragraph (a) of subsection (2) above, any person appearing to him to be performing regulatory, supervisory, investigative or registration functions.

(4) The categories of person prescribed by the Secretary of State, for the purpose of paragraph (b) of subsection (2) above, shall be such categories of person connected with the performance by any designated person of regulatory, supervisory, investigative or registration functions as he considers it appropriate to prescribe.

(5) In this section—

"the Crown" includes the Crown in right of Her Majesty's Government in Northern Ireland; and

"prescribed" means prescribed by regulations made by the Secretary of State.

(6) The power to make regulations under this section shall be exercisable by statutory instrument.

(7) Any such instrument shall be subject to annulment in pursuance of a resolution of either House of Parliament.

Interpretation of Part V

43.—(1) In this Part of this Act (except where the context otherwise requires)—

"authorised government department" means a government department which is an authorised department for the purposes of the Crown Proceedings Act 1947;

"confiscation order" means an order under section 1(1), 11(4), 12(3) or 13 of the Proceeds of Crime (Scotland) Act 1995; and

"drug trafficking" has the same meaning as in the said Act of 1995.

(2) This Part of this Act shall (except where the context otherwise requires) be construed as one with the Criminal Procedure (Scotland) Act 1995.

(3) This Part of this Act applies to property whether it is situated in Scotland or elsewhere.

(4) References in this Part of this Act—

(a) to offences include a reference to offences committed before the commencement of section 1 of the Criminal Justice (Scotland) Act 1987; but nothing in this Act imposes any duty or confers any power on any court in or in connection with proceedings against a person for an offence to which that section relates instituted before the commencement of that section;

(b) to anything received in connection with drug trafficking include a reference to anything received both in that connection and in some other connection; and

(c) to property held by a person include a reference to property vested in the interim or permanent trustee sequestration or in his trustee in bankruptcy or liquidator.

PROCEEDS OF CRIME (SCOTLAND) ACT 1995

(1995 c. 43)

ARRANGEMENT OF SECTIONS

PART I

CONFISCATION OF THE PROCEEDS OF CRIME

Confiscation orders

. . .

PART III

RESTRAINT ORDERS

PART IV

RECIPROCAL ARRANGEMENTS FOR ENFORCEMENT OF ORDERS

PART V

MISCELLANEOUS AND GENERAL

SCHEDULES:

An Act to consolidate as regards Scotland certain enactments relating to the confiscation of the proceeds of, and forfeiture of property used in, crime.

[November 8, 1995]

PART I

CONFISCATION OF THE PROCEEDS OF CRIME

Confiscation orders

General provision

1.—(1) Subject to the provisions of this Part, where in respect of any offence to which this Part applies—

(a) the accused is convicted, whether in solemn or summary proceedings; or

(b) in the case of summary proceedings (without proceeding to conviction) an order is made discharging him absolutely,

the court, on the application of the prosecutor, may make an order (a "confiscation order") requiring the accused to pay such sum as the court thinks fit.

(2) This Part applies to any offence which has been prosecuted—

(a) on indictment; or

(b) on summary complaint if the offence is punishable by a fine of an amount greater than the amount corresponding to level 5 on the standard scale or by imprisonment for a period longer than 3 months or by both such fine and imprisonment.

but it does not apply to an offence under Part III of the 1989 Act (financial assistance for terrorism).

(3) A confiscation order shall not be made unless the court orders some other disposal (including an absolute discharge) in respect of the accused.

(4) Except where the offence is a drug trafficking offence, the court may make a confiscation order against an accused only if it is satisfied that he has benefited from the commission of the offence concerned.

(5) The sum which a confiscation order requires an accused to pay in the case of a drug trafficking offence shall be an amount not exceeding—

(a) subject to paragraph (b) below, what the court assesses to be the value of the proceeds of the person's drug trafficking; or

(b) if the court is satisfied that the amount that might be realised in terms of this Act at the time the confiscation order is made has a value less than that of the proceeds of the person's drug trafficking, what it assesses to be that amount.

(6) The sum which a confiscation order requires an accused to pay in the case of an offence not mentioned in subsection (5) above, must not exceed the lesser of—

(a) the amount of the benefit—

   (i) from the commission of the offence; or
   (ii) where section 2(4) of this Act applies, from the commission of the offence and any other offence, not being a drug trafficking offence, to which this Part of this Act applies; and

(b) the amount that might be realised at the time the order is made.

(7) Any application under this section shall be made—

(a) in proceedings on indictment, when the prosecutor moves for sentence or, if the accused is remitted for sentence under section 195 of the 1995 Act, before sentence is pronounced; and

(b) in summary proceedings, following the conviction of the accused.

(8) For the purposes of any appeal or review, a confiscation order is a sentence.

Benefit from commission of offence

2.—(1) For the purposes of this Part of this Act, an accused shall be held to have benefited from the commission of an offence if in connection with its commission he has obtained, directly or indirectly, any property or other economic advantage.

(2) Subject to subsection (4) below, in determining whether an accused has benefited from the commission of an offence and, if he has, the amount referred to in section 1(6)(a)(i) of this Act, the court may make the following assumptions, except in so far as he proves either of them, on the balance of probabilities, to be incorrect—

(a) that any property or other economic advantage which has been obtained by him since the relevant date has been obtained in connection with the commission of the offence; and

(b) that any expenditure by him since the relevant date was met out of property or other economic advantage obtained in connection with the commission of the offence.

(3) In subsection (2) above "the relevant date" means—

(a) the date of the offence; or

(b) if the offence is found to have been committed over a period of time, the date occurring at the beginning of that period.

(4) Where—

(a) the application for the confiscation order has been made in respect of two or more offences; or

(b) during the relevant period the accused has been convicted of at least one other offence to which this Part of this Act applies,

the court may, in determining the amount referred to in section 1(6)(a)(ii) of this Act, make the assumptions set out in subsection (5) below, except in so far as the accused proves either of those assumptions, on the balance of probabilities, to be incorrect.

(5) Those assumptions are—

(a) that any property or economic advantage which has been obtained by the accused during the relevant period has been obtained in connection with the commission of an offence to which this Part of this Act applies; and

(b) that any expenditure by him during the relevant period was met out of property or other economic advantage obtained in connection with the commission of such an offence.

(6) In subsections (4) and (5) above, "the relevant period" means the period of six years ending with the date on which proceedings were instituted against the accused for the offence in respect of which the application for the confiscation order has been made.

(7) In this Act, "property" means any property wherever situated, whether heritable or moveable or whether corporeal or incorporeal.

Assessing the proceeds of drug trafficking

3.—(1) For the purposes of this Act—

(a) any payments or other rewards received by a person at any time (whether before or after the commencement of this Act) in connection with drug trafficking carried on by him or another are his proceeds of drug trafficking, and

(b) the value of his proceeds of drug trafficking is the aggregate of the values of the payments or other rewards.

(2) Without prejudice to section 9 of this Act the court may, in making an assessment as regards a person under section 1(5) of this Act, make the following assumptions, except in far as any of them may be shown to be incorrect in that person's case—

(a) that any property appearing to the court—

(i) to have been held by him at any time since his conviction; or, as the case may be,

    (ii) to have been transferred to him at any time since a date six years before his being indicted, or being served with the complaint, was received by him, at the earliest time at which he appears to the court to have held it, as a payment or reward in connection with drug trafficking carried on by him;

  (b) that any expenditure of his since the date mentioned in paragraph (a)(ii) above was met out of payments received by him in connection with drug trafficking carried on by him, and

  (c) that, for the purpose of valuing any property received or assumed to have been received by him at any time as such a reward, he received the property free of any other interests in it.

(3) Subsection (2) above does not apply if the only offence by virtue of which the assessment is being made is an offence under section 14 of the Criminal Justice (International Co-operation) Act 1990 or section 37 or 38 of the Criminal Law (Consolidation) (Scotland) Act 1995.

(4) The court shall, in making an assessment as regards a person under section 1(5) of this Act, leave out of account any of his proceeds of drug trafficking that are shown to the court to have been taken into account in a case where a confiscation order (whether under this Act or under and within the meaning of—

  (a) section 2 of the 1994 Act; or

  (b) any corresponding provision in Northern Ireland), has previously been made against him.

Realisable property

4.—(1) In this Act "realisable property" means, subject to subsection (2) below—

  (a) the whole estate wherever situated of a person—

    (i) against whom proceedings have been instituted for an offence to which this Part of this Act applies; or
    (ii) in respect of whom a restraint order has been made by virtue of section 29(3) of this Act;

  (b) the whole estate wherever situated of a person to whom any person whose whole estate is realisable by virtue of paragraph (a) above has (directly or indirectly and whether in one transaction or in a series of transactions) made a gift caught by this Part of this Act or, as the case may be, an implicative gift;

  (c) any other property in the possession or under the control of a person mentioned in paragraph (a) or (b) above; and

  (d) any income or vesting in a person mentioned in paragraph (a) or (b) above.

(2) Property is not realisable if—

  (a) held on trust by a person mentioned in subsection (1)(a) or (b) above for a person not so mentioned;

  (b) a suspended forfeiture order is in force in respect of the property; or

  (c) it is, for the time being, a restraint order made in respect of other proceedings.

(3) For the purposes of this Part of this Act, the amount that might be realised at the time a confiscation order is made in respect of a person is—

    (a) in relation to an offence which is not a drug trafficking offence, subject to section 7(5) of this Act, the total value at that time of all his realisable property, and of all gifts caught by this Part which have been made by him, less any amount due by him at that time in respect of any compensation order under section 249 of the 1995 Act made before the confiscation order; and

    (b) in relation to a drug trafficking offence, the total value at that time of all his realisable property, and of all implicative gifts which have been made by him.

(4) In assessing the value of realisable property (other than money) of a person in respect of whom it proposes to make a confiscation order, the court shall have regard to the likely market value of the property at the date on which the order would be made; but it may also have regard to any security or real burden which would require to be discharged in realising the property or to any other factors which might reduce the amount recoverable by such realisation.

(5) In assessing the value of realisable property of a person whose estate has been sequestrated, or who has been adjudged bankrupt in England and Wales or Northern Ireland, the court shall take into account the extent to which the property is subject to, as the case may be, sequestration or bankruptcy procedure by virtue of paragraph 1 or 2 of Schedule 2 to this Act.

(6) Without prejudice to section 2(7) of this Act, the court may, for the purposes of section 1(5)(b) of this Act, disregard the amount (or part of the amount) of an implicative gift if it considers it improbable that such amount (or part) could be realised.

Gifts caught by Part I

5.—(1) A gift is caught by this Part of this Act if—

    (a) it was made by the accused—

        (i) in contemplation of, or after, the commission of the offence; or, if more than one,

        (ii) in contemplation of any of the offences or after the commission of the earlier or the earliest of the offences,

    to which the proceedings mentioned in section 4(1)(a)(i) of this Act for the time being relate, not being drug trafficking offences; or

    (b) where subsection (4) of section 2 of this Act applies, it was made by the accused within the relevant period within the meaning of subsection (6) of that section.

(2) The value of a gift caught by this Part of this Act shall be assessed in accordance with section 7 of this Act.

(3) At any time before the realisation of property which is or represents a gift caught by this Part of this Act, the recipient of the gift may apply to the court for an order under this subsection and, if the court is satisfied, on the balance of probabilities—

    (a) that the person received the gift not knowing, not suspecting and not having reasonable grounds to suspect that the gift was made in contemplation of, or after, the commission of the offence or, if more than one, in contemplation of any of the offences or after the commission of the earlier or the earliest of the offences to which the proceedings for the time being relate; and

(b) that he was not associated with the giver in the commission of the offence; and

(c) that he would suffer hardship if the application were not granted, it may make an order declaring that the gift or a part of the gift shall not be caught by this Part of this Act and that the property or part of the property of the recipient of the gift shall not be, or shall cease to be, realisable for the purposes of this Part of this Act and, if a confiscation order has already been made, varying that order accordingly, where necessary.

(4) An appeal shall lie to the High Court at the instance of—

(a) the applicant against the refusal;

(b) the prosecutor against the granting,

of an application under subsection (3) above, and the High Court in determining such an appeal may make such order as could have been made by the court on an application under that subsection.

(5) The procedure in an appeal under this section shall be the same as the procedure in an appeal against sentence.

Implicative gifts

6.—(1) In this Act references to an "implicative gift" are references to a gift (whether made before or after the commencement of this Act)—

(a) made not more than six years before the date on which, in respect a person suspected of, or charged with, a drug trafficking offence, the proceedings were commenced or a restraint order was made (whichever first occurs); or

(b) made at any time if the gift was of property—

    (i) received by the giver in connection with drug trafficking carried on by him or another, or

    (ii) which, in whole or in part, directly or indirectly represented in the giver's hands property received by him in that connection.

(2) The value of an implicative gift shall be assessed in accordance with section 7 of this Act.

(3) Where the court is satisfied, on the application of a person in receipt of an implicative gift made before or after a confiscation order has been made—

(a) that the person received the gift not knowing, not suspecting and not having reasonable grounds to suspect that the giver was in any way concerned in drug trafficking; and

(b) that he is not, and has never been, associated with the giver in drug trafficking; and

(c) that he would suffer hardship if the application were not granted, it may make an order declaring that the gift or a part of the gift shall not be an implicative gift and that the property or part of the property of the recipient of the gift shall not be, or shall cease to be, realisable for the purposes of this Part of this Act and, if a confiscation order has already been made, varying that order accordingly, where necessary.

(4) An appeal shall lie to the High Court at the instance of—

(a)   the applicant against the refusal;

(b)   the prosecutor against the granting,

of an application under subsection (3) above on the ground that there has been a miscarriage of justice.

(5) The procedure in an appeal under this section shall be the same as the procedure in an appeal against sentence.

Gifts: valuation

7.—(1) In assessing the value of—

(a)   a gift caught by this Part of this Act; or

(b)   an implicative gift,

the court shall, subject to sub-sections (4) to (6) below, take it to be the greater of the values specified in subsections (2) and (3) below.

(2) The value specified in this subsection is the value of the gift when received adjusted to take account of subsequent changes in the value of money.

(3) The value specified in this subsection is both of the following—

(a)   the likely market value, on the date on which the confiscation order is to be made, of—

    (i)   the gift, if retained; or

    (ii)   where the recipient of the gift retains only part of it, the retained part, and any property or part of any property which, directly or indirectly, represents the gift; or

    (iii)   where the recipient of the gift retains no part of it, any property or part of any property which directly or indirectly, represents the gift; and

(b)   the value of any other property and any other economic advantage which by reason of the making of the gift the recipient of the gift has obtained, directly or indirectly, prior to the date on which the confiscation order is to be made, adjusted to take account of subsequent changes in the value of money.

(4) The circumstances in which the accused is to be treated as making a gift include those where he transfers an interest in property to another person directly or indirectly for a consideration the value of which is significantly less than the value of that interest at the time of transfer; and in those circumstances the value of the gift shall be the difference between the value of that consideration and the value of that interest at the time of transfer, adjusted to take account of subsequent changes in the value of money.

(5) Where a gift was in the form of money and the recipient of the gift shows that, on the balance of probabilities, the money or any of it has not been used to purchase goods or services or to earn interest or any other return, the value of the gift or such part of it as has not been so used shall be taken to be the face value of the money or, as the case may be, unused amount of the money.

(6) The court may, notwithstanding the foregoing provisions of this section, disregard the amount (or part of the amount) of a gift caught by this Part of this Act if it considers it improbable that such amount (or part) could be realised.

Making of confiscation orders

8.—(1) If the court decides to make a confiscation order, it shall determine the amount to be payable thereunder before making any decision as to—

(a) imposing a fine on the accused;

(b) making any order involving any payment by him.

(2) Where a court makes a confiscation order against an accused in any proceedings, it shall, in respect of any offence of which he is convicted in those proceedings, take account of the order before—

(a) imposing any fine on him;

(b) making any order involving any other payment by him,

but subject to that, the court shall leave the order out of account in determining the appropriate sentence or other manner of dealing with the accused.

(3) No enactment restricting the power of a court which deals with an accused in a particular way from dealing with him also in any other way shall, by reason only of the making of a confiscation order (or the postponement of a decision as regards making such an order), have the effect of restricting the court in dealing with the accused in any way it considers appropriate in respect of an offence.

(4) Where a court makes both a confiscation order and a compensation order under section 249 of the 1995 Act against the same person in the same proceedings in relation to the same offence and the offence involves the misappropriation of property, it shall direct that the compensation shall be paid first out of any sums applied towards the satisfaction of the confiscation order.

Statements relevant to making confiscation orders

9.—(1) Where the prosecutor applies for the making of a confiscation order, the prosecutor may lodge with the clerk of court a statement as to any matters relevant—

(a) in connection with a drug trafficking offence, to the assessment of the value of the accused's proceeds of drug trafficking; and

(b) in connection with any other offence—

    (i) to determining whether the accused has benefited for the purposes of section 1(6)(a) of this Act; or

    (ii) to an assessment of the value of the accused's benefit from the commission of the offence.

(2) Without prejudice to section 256 of the 1995 Act, if the accused accepts to any extent any allegation in the statement lodged under subsection (1) above, the court may, for the purpose of such determination or assessment as is mentioned in paragraph (a) or (b) of that subsection, treat his acceptance as conclusive of the matters to which it relates.

(3) Where—

(a) a statement is lodged under subsection (1) above; and

(b) the court is satisfied that a copy of that statement has been served on the accused,

the court may require the accused to indicate, within such period as the court may specify, to what extent he accepts each allegation in the statement and, in so far as he does not accept any such allegation, to indicate the basis of such non-acceptance.

(4) If the accused fails in any respect to comply with a requirement under subsection (3) above, he may be treated for the purposes of this section as accepting every allegation in the statement apart from any allegation in respect of which he has complied with the requirement.

(5) Without prejudice to section 256 of the 1995 Act, where—

(a) there is lodged with the clerk of court by the accused a statement as to any matters relevant to determining the amount that might be realised at the time the confiscation order is made; and

(b) the prosecutor accepts to any extent any allegation in the statement, the court may, for the purposes of that determination, treat that acceptance as conclusive of the matters to which it relates.

(6) Without prejudice to section 10(1) of this Act, where—

(a) any allegation in the statement lodged under subsection (1) above is challenged by the accused, or

(b) the basis of the non-acceptance by the accused of any such allegation is challenged by the prosecutor,

the court shall consider the matters being challenged at a hearing.

(7) Where the judge presiding at a hearing held under subsection (6) above is not the trial judge he may, on the application of either party, if he considers that it would be in the interests of justice to do so, adjourn the hearing to a date when the trial judge is available.

(8) No acceptance by a person under this section that any payment or other reward was received by him in connection with drug trafficking carried on by him or another shall be admissible in evidence in any proceedings, whether in Scotland or elsewhere, in respect of an offence.

Postponed confiscation orders

10.—(1) If the court considers—

(a) that it has some, but not sufficient, relevant information for the purpose of enabling it to come to a decision as to whether to make a confiscation order; or

(b) that it does not have sufficient relevant information to enable it to come to a decision as to the amount to be payable under the confiscation order,

it may, subject as the case may be to subsection (6) or (10) below, postpone that decision for a period not exceeding 6 months after the date of conviction for the purpose of enabling further information to be obtained.

(2) Without prejudice to sections 201 and 202 of the 1995 Act, the court may notwithstanding postponement under subsection (1) above and subject to subsection (3) below, proceed, on the prosecutor's motion therefor, to sentence or to otherwise deal with the accused in respect of the conviction.

(3) Where the court proceeds as mentioned in subsection (2) above—

(a) no fine shall be imposed on the accused; and

(b) no order shall be made involving any other payment by him, in relation to the conviction before the decision whether to make a confiscation order is taken.

(4) Where in the case of conviction on indictment a decision has been postponed under subsection (1) above for a period, any intention to appeal under section 106 of the 1995 Act against conviction or against both conviction and any sentence passed during that period in respect of the conviction, shall be intimated under section 109(1) of the 1995 Act not within 2 weeks of the final determination of the proceedings but within 2 weeks of—

(a) in the case of an appeal against conviction where there has been no such sentence, the day on which the period of postponement commences;

(b) in any other case, the day on which such sentence is passed in open court.

(5) Notwithstanding any appeal of which intimation has been given by virtue of subsection (4) above, a person may appeal under section 106 of the 1995 Act against the confiscation order (if the decision is to make one) or against any other sentence passed, after the period of postponement, in respect of the conviction.

(6) If during the period of postponement intimation is given by virtue of subsection (4) above by the person, the High Court may, on the application of the prosecutor, extend that period to a date up to 3 months after the date of disposal of the appeal.

(7) This subsection applies where in the case of summary conviction a decision has been postponed under subsection (1) above for a period.

(8) Where subsection (7) above applies and the offender appeals under section 175 of the 1995 Act against conviction or against both conviction and any sentence passed during the period of postponement—

(a) his application for a stated case shall be made not within one week of the final determination of the proceedings but within one week of the day mentioned in paragraph (a) or (b) of subsection (4) above;

(b) his draft stated case shall be prepared and issued not within 3 weeks of the final determination of the proceedings but within 3 weeks of the said day.

(9) Where subsection (7) above applies, then, notwithstanding any appeal against conviction or sentence or both, the offender may appeal under section 175(2)(b), and the prosecutor may appeal under section 175(3)(b), of the 1995 Act against any confiscation order or against any other sentence passed, after the period of postponement, in respect of the conviction.

(10) Where subsection (7) above applies, then, if during the period of postponement the offender applies for a stated case or lodges a note of appeal, the High Court may, on the application of the prosecutor, extend the period of postponement to a date up to 3 months after the date of disposal of the appeal.

Increase in benefit or realisable property

11.—(1) This section applies where the court which made a confiscation order is satisfied, on an application made by the prosecutor, that at the time the application is made—

(a) in the case of a drug trafficking offence, the value of the proceeds of the person's drug trafficking, or the amount that might be realised, is greater than—

(i) the value of the proceeds of his drug trafficking; or, as the case may be,

(ii) the amount that might be realised; or

(b) in any other case, the benefit for the purposes of section 1(6)(a) of this Act, or the amount that might be realised, is greater than—

(i) the benefit; or, as the case may be,

(ii) the amount that might be realised,

which was taken into account when the order was made.

(2) The considerations by reference to which the court may be satisfied as mentioned in subsection (1) above shall include—

(a) the value of the proceeds of the person's drug trafficking or, as the case may be, the benefit was greater than was taken into account when the confiscation order was made or has increased in value since the confiscation order was made; or

(b) further proceeds of drug trafficking have or benefit has been obtained since the confiscation order was made; or

(c) the value of realisable property was greater than was taken into account when the confiscation order was made; or

(d) any realisable property taken into account at the time when the confiscation order was made has subsequently increased in value; or

(e) that the amount, or part of the amount, of a gift which was disregarded under section 7(6) of this Act could now be realised.

(3) An application under subsection (1) above shall be made as soon as is reasonably practicable after the relevant information becomes available to the prosecutor but in any event within 6 years commencing with the date when the person was convicted of the offence.

(4) Where this section applies—

(a) the court may make a new confiscation order for the payment of such sum as appears to the court to be appropriate having regard to what is now shown to be the benefit or the amount that might be realised; and

(b) if the earlier confiscation order has not been satisfied then the court, in making the new confiscation order, shall recall the earlier order and may take into account the amount unpaid (including any interest· payable by virtue of section 15(1) of this Act) under the earlier order.

(5) Subsection (4) above applies to an offence which is not a drug trafficking offence notwithstanding that any matters in relation to the making of the confiscation order are, by virtue of section 9(2) or (5) of this Act, to be treated as conclusive.

(6) Section 9 of this Act shall, subject to any necessary modifications, apply in relation to the making of a new confiscation order in pursuance of this section as it applies where the prosecutor has applied for the making of a confiscation order under section 1 of this Act.

(7) The assumptions mentioned in, as the case may be, section 3(2) or 2(2) and (5) of this Act shall not apply for the purposes of this section.

Realisable property inadequate to meet payments under confiscation order

12.—(1) This section applies where the court which made a confiscation order is satisfied on the balance of probabilities, on an application made to it by the accused or the prosecutor, that the value of the realisable property is inadequate to meet any amount unpaid (including any interest payable by virtue of section 15(1) of this Act) under the confiscation order.

(2) When considering whether the value of the realisable property is inadequate the court—

(a) shall, unless already taken into account under section 4(5) of this Act, take into account the extent to which property of a person whose estate has been sequestrated or who has been adjudged bankrupt is or has been included in the bankrupt's estate for the purposes of the Bankruptcy (Scotland) Act 1985 or Part IX of the Insolvency Act 1986; and

(b) may disregard any inadequacy which appears to it to be attributable, wholly or partly, to anything done by the accused for the purpose of protecting the realisable property from realisation.

(3) Where this section applies, the court shall recall the confiscation order and make a new confiscation order for the payment of such sum of a lesser amount than that for which the original order was made which appears to the court to be appropriate having regard to—

(a) the value of the realisable property as determined under subsection (1) above; and

(b) any amount paid in pursuance of the original order.

(4) Section 9 of this Act shall, subject to any necessary modifications, apply in relation to an application under this section as it applies where the prosecutor has applied for the making of a confiscation order under section 1 of this Act.

Confiscation orders where proceeds of crime discovered at later date

13.—(1) This section applies where no confiscation order has been made in relation to an offence under section 1 or 10 of this Act.

(2) Where the court, on an application made to it by the prosecutor under this section, is satisfied—

(a) that a person convicted of—

   (i) an offence other than a drug trafficking offence has benefited in connection with the commission of the offence concerned; or

   (ii) a drug trafficking offence was in receipt of the proceeds of drug trafficking in respect of that offence;

(b) that the information necessary to enable a confiscation order to be made on the date on which an application under section 1 of this Act was or could have been made was not available to the prosecutor,

it may make a confiscation order in relation to that person.

(3) An application under this section shall be made as soon as is reasonably practicable after the relevant information becomes available to the prosecutor but in any event not later than 6 years after the date when the person was convicted of the offence.

(4) In determining the sum to be payable under a confiscation order made in pursuance of this section, the court shall take into account—

(a) any order involving any payment by the offender;

(b) any suspended forfeiture order or an order for forfeiture under any other enactment made in respect of the offender,

which forms part of the sentence already imposed for the offence concerned.

(5) Sections 1(3) and 8(1), (2) and (4) of this Act shall not apply in relation to a confiscation order made in pursuance of this section.

(6) Section 9 of this Act shall, subject to any necessary modifications, apply in relation to the making of a confiscation order in pursuance of this section as it applies where the prosecutor has applied for the making of a confiscation order under section 1 of this Act.

(7) Where the court makes a confiscation order in pursuance of this section and a compensation order has been made under section 249 of the 1995 Act in respect of misappropriation of property by the offender, the court shall direct that compensation shall first be paid out of any sums applied towards the satisfaction of the confiscation order to the extent of any sums outstanding in respect of the compensation order.

(8) The assumptions mentioned in, as the case may be, section 2(2) and (5) or 3(2) of this Act shall not apply for the purposes of this section.

(9) In determining the sum to be payable as mentioned in subsection (4) above in connection with a drug trafficking offence, the court may take into account any payment or other reward received by the offender on or after the date of conviction, but only if the prosecutor satisfies the court that it was received by the offender in connection with drug trafficking carried on by the offender or another on or before that date.

(10) In this section "the court" means the court which had jurisdiction in respect of the offence concerned to make a confiscation order under section 1 of this Act.

Application of provisions relating to fines to enforcement of confiscation orders

14.—(1) Section 211(3) to (6) of the 1995 Act and the other provisions of that Act specified in subsection (2) below shall, subject to the qualifications mentioned in that subsection, apply in relation to confiscation orders as they apply in relation to fines; and section 91 of the Magistrates' Courts Act 1980 and Article 96 of the Magistrates' Courts (Northern Ireland) Order 1981 (provisions relating to transfer of fines from Scotland etc.) shall be construed accordingly.

(2) The provisions of the 1995 Act mentioned in subsection (1) above are—

(a) section 214, provided that—

  (i) any allowance under that section of time (or further time) for payment; or
  (ii) any order of payment by instalments,

  shall be without prejudice to the exercise by any administrator appointed in relation to the confiscation order of his powers and duties under this Act; and the court may, pending such exercise, any decision as to refusing or allowing time (or further time) for payment or, as the case may be, making an order of payment by instalments;

(b) section 215, subject to the like proviso as in paragraph (a) above;

(c) section 216, but as if subsection (1)—

  (i) gave the prosecutor an opportunity to be heard at any enquiry thereunder; and
  (ii) applied whether the offender was in prison or not;

(d) section 217;

(e) section 218(2) and (3);

(f) section 219, provided that—

  (i) where a court imposes a period of imprisonment both in respect of a fine and of a confiscation order the amounts in respect of which the period is imposed shall, for the purposes of subsection (2) of that section, be aggregated; and
  (ii) before imposing a period of imprisonment to which there is a liability by virtue of that section the court shall, if an administrator has been appointed in relation to the confiscation order,

require a report from him as to whether and in what way he is likely to exercise his powers and duties under this Act and shall take that report into account; and the court may, pending such exercise, postpone any decision as to such imposition;

(g) section 220, except that the reference in subsection (1) of that section to the person paying a sum to the governor of the prison under conditions prescribed by rules made under the Prisons (Scotland) Act 1989 shall be construed as including a reference to an administrator appointed in relation to the confiscation order making such payment under this Act in respect of the person;

(h) section 221, provided that an order of recovery by civil diligence shall not be made under the section where an administrator is appointed in relation to the confiscation order;

(i) section 222; except that for the purposes of that section "confiscation order" in subsection (1) above shall be construed as including such an order within the meaning of the 1994 Act or of any corresponding provision in Northern Ireland;

(j) section 223;

(k) section 224.

(3) Where a court, by virtue of subsection (1) above, orders the sum due under a confiscation order to be recovered by civil diligence under section 221 of the 1995 Act, any arrestment executed by a prosecutor under subsection (2) of section 33 of this Act shall be deemed to have been executed by the court as if that subsection authorised such execution.

(4) Where in any proceedings a confiscation order has been made as regards a person and a period of imprisonment or detention is imposed on him in default of payment of its amount (or as the case may be of an instalment thereof), that period shall run from the expiry of any other period of imprisonment or detention (not being one of life imprisonment or detention for life) imposed on him in the proceedings.

(5) The reference in subsection (4) above to "any other period of imprisonment or detention imposed" includes (without prejudice to the generality of the expression) a reference to such a period on default of payment of a fine (or instalment thereof); but only where that default had occurred before the warrant for imprisonment is issued for the default in relation to the order.

Interest on sums unpaid under confiscation orders

15.—(1) If any sum required to be paid by a person under a confiscation order is not paid when it is required to be paid (whether forthwith on the making of the order or at a time specified under section 214(1) of the 1995 Act) that person shall be liable to pay interest on that sum for the period for which it remains unpaid and the amount of the interest shall for the purposes of enforcement be treated as part of the amount to be recovered from him under the confiscation order.

(2) The sheriff may, on the application of the prosecutor, increase the term of imprisonment or detention fixed in respect of the confiscation order under section 214(2) of the 1995 Act if the effect of subsection (1) above is to increase the maximum period applicable in relation to the order under section 219(2) of the 1995 Act.

(3) The rate of interest under subsection (1) above shall be the rate payable under a decree of the Court of Session.

Exercise of powers

Exercise of powers by court or administrator

16.—(1) This section applies to the powers as regards realisable property conferred on the court by sections 28, 29, 31, 32 and 33 of and paragraphs 1, 4, and 12 of Schedule 1 to this Act in relation to confiscation orders and on an administrator by that Schedule.

(2) Subject to the following provisions of this section, the powers shall be exercised with a view to making available for satisfying the confiscation order or, as the case may be, any confiscation order that may be made in the case of a person mentioned in section 4(1)(a) of this Act the value for the time being of realisable property held by any person by the realisation of such property.

(3) In the case of realisable property held by a person by virtue only of having received a gift made directly or indirectly by the accused which is caught by this Part of this Act, the powers shall be exercised with a view to realising no more than the value of the gift as assessed under section 7 of this Act.

(4) The powers shall be exercised with a view to allowing any person other than a person mentioned in paragraph (a) and, in relation to a drug trafficking offence, paragraph (b) of section 4(1) of this Act or the recipient of any such gift to retain or recover the value of any property held by him.

(5) An order may be made or other action taken in respect of a debt owed by the Crown.

(6) In exercising those powers, no account shall be taken of any obligations of such a person or of the recipient of any such gift which conflict with the obligation to satisfy the confiscation order.

(7) Subsections (2) to (6) of section 31 of the 1994 Act (exercise of powers by High Court etc.) shall apply as regards the powers conferred on the court by sections 35, 36, 37 and 38 of this Act as those subsections apply as regards the powers conferred on the High Court (within the meaning that expression has in relation to England and Wales) by the sections mentioned in subsection (1) of the said section 31.

Compensation

Compensation

17.—(1) Subject to subsection (3) below, if proceedings are instituted against a person for an offence to which this Part of this Act applies, and either—

(a) the proceedings do not result in his conviction for any such offence, or

(b) where he is convicted of one or more such offences—

(i) the conviction or convictions concerned are quashed (and no conviction for any such offence is substituted); or

(ii) he is pardoned by Her Majesty in respect of the conviction or convictions concerned,

the court may, on an application by a person who held property which was realisable property, order compensation to be paid to the applicant if, having regard to all the circumstances, it considers it appropriate to do so.

(2) Subsection (1) above is without prejudice to any right which may otherwise exist to institute proceedings in respect of delictual liability disclosed by such circumstances as are mentioned in paragraphs (a) and (b) of subsection (3) below.

(3) The court shall not order compensation to be paid under subsection (1) above in any case unless satisfied—

(a) that there has been some serious default on the part of a person concerned in the investigation of the offence or offences concerned, being a person mentioned in subsection (5) below, and that, but for that default, the proceedings would not have been instituted or continued; and

(b) that the applicant has suffered loss or damage in consequence of anything done in relation to the property under section 28, 29, 31, 32, 33 or 42 of or Schedule 1 to this Act or by virtue of section 37 of the 1994 Act (recognition and enforcement in England and Wales of orders and functions under this Act).

(4) The amount of compensation to be paid under this section shall be such as the court thinks just in all the circumstances of the case.

(5) Compensation payable under this section shall he paid, where the person in default was—

(a) a constable of a police force within the meaning of the Police (Scotland) Act 1967, by the police authority or joint police board for the police area for which that force is maintained;

(b) a constable other than is mentioned in paragraph (a) above, but with the powers of such a constable, by the body under whose authority he acts;

(c) a procurator fiscal or was acting on behalf of the Lord Advocate, by the Lord Advocate;

(d) a person commissioned by the Commissioners of Customs and Excise, by those Commissioners; and

(e) an officer of the Commissioners of Inland Revenue, by those Commissioners.

(6) An application for compensation under this section shall be made not later than three years after the conclusion of the proceedings in respect of which the Confiscation order was made; and subsection (6) of section 29 of this Act shall apply for the purpose of determining when proceedings are concluded for the purposes of this subsection as it applies for the purposes of that section.

(7) In this section, "the court" means the Court of Session or the sheriff exercising his civil jurisdiction.

Investigation and disclosure of information

Order to make material available

18.—(1) The procurator fiscal may, for the purpose of an investigation into whether a person has benefited from the commission of an offence to which this Part of this Act applies and as to the amount of that benefit, apply to the sheriff for an order under subsection (2) below in relation to particular material or material of a particular description.

(2) If on such an application the sheriff is satisfied that the conditions in subsection (4) below are fulfilled, he may, subject to section 20(11) of this Act, make an order that the person who appears to him to be in possession of the material to which the application relates shall—

(a) produce it to a constable for him to take away; or

(b) give a constable access to it, within such period as the order may specify.

(3) The period to be specified in an order under subsection (2) above shall be seven days unless it appears to the sheriff that a longer or shorter period would be appropriate in the particular circumstances of the application.

(4) The conditions referred to in subsection (2) above are—

(a) that there are reasonable grounds for suspecting that a specified person has benefited from the commission of an offence to which this Part of this Act applies;

(b) that there are reasonable grounds for suspecting that the material to which the application relates—

(i) is likely to be of substantial value (whether by itself or together with other material) to the investigation for the purpose of which the application is made; and

(ii) does not consist of or include items subject to legal privilege; and

(c) that there are reasonable grounds for believing that it is in the public interest, having regard—

(i) to the benefit likely to accrue to the investigation if the material is obtained; and

(ii) to the circumstances under which the person in possession of the material holds it,

that the material be produced or that access to it should be given.

(5) where the sheriff makes an order under subsection (2)(b) above in relation to material on any premises he may, on the application of the procurator fiscal, order any person who appears to him to be entitled to grant entry to the premises to allow a constable to enter the premises to obtain access to the material.

(6) An application under subsection (1) or (5) above may be made *ex parte* in chambers.

(7) Provision may be made by rules of court as to—

(a) the discharge add variation of orders under this section, and

(b) proceedings relating to such orders.

(8) Where the material to which an application under this section relates consists of information contained in a computer—

(a) an order under subsection (2)(a) above shall have effect as an order to produce the material in a form in which it can be taken away and in which it is visible and legible; and

(b) an order under subsection (2)(b) above shall have effect as an order to give access to the material in a form in which it is visible and legible.

(9) An order under subsection (2) above—

(a) shall not confer any fight to production of, or access to, items subject to legal privilege;

(b) shall have effect notwithstanding any obligation as to secrecy or other restriction upon the disclosure of information imposed by statute or otherwise; and

(c) may be made in relation to material in the possession of an authorised government department;

and in this subsection "authorised government department" means a government department which is an authorised department for the purposes of the Crown Proceedings Act 1947.

(10) In this section—

  (a) "items subject to legal privilege" and "premises" have the same meanings as in section 33 of the Criminal Law (Consolidation) (Scotland) Act 1995; and

  (b) references to a person from the commission of an offence to which this Part of this Act applies, in relation to conduct which is not such an offence but which would have been if it had occurred in Scotland, shall be construed in accordance with section 2 of this Act as if that conduct had so occurred.

(11) This section and sections 19 and 20 of this Act do not apply to investigations into drug trafficking.

[1](12) In this section "constable" includes a person commissioned by the Commissioners of Customs and Excise.

NOTE
[1]Inserted by the Crime and Disorder Act 1998 (c. 37), Sched. 8, para. 115 (effective September 30, 1998: S.I. 1998 No. 2327).

Authority for search

19.—(1) The procurator fiscal may, for the purpose of an investigation into whether a person has benefited from the commission of an offence to which this Part of this Act applies and as to the amount of that benefit, apply to the sheriff for a warrant under this section in relation to specified premises.

(2) On such application the sheriff may issue a warrant authorising a constable to enter and search the premises if the sheriff is satisfied—

  (a) that an order made under section 18 of this Act in relation to material on the premises has not been complied with; or

  (b) that the conditions in subsection (3) below are fulfilled; or

  (c) that the conditions in subsection (4) below are fulfilled.

(3) The conditions referred to in subsection (2)(b) above are—

  (a) that there are reasonable grounds for suspecting that a specified person has benefited from the commission of an offence to which this Part of this Act applies; and

  (b) that the conditions in section 18(4)(b) and (c) of this Act are fulfilled in relation to any material on the premises; and

  (c) that it would not be appropriate to make an order under that section in relation to the material because—

    (i) it is not practicable to communicate with any person entitled to produce the material; or

    (ii) it is not practicable to communicate with any person entitled to grant access to the material or entitled to grant entry to the premises on which the material is situated; or

    (iii) the investigation for the purposes of which the application is made might be seriously prejudiced unless a constable could secure immediate access to the material.

(4) The conditions referred to in subsection (2)(c) above are—

  (a) that there are reasonable grounds for suspecting that a specified person has benefited from the commission of an offence to which this Part of this Act applies; and

(b) that there are reasonable grounds for suspecting that there is on the premises material relating to the specified person, or to the question whether that person has so benefited or the amount of that benefit, which is likely to be of substantial value (whether by itself or together with other material) to the investigation for the purpose of which the application is made, but that the material cannot at the time of the application be particularised; and

(c) that—

    (i) it is not practicable to communicate with any person entitled to grant entry to the premises; or

    (ii) entry to the premises will not be granted unless a warrant is produced; or

    (iii) the investigation for the purpose of which the application is made might be seriously prejudiced unless a constable arriving at the premises could secure immediate entry to them.

(5) Where a constable has entered premises in the execution of a warrant issued under this section, he may seize and retain any material, other than items subject to legal privilege, which is likely to be of substantial value (whether by itself or together with other material) to the investigation for the purpose of which the warrant was issued.

[1](6) Subsections (10) and (12) of section 18 of this Act shall apply for the purposes of this section as they apply for the purposes of that section.

NOTE
[1]Amended by the Crime and Disorder Act 1998 (c. 37), Sched. 8, para. 116 (effective September 30, 1998: S.I. 1998 No. 2327).

Disclosure of information held by government departments

20.—(1) Subject to subsection (4) below, the Court of Session may on an application by the Lord Advocate order any material mentioned in subsection (3) below which is in the possession of an authorised government department to be produced to the Court within such period as the Court may specify.

(2) The power to make an order under subsection (1) above is exercisable if—

(a) the powers conferred on the Court by section 28(1)(a) of this Act are exercisable by virtue of section 29(2) of this Act; or

(b) those powers are exercisable by virtue of section 29(3) of this Act and the Court has made a restraint order which has not been recalled.

(3) The material referred to in subsection (1) above is any material which—

(a) has been submitted to an officer of an authorised government department by a person who holds, or has at any time held, realisable property;

(b) has been made by an officer of an authorised government department in relation to such a person; or

(c) is correspondence which passed between an officer authorised government department and such a person;

and an order under that subsection may require the production of all such material or of a particular description of such material, being material in the possession of the department concerned.

(4) An order under subsection (1) above shall not require the production of any material unless it appears to the Court of Session that the material is likely

to contain information that would facilitate the exercise of the powers conferred on the Court by section 28(1)(a) of or paragraph 1 or 12 of Schedule 1 to this Act or on an administrator appointed under paragraph 1(1) of that Schedule.

(5) The Court may by order authorise the disclosure to such an administrator of any material produced under subsection (1) above or any part of such material; but the Court shall not make an order under this subsection unless a reasonable opportunity has been given for an officer of the department to make representations to the Court.

(6) Material disclosed in pursuance of an order under subsection (5) above may, subject to any conditions contained in the order, be further disclosed for the purposes of the functions under this Act of the administrator or the High Court.

(7) The Court of Session may by order authorise the disclosure to a person mentioned in subsection (8) below of any material produced under subsection (1) above or any part of such material but the Court shall not make an order under this subsection unless—

(a) a reasonable opportunity has been given for an officer of the department to make representations to the Court; and

(b) it appears to the Court that the material is likely to be of substantial value in exercising functions relating to the investigation of crime.

(8) The persons referred to in subsection (7) above are—

(a) a constable;

(b) the Lord Advocate or any procurator fiscal; and

(c) an officer within meaning of the Customs and Excise Management Act 1979.

(9) Material disclosed in pursuance of an order under subsection (7) above may, subject to any conditions contained in the order, be further disclosed for the purposes of functions relating to the investigation of crime or whether any person has benefited from the commission of an offence to which this Part of this Act applies or the amount of that benefit.

(10) Material may be produced or disclosed in pursuance of this section notwithstanding any obligation as to secrecy or other restriction upon the disclosure of information imposed by statute or otherwise.

(11) An order under subsection (1) above and, in the case of material in the possession of an authorised government department, an order under section 18(2) of this Act may require any officer of the department (whether named in the order or not) who may for the time being be in possession of the material concerned to comply with such order; and any such order shall be served as if the proceedings were civil proceedings against the department.

(12) Where any requirement is included in any order by virtue of subsection (11) above, the person on whom the order is served—

(a) shall take all reasonable steps to bring it to the attention of the officer concerned; and

(b) if the order is not brought to that officer's attention within the period referred to in subsection (1) above, shall report the reasons for the failure to the Court of Session,

and it shall also be the duty of any other officer of the department in receipt of the order to take such steps as are mentioned in paragraph (a) above.

(13) In this section "authorised government department" means a government department which is an authorised department for the purposes of the

Crown Proceedings Act 1947; and subsection (10) of section 18 of this Act shall apply for the purposes of this section as it applies for the purposes of that section.

PART III

RESTRAINT ORDERS

Restraint orders

28.—(1) The court may, on the application of the prosecutor, make an order (in this Part of this Act referred to as a "restraint order") in the circumstances mentioned in—

   (a)   section 29(2) or (3) of this Act interdicting—

      (i)   any person named in the order from dealing with his realisable property; or

      (ii)   that person and any person named in the order as appearing to the court to have received from him a gift caught by Part I of this Act or, as the case may be, an implicative gift from dealing with their own, or the other's, realisable property,

   (whenever that property was acquired and whether it is described in the order or not); and

   (b)   section 30(1) of this Act interdicting any person named in the order from dealing with any property which is, or is liable to be, the subject of a suspended forfeiture order.

(2) A restraint order made under subsection (1)(a) above may contain conditions and exceptions to which the interdict shall be subject and in particular—

   (a)   may provide for the release to the person named in the order of such reasonable living expenses as the court thinks fit; and

   (b)   shall provide for the release of property in so far as it is required to meet reasonable legal expenses payable or likely to be payable in relation to proceedings—

      (i)   as regards the offence by virtue of which the restraint order has been made; or

      (ii)   as regards a confiscation order made on conviction of the offence.

(3) A restraint order shall—

   (a)   be made on an *ex parte* application which shall be heard in chambers; and

   (b)   without prejudice to the time when it becomes effective, be intimated to each person affected by it.

(4) For the purposes of this Part of this Act, dealing with property includes (without prejudice to the generality of the expression)—

   (a)   making a payment to any person in reduction of the amount of a debt;

(b)   removing the property from the jurisdiction of the court; and

(c)   transferring or disposing of the property.

(5) Where the court has made a restraint order (including a restraint order made under and within the meaning of the 1994 Act), a constable or a person commissioned by the Commissioners of Customs and Excise may, for the purpose of preventing any property subject to the order being removed—

(a)   in the case of a restraint order made in connection with a drug trafficking offence (including a drug trafficking offence within the meaning of the 1994 Act) from Great Britain;

(b)   in any other case, the jurisdiction of the court,

seize that property.

(6) Property seized under subsection (5) above shall be dealt with in accordance with the directions of the court which made the order.

(7) In this Part of this Act, "the court" means where, as regards the criminal proceedings in question, a trial diet or a diet fixed for the purposes of section 76 of the 1995 Act is intended to be held, is being or has been held—

(a)   in the High Court of Justiciary, the Court of Session;

(b)   in the sheriff court, a sheriff of that court exercising his civil jurisdiction.

(8) The court may, where it has granted a restraint order, interdict a person not subject to that order from dealing with property affected by it while it is in force.

(9) Subsections (2)(a) and (3)(a) above shall apply in relation to an interdict under subsection (8) above as they apply in relation to subsection (1) above; and subsections (1), (2), (4) and (5) of section 31 of this Act shall apply in relation to an interdict under subsection (8) above as they apply in relation to a restraint order.

(10) Without prejudice to the time when it becomes effective, an interdict under subsection (8) above shall be intimated to each person affected by it.

Restraint orders in relation to realisable property

29.—(1) A restraint order under section 28(1)(a) of this Act may be made in the circumstances mentioned in either subsection (2) or (3) below.

(2) For the purposes of this subsection, the circumstances are—

(a)   proceedings have been instituted against an accused in Scotland for an offence to which Part I of this Act applies;

(b)   the proceedings have not been concluded; and

(c)   either a confiscation order has been made or it appears to the court that, in the event of his conviction of the offence, there are reasonable grounds for thinking that a confiscation order may be made in those proceedings.

(3) For the purposes of this subsection, the circumstances are that the court is satisfied that—

(a)   it is proposed to institute proceedings within 28 days against a person suspected of such an offence and it appears to the court that, in the event of his conviction of the offence, there are reasonable grounds for thinking that a confiscation order may be made in those proceedings; or

(b) the prosecutor has made, or proposes within 28 days to make, an application under section 11 or, as the case may be, section 13 of this Act in relation to that person in respect of the offence, and it appears to the court that there are reasonable grounds for thinking that the application may be granted.

(4) Where the court has made a restraint order in the circumstances mentioned in subsection (3)(a) or (b) above and no proceedings have been instituted or application made within 28 days as mentioned in that subsection, the prosecutor shall forthwith apply to the court for the recall of the order and the court shall grant the application.

(5) When proceedings for the offence or, as the case may be, proceedings on an application under section 11 or 13 of this Act are concluded, the prosecutor shall forthwith apply to the court for recall of the order and the court shall grant the application.

(6) For the purposes of this section, proceedings are concluded as regards an offence where—

(a) the trial diet is deserted *simpliciter*;

(b) the accused is acquitted or, under section 65 or 147 of the 1995 Act, discharged or liberated;

(c) the High Court of Justiciary or, as the case may be, the sheriff sentences or otherwise deals with him without making a confiscation order and without postponing a decision as regards making such an order;

(d) after such postponement as is mentioned in paragraph (c) above, the High Court of Justiciary or, as the case may be, the sheriff decides not to make a confiscation order;

(e) his conviction is quashed; or

(f) a confiscation order made in the proceedings is satisfied (whether by payment of the amount due under the order or by the accused serving imprisonment in default).

(7) For the purposes of this section, proceedings on an application under section 11 or 13 of this Act are concluded—

(a) when the application is refused; or

(b) where the application is granted, when a confiscation order made in the proceedings is satisfied (whether by payment of the amount due under the order or by the accused serving imprisonment in default).

Restraint orders in relation to forfeitable property

30.—(1) A restraint order may be made in respect of a person under section 28(1)(b) where—

(a) proceedings have been instituted against him in Scotland for an offence;

(b) the proceedings have not been concluded; and

(c) a suspended forfeiture order has been made in respect of the property concerned or it appears to the court that, in the event of his conviction of the offence, there are reasonable grounds for thinking that a suspended forfeiture order may be made in those proceedings.

(2) A restraint order may also be made where the court is satisfied that it is proposed to institute proceedings in respect of an offence within 28 days and it appears to the court that, in the event of his conviction of the offence, there are reasonable grounds for thinking that a suspended forfeiture order may be made in those proceedings.

(3) Where the court has made a restraint order by virtue of subsection (2) above, and no proceedings have been instituted within 28 days as mentioned in that subsection, the prosecutor shall forthwith apply to the court for the recall of the order and the court shall grant the application.

(4) When proceedings for the offence are concluded, the prosecutor shall forthwith apply to the court for recall of the order and the court shall grant the application.

(5) For the purpose of this section, proceedings are concluded as regards an offence where—

(a) the trial is deserted *simpliciter*;

(b) the accused is acquitted or, under section 65 or 147 of the 1995 Act, discharged or liberated;

(c) the High Court of Justiciary or, as the case may be, the sheriff sentences or otherwise deals with him without making a suspended forfeiture order;

(d) his conviction is quashed;

(e) a suspended forfeiture order made in the proceedings is recalled or varied so as to exclude from forfeiture any property to which the restraint order relates; or

(f) the property, or part of the property, to which the restraint order relates is forfeited.

Variation and recall of restraint orders

31.—(1) Subject to subsections (2) and (3) below, the court may, at the instance of—

(a) the prosecutor, at any time vary or recall a restraint order in relation to any person or to any property;

(b) any person having an interest, at any time vary or recall a restraint order in relation to the person or to any property.

(2) On an application made under subsection (1)(b) above by a person named in a restraint order as having received a gift caught by Part I of this Act or, as the case may be, an implicative gift, the court may recall the order in relation to that person if it is satisfied on the balance of probabilities—

(a) that he received the gift not knowing, not suspecting and not having reasonable grounds to suspect that the gift was made in contemplation of, or after, the commission of the offence or if more than one, in contemplation of any of the offences or after the commission of the earlier or the earliest of the offences to which the proceedings for the time being relate; and

(b) that he was not associated with the giver in the commission of the offence; and

(c) that he would suffer hardship if the order were not recalled.

(3) Where an application has been made under subsection (1) above for the variation or recall of a restraint order, any property in relation to which the

restraint order was made shall not be realised during the period beginning with the making of the application and ending with the determination of the application by the court.

(4) The court may, where it has recalled a restraint order as mentioned in subsection (1)(b) or (2) above, order that property of the person at whose instance it was recalled shall cease to be realisable or, as the case may be, liable to forfeiture.

(5) The prosecutor or any person having an interest may reclaim or appeal to the Court of Session against an interlocutor refusing, varying or recalling or refusing to vary or recall a restraint order, within such period as may be prescribed by Act of Sederunt.

(6) Where, in relation to a restraint order which is recalled, interdict has been granted under section 28(8) of this Act, the clerk of court shall, on the restraint order being recalled, forthwith so inform each person so interdicted.

Inhibition of property affected by restraint order or by interdict

32.—(1) On the application of the Lord Advocate, the Court of Session may in respect of heritable realisable property in Scotland affected by a restraint order (whether such property generally or particular such property) grant warrant for inhibition against any person interdicted by the order or, in relation to that property, under section 28(8) of this Act; and subject to the provisions of this Part of this Act, the warrant—

(a) shall have effect as if granted on the dependence of an action for debt at the instance of the Lord Advocate against the person and may be executed, recalled, loosed or restricted accordingly; and

(b) shall have the effect of letters of inhibition and shall forthwith be registered by the Lord Advocate in the Register of Inhibitions and Adjudications.

(2) Section 155 of the Titles to Land Consolidation (Scotland) Act 1868 (effective date of inhibition) shall apply in relation to an inhibition for which warrant has been granted under subsection (1) above as that section applies to an inhibition by separate letters or contained in a summons.

(3) In the application of section 158 of that Act of 1868 (recall of inhibition) to such an inhibition as is mentioned in subsection (2) above, that section to a particular Lord Ordinary shall be construed as references to any Lord Ordinary.

(4) The fact that an inhibition has been executed under subsection (1) above in respect of property shall not prejudice the exercise of an administrator's powers under or for the purposes of this Part of this Act in respect of that property.

(5) No inhibition executed under subsection (1) above shall have effect once, or in so far as, the restraint order affecting the property in respect of which the warrant for the inhibition has been granted has ceased to have effect in respect of that property; and the Lord Advocate shall—

(a) apply for the recall, or as the case may be restriction, of the inhibition; and

(b) ensure that the recall, or restriction, of an inhibition on such application is reflected in the Register of Inhibitions and Adjudications.

Arrestment of property affected by restraint order

33.—(1) On the application of the prosecutor, the court may, in respect of moveable property affected by a restraint order (whether such property generally or particular such property), grant warrant for arrestment if the property would be arrestable if the person entitled to it were a debtor.

(2) A warrant under subsection (1) above shall have effect as if granted on the dependence of an action for debt at the instance of the prosecutor against the person and may be executed, recalled, loosed or restricted accordingly.

(3) The fact that an arrestment has been executed under subsection (2) above in respect of property shall not prejudice the exercise of an administrator's powers under or for the purposes of this Act in respect of that property.

(4) No arrestment executed under subsection (2) above shall have effect once, or in so far as, the restraint order affecting the property in respect of which the warrant for such arrestment has been granted has ceased to have effect in respect of that property; and the prosecutor shall apply to the court for an order recalling, or as the case may be, restricting the arrestment accordingly.

Administrators

34. Schedule 1 to this Act shall have effect as regards the appointment of administrators under this Act.

PART IV

RECIPROCAL ARRANGEMENTS FOR ENFORCEMENT OF ORDERS

Recognition and enforcement of orders made in England and Wales

35.—(1) An order to which this section applies shall, subject to this section and section 36 of this Act, have effect in the law of Scotland but shall be enforced in Scotland only in accordance with this section and that section.

(2) A receiver's functions under or for the purposes of section 77, 80 or 81 of the 1988 Act or section 26, 29 or 30 of the 1994 Act shall, subject to this section and section 36 of this Act, have effect in the law of Scotland.

(3) If an order to which this section applies is registered under this section—

(a) the Court of Session shall have in relation to its enforcement, the same power;

(b) proceedings for or with respect to its enforcement may be taken, and

(c) proceedings for or with respect to any contravention of such an order (whether before or after such registration) may be taken,

as if the order had originally been made in that Court.

(4) Nothing in this section enables any provision of an order which empowers a receiver to do anything in Scotland under section 80(3)(a) of the 1988 Act or section 29(3)(a) of the 1994 Act to have effect in the law of Scotland.

(5) The orders to which this section applies are orders of the High Court—

(a) made under section 77, 78 or 81 of the 1988 Act or section 26, 29, 30 or 59 of the 1994 Act;

(b) relating to the exercise by that Court of its powers under those sections; or

(c) relating to receivers in the performance of their functions under the said section 77, 78 or 81 of the 1988 Act or the said section 26, 29 or 30 of the 1994 Act,

but not including an order in proceedings for enforcement of any such order.

(6) References in this section to an order under—

(a) section 77 of the 1988 Act include references to a discharge under section 76(4) of that Act; or

(b) section 26 of the 1994 Act include references to a discharge under section 25(5) of that Act,

of such an order.

(7) In this section and in section 36 of this Act, "order" means any order, direction or judgment (by whatever name called).

(8) Nothing in any order of the High Court under section 80(6) of the 1988 Act or section 29(6) of the 1994 Act prejudices any enactment or rule of law in respect of the recording of deeds relating to heritable property in Scotland or the registration of interests in such property.

(9) In this Part, "High Court" means the High Court of England and Wales.

Provisions supplementary to section 35

36.—(1) The Court of Session shall, on application made to it in accordance with rules of court for registration of an order to which section 35 of this Act applies, direct that the order shall, in accordance with such rules, be registered in that Court.

(2) Subsections (1) and (3) of section 35 of this Act and subsection (1) above are subject to any provision made by rules of court—

(a) as to the manner in which and conditions subject to which that section applies are to be enforced in Scotland;

(b) for the sisting of proceedings for enforcement of such an order;

(c) for the modification or cancellation of the registration of such order if the order is modified or revoked or ceases to have effect.

(3) This section and section 35 of this Act are without prejudice to any enactment or rule of law as to the effect of notice or the want of it in relation to orders of the High Court.

(4) The Court of Session shall have the like power to make an order under section 1 of the Administration of Justice (Scotland) Act 1972 (extended power to order inspection of documents etc.) in relation to proceedings brought or likely to be brought under—

(a) Part VI of the 1988 Act, or;

(b) the 1994 Act,

in the High Court as if those proceedings were brought or were likely to be brought in the Court of Session.

(5) The Court of Session may, additionally, for the purpose of—

(a) assisting the achievement in Scotland of the purposes of orders to which section 35 of this Act applies;

(b) assisting receivers performing functions thereunder or for the purposes of section 77, 80 or 81 of the 1988 Act or section 26, 29 or 30 of the 1994 Act,

make such orders and do otherwise as seems to it appropriate.

(6) A document purporting to be a copy of an order under or for the purposes of—

(a) Part VI of the 1988 Act; or

(b) the 1994 Act,

by the High Court and to be certified as such by a proper office of that Court shall, in Scotland, be sufficient evidence of the order.

Inhibition of Scottish property affected by order registered under section 35

37.—(1) On the application of the Lord Advocate, the Court of Session may in respect of heritable realisable property in Scotland affected by a restraint order registered under section 35 of this Act (whether such property generally or particular such property) grant warrant for inhibition against any person with an interest in that property; and the warrant—

(a) shall have effect as if granted on the dependence of an action for debt at the instance of the Lord Advocate against the person and may be executed, recalled, loosed or restricted accordingly;

(b) shall have the effect of letters of inhibition and shall forthwith be registered by the Lord Advocate in the Register of Inhibitions and Adjudications.

(2) Section 155 of the Titles to Land Consolidation (Scotland) Act 1868 (effective date of inhibition) shall apply in relation to an inhibition for which warrant has been granted under subsection (1) above as that section applies to an inhibition by separate letters or contained in a summons.

(3) In the application of section 158 of that Act of 1868 (recall of inhibition) to such an inhibition as is mentioned in subsection (2) above, references in that section to a particular Lord Ordinary shall be construed as references to any Lord Ordinary.

(4) The fact that an inhibition has been executed under subsection (1) above, in respect of property shall not prejudice the exercise of a receiver's powers under or for the purposes of—

(a) section 77, 80 or 81 of the 1988 Act; or

(b) section 26, 29 or 30 of the 1994 Act,

in respect of that property.

(5) No inhibition executed under subsection (1) above shall have effect once, or in so far as, the restraint order affecting the property in respect of which the warrant for the inhibition has been granted has ceased to have effect in respect of that property; and the Lord Advocate shall—

(a) apply for the recall, or as the case may be restriction, of the inhibition; and

(b) ensure that the recall, or restriction, of an inhibition on such application is reflected in the the the Register of Inhibitions and Adjudications.

(6) Any power of the Court of Session to recall, loose or restrict inhibitions shall, in relation to an order containing an inhibition under subsection (1) above and without prejudice to any other consideration lawfully applying to the exercise of the power, be exercised with a view to achieving the purposes specified in section 80 of the 1988 Act or, as the case may be, section 31 of the 1994 Act.

Arrestment of Scottish property affected by order registered under section 35

38.—(1) On the application of the Lord Advocate, the Court of Session may, in respect of moveable property affected by a restraint order registered under section 35 of this Act (whether such property generally or particular such property), grant warrant for arrestment if the property would be arrestable if the person entitled to it were a debtor.

(2) A warrant under subsection (1) above shall have effect as if granted on the dependence of an action for debt at the instance of the Lord Advocate against the person and may be executed, recalled, loosed or restricted accordingly.

(3) The fact that an arrestment has been executed under subsection (2) above in respect of property shall not prejudice the exercise of a receiver's powers under or for the purposes of —

    (a)   section 77, 80 or 81 of the 1988 Act; or

    (b)   section 26, 29 or 30 of the 1994 Act,

in respect of that property.

(4) No arrestment executed under subsection (2) above shall have effect once, or in so far as, the restraint order affecting the property in respect of which the warrant for such arrestment has been granted has ceased to have effect in respect of that property; and the Lord Advocate shall apply to the Court of Session for an order recalling, or as the case may be, restricting the arrestment accordingly.

(5) Any power of the Court of Session to recall, loose or restrict arrestments shall, in relation to an arrestment proceeding upon a warrant under subsection (1) above and without prejudice to any other consideration lawfully applying to the exercise of the power, be exercised with a view to achieving the purposes specified in section 80 of the 1988 Act or, as the case may be, section 31 of the 1994 Act.

Enforcement of Northern Ireland orders

39.—(1) Her Majesty may by Order in Council provide that, for the purposes of Part III of and Schedules 1 and 2 to this Act, this Act shall have effect as if—

    (a)   references to confiscation orders included a reference to orders made by courts in Northern Ireland which appear to Her Majesty to correspond to confiscation orders;

    (b)   references to—

        (i)   offences to which Part I of this Act applies; or

        (ii)   drug trafficking offences,

        included a reference to any offence under the law of Northern Ireland (not being an offence to which that Part applies) which appears to Her Majesty to correspond to such an offence; and

    (c)   such other modifications were made as may be specified in the Order in Council, being modifications which appear to Her Majesty to be requisite or desirable having regard to procedural differences which may for the time being exist between Scotland and Northern Ireland; and without prejudice to the generality of this paragraph modifications may include provision as to the circumstances in which proceedings in Northern Ireland are to be treated for the purposes of those sections as instituted or as concluded.

(2) An Order in Council under this section may provide provisions mentioned in subsection (1) above to have effect in relation to anything done or to be done in Northern Ireland subject to such further modifications as may be specified in the Order.

(3) An Order in Council under this section may contain such incidental, consequential and transitional provisions as Her Majesty considers expedient.

(4) An Order in Council under this section may, in particular, provide for section 18 of the Civil Jurisdiction and Judgements Act 1982 (enforcement of United Kingdom judgments in other parts of the United Kingdom) not to apply in relation to such orders made in connection with drug trafficking offences as may be prescribed by the Order

(5) An Order in Council under this section shall be subject to annulment in pursuance of a resolution of either House of Parliament.

Enforcement of orders made outside United Kingdom

40.—(1) Her Majesty may by Order in Council—

(a) direct in relation to a country or territory outside the United Kingdom designated by the Order that, subject to such modifications as may be specified, Part I of this Act and Part III of this Act so far as it relates to realisable property shall apply in relation to external confiscation orders and to proceedings which have been or are to be instituted in the designated country and may result in an external confiscation order being made there;

(b) make—

(i) such provision as to evidence or proof of any matter for the purposes of this section and section 41 of this Act; and

(ii) such incidental, consequential and transitional provision,

as appears to Her Majesty to be expedient.

(2) In this Part of this Act—

"designated country" means a country or territory designated by an Order in Council made under this section; and

"external confiscation order" means an order made by a court in a designated country for the purpose of recovering payments or other rewards or property or other economic advantage received in connection with—

(a) an offence corresponding with or similar to an offence to which Part I of this Act applies; or

(b) drug trafficking,

or the value of such payments, property, reward or economic advantage.

(3) An Order in Council under this section may make different provision for different cases or classes of case.

(4) The power to make an Order in Council under this section includes power to modify Part I of this Act or Part III of this Act so far as it relates to realisable property in such a way as to confer power on a person to exercise a discretion.

(5) An Order in Council under this section shall be subject to annulment in pursuance of a resolution of either House of Parliament.

Registration of external confiscation orders

41.—(1) On an application made by or on behalf of the Government of a designated country, the Court of Session may register an external confiscation order made there if—

(a) it is satisfied that at the time of registration the order is in force and not subject to appeal;

(b) it is satisfied, where the person against whom the order is made did not appear in the proceedings, that he received notice of the proceedings in sufficient time to enable him to defend them; and

(c) it is of the opinion that enforcing the order in Scotland would not be contrary to the interests of justice.

(2) In subsection (1) above "appeal" includes—

(a) any proceedings by way of discharging or setting aside a judgment; and

(b) an application for a new trial or a stay of execution.

(3) The Court of Session shall cancel the registration of an external confiscation order if it appears to the court that the order has been satisfied by payment of the amount due under it or by the person against whom it was made serving imprisonment in default of payment or by any other means.

Enforcement of Scottish orders in England and Wales

42.—(1) Her Majesty may by Order in Council make such provision as Her Majesty considers expedient for the purpose—

(a) of enabling property in England and Wales which is realisable property to be used or realised for the payment of any amount payable under a confiscation order made in connection with an offence to which Part I of this Act applies;

(b) of securing that, where no such confiscation order has been made, property in England and Wales which is realisable property is available, in the event that such an order is so made, to be used or realised for the payment of any amount payable under it; and

(c) of enabling the enforcement in England and Wales of restraint orders, suspended forfeiture orders and forfeiture orders under any enactment other than the 1989 Act.

(2) Without prejudice to the generality of the power conferred by subsection (1) above, an Order in Council under this section may—

(a) provide that, subject to any specific conditions, such description of orders made under or for the purposes of Part I, II or III of this Act so far as it relates to realisable property shall have effect in the law of England and Wales;

(b) provide that, subject to any specified conditions, the functions of a person appointed under Schedule 1 to this Act shall have effect in the law of England and Wales;

(c) make provision—

(i) for the registration in the High Court of such descriptions of orders made under or for the purposes of Part I, II or III of this Act so far as it relates to realisable property as may be specified; and

(ii) for the High Court to have, in relation to the enforcement of orders made under or for the purposes of Part 1,11 or III of this Act so far as it so relates which are so registered, such powers as may be specified; and

(d) make provision as to the proof in England and Wales of orders made under or for the purposes of Part I, II or III of this Act so far as it so relates.

(3) In subsection (2) above "specified" means specified in an Order in Council under this section.

(4) An Order in Council under this section may amend or apply, with or without modifications, any enactment.

(5) An Order in Council under this section may contain such incidental, consequential and transitional provisions as Her Majesty considers expedient.

(6) An Order in Council under this section shall be subject to annulment in pursuance of a resolution of either House of Parliament.

Order in council as regards taking of action in designated country

43.—(1) Her Majesty may by Order in Council make such provision in connection with the taking of action in a designated country in consequence of the making of a restraint order, confiscation order or suspended forfeiture order under this Act or a forfeiture order under any other enactment as appears to Her Majesty to be expedient.

(2) Without prejudice to the generality of subsection (1) above, the provision contained in an Order in Council made under this section may include a direction that in such circumstances as may be specified proceeds arising out of action taken in a designated country with a view to satisfying a confiscation order which are retained there shall nevertheless be treated as reducing the amount payable under the confiscation order to such extent as may be specified.

(3) An Order in Council under this section may amend or apply, with or without modifications, any enactment.

(4) Subsections (1)(b), (3) and (5) of section 40 of this Act shall apply in respect of Orders in Council under this section as they apply in respect of Orders in Council under that section.

PART V

MISCELLANEOUS AND GENERAL

Sequestration etc. of person holding realisable or forfeitable property

44.—(1) Schedule 2 to this Act shall have effect in relation to the sequestration, bankruptcy, winding up or receivership of persons or, as the case may be, companies holding realisable or forfeitable property.

(2) In this section and in that Schedule "forfeitable property" means property which is or is liable to be the subject of a suspended forfeiture order.

Disposal of family home under Part I or II

45.—(1) This section applies where—

    (a) a confiscation order has been made in relation to any person and the prosecutor has not satisfied the court that—

        (i) in the case of an order made in connection with a drug trafficking offence, the person's interest in his family home has been acquired by means of the proceeds of drug trafficking; or

        (ii) in any other case, the person's interest in his family home has been acquired by means of the benefit derived from the commission of the offence concerned; or

    (b) a person's family home has been forfeited to the Crown under section 24 of this Act.

(2) Where this section applies, then, before the Crown disposes of any right or interest in the person's family home it shall—

    (a) obtain the relevant consent; or

    (b) where it is unable to do so, apply to the court for authority to carry out the disposal.

(3) On an application being made to it under subsection (2)(b) above, the court, after having regard to all the circumstances of the case including—

(a) the needs and financial resources of the spouse or former spouse of the person concerned;

(b) the needs and financial resources of any child of the family;

(c) the length of the period during which the family home has been used as a residence of the persons referred to in paragraph (a) or (b) above,

may refuse to grant application or may postpone the granting of the application for such period (not exceeding 12 months) as it may consider reasonable in the circumstances or may grant the application subject to such conditions as it may prescribe.

(4) Subsection (3) above shall apply—

(a) to an action for division and sale of the family home of the person concerned; or

(b) to an action for the purpose of obtaining vacant possession of that home,

brought by the Crown as it applies to an application under subsection (2)(b) above and, for the purposes of this subsection, any reference in the said subsection (3) to the granting of the application shall be construed as a reference to the granting of decree in the action.

(5) In this section—

"family home", in relation to any person (in this subsection referred to as "the relevant person") means any property in which the relevant person has or had (whether alone or in common with any other person) a right or interest, being property which is occupied as a residence by the relevant person and his or her spouse or by the relevant person's spouse or former spouse (in any case with or without a child of the family) or by the relevant person with a child of the family;

"child of the family" includes any child or grandchild of either the relevant person or his or her spouse or former spouse, and any person who has been treated by either the relevant person or his or her spouse or former spouse as if he or she were a child of the relevant person, spouse or former spouse, whatever the age of such a child, grandchild or person may be; and

"relevant consent" means in relation to the disposal of any fight or interest in a family home—

(a) in a case where the family home is occupied by the spouse or former spouse of the relevant person, the consent of the spouse or, as the case may be, of the former spouse, whether or not the family home is also occupied by the relevant person;

(b) where paragraph (a) above does not apply, in a case where the family home is occupied by the relevant person with a child of the family, the consent of the relevant person.

Forfeiture of property where accused has died

46.—(1) This section applies where at any time after criminal proceedings have been instituted against an accused for an offence to which Part I of this Act applies and before the accused has been sentenced or otherwise dealt with in the proceedings he dies.

(2) The Court of Session, if it is satisfied beyond reasonable doubt on an application being made to it by the Lord Advocate—

    (a) that the accused committed the offence; and

    (b) that there is property—

        (i) which the accused had obtained, directly or indirectly, in connection with the commission of the offence or, as the case may be, in connection with drug trafficking; or

       (ii) which is a gift caught by Part I of this Act or, as the case may be, an implicative gift,

may, subject to subsection (5) below, make an order which shall have the effect of forfeiting that property.

(3) The Court of Session may, without prejudice to any other power available to it, at any time before the determination of the case, allow an amendment of the application under subsection (2) above if the amendment is of a type which could competently have been made in an indictment or complaint under section 96 or 159 of the 1995 Act in the criminal proceedings.

(4) An application under subsection (2) above shall be made as soon as is reasonably practicable after the relevant information becomes available to the Lord Advocate, but, in any event, within 6 years commencing with the date of death of the accused.

(5) An application under subsection (2) above in relation to property such as is mentioned in paragraph (b)(ii) of that subsection shall be served on the recipient of the gift and, if he satisfies the Court on the balance of probabilities—

    (a) that he received the gift not knowing, not suspecting and not having reasonable grounds to suspect that the gift was made in contemplation of, or after, the commission of the offence or, if more than one, in contemplation of any of the offences or after the commission of the earlier or the earliest of the offences to which the proceedings for the time being relate; and

    (b) that he was not associated with the giver in the commission of the offence; and

    (c) that he would suffer hardship if the application were granted,

the Court may refuse to make an order as mentioned in that subsection; and in the application of this subsection to an implicative gift, any reference to the commission of the offence shall be construed as a reference to the drug trafficking and the reference in paragraph (b) above to the earlier or earliest of more than one offence shall be construed as a reference to the beginning of the drug trafficking.

(6) Where property has been forfeited under this section, then, if the Court of Session, on an application being made to it is satisfied by the applicant on the balance of probabilities that he was the owner of, or otherwise had an interest in, the property immediately before such forfeiture, it shall make an order under subsection (7) below.

(7) An order under this subsection shall direct the Crown, if the applicant—

    (a) was the owner of the property, to return it to him if it is reasonably practicable to do so or, if not, to pay compensation to him of an amount determined under subsection (8) below; or

(b) otherwise had an interest in the property, to pay compensation of an amount corresponding to the value of such interest.

(8) For the purposes of subsection (7) above, the amount determined under this subsection shall be an amount equal to the amount of any consideration received for the property or the value of any such consideration at the time of the disposal, or, if no consideration was received, an amount equal to the value of the property at the time of the disposal.

(9) Property which has been forfeited under this section shall be dealt with by the Crown in such manner as seems to it to be appropriate.

(10) Where a restraint order is not in force in respect of a person when he dies in the circumstances mentioned in subsection (1) above, the Court of Session may, on the application of the Lord Advocate, in so far as the property is concerned is—

(a) heritable property in Scotland, make an order inhibiting any person; and

(b) moveable property, grant warrant for arrestment if the property would be arrestable if the person entitled to it were a debtor.

(11) Paragraphs (a) and (b) of subsection (1) and subsections (2) to (5) of section 32 of this Act shall, subject to any necessary modifications, apply for the purposes of subsection (10)(a) above as they apply for the purposes of that section.

(12) Subsections (2) to (4) of section 33 of this Act shall, subject to any necessary modifications, apply for the purposes of subsection (10)(b) above as they apply for the purposes of that section.

(13) Proceedings under this section are civil proceedings for the purposes of section 10 of the Law Reform (Miscellaneous Provisions) (Scotland) Act 1968.

Construction of certain enactments

47.—(1) Section 28 of the Bankruptcy Act 1914 (effect of order of discharge) shall have effect as if amounts payable under confiscation orders were debts excepted under subsection (1)(a) of that section.

(2) In section 1(2)(a) of the Rehabilitation of Offenders Act 1974 (failure to pay fines etc. not to prevent person becoming rehabilitated) the reference to a fine or other sum adjudged to be paid by or on a conviction does not include a reference to an amount payable under a confiscation order.

(3) Section 55(2) of the Bankruptcy (Scotland) Act 1985 (discharge of debtor not to release him from liabilities in respect of fines, etc.) shall have effect as if the reference to a fine included a reference to a confiscation order.

(4) Section 281(4) of the Insolvency Act 1986 (discharge of bankrupt not to release him from liabilities in respect of fines, etc.) shall have effect as if the reference to a fine included a reference to a confiscation order.

Service and notice

48. Subject to the provisions of this Act, provision may be made by rules of court as to the giving of notice required for the purposes of this Act in so far as it is connected with drug trafficking or the effecting of service so required; and different provision may be so made for different cases or classes of case and for different circumstances or classes of circumstance.

Interpretation

49.—(1) In this Act, unless the context otherwise requires—

"the 1988 Act" means the Criminal Justice Act 1988;

"the 1989 Act" means the Prevention of Terrorism (Temporary Provisions) Act 1989;

"the 1994 Act" means the Drug Trafficking Act 1994;

"the 1995 Act" means the Criminal Procedure (Scotland) Act 1995;

"accused" includes a person against whom criminal proceedings have been instituted in relation to the commission of an offence and a person convicted of an offence;

"clerk of court" includes the sheriff clerk;

"confiscation order" means an order made under section 1(1), 11(4), 12(3) or 13 of this Act;

"interest", in relation to property, includes right;

"property" has the meaning assigned by section 2 of this Act;

"realisable property" has the meaning assigned by section 4 of this Act;

"restraint order" means an order made under section 28 of this Act;

"suspended forfeiture" means an order made under section 21(2) of this Act.

(2) In this Act, "drug trafficking" means, subject to subsections (3) and (4) below, doing or being concerned in any of the following, whether in Scotland or elsewhere—

(a) producing or supplying a controlled drug where the production or supply contravenes section 4(1) of the Misuse of Drugs Act 1971;

(b) transporting or storing such a drug where possession of it contravenes section 5(1) of that Act;

(c) importing or exporting such a drug where the importation or exportation is prohibited by section 3(1) of that Act;

(d) producing, supplying, transporting, storing, importing or exporting such a drug in contravention of a corresponding law ("corresponding law" having the meaning assigned by section 36(1) of that Act);

(e) manufacturing or supplying a scheduled substance within the meaning of section 12 of the Criminal Justice (International Co-operation) Act 1990 where the manufacture or supply is an offence under that section;

(f) acquiring, having possession of or using property in contravention of section 37 of the Criminal Law (Consolidation) (Scotland) Act 1995;

(g) concealing or transferring the proceeds of drug trafficking in contravention of section 14 of the said Act of 1990;

(h) using any ship for illicit traffic in controlled contravention of section 19 of the said Act of 1990.

(3) Drug trafficking also includes, whether in Scotland or elsewhere, entering into or being otherwise concerned in any arrangement whereby—

(a) the retention or control by or on behalf of another person of the other person's proceeds of drug trafficking is facilitated, or

(b) the proceeds of drug trafficking by another person are used to secure that funds are placed at the other person's disposal or are used for the other person's benefit to acquire property by way of investment.

(4) In paragraphs (e) to (g) of subsection (2) above, references to conduct contravention of the enactments mentioned in those paragraphs include conduct which would contravene the enactments if it took place in Scotland.

(5) In this Act a "drug trafficking offence" means any of the following—

(a) an offence under—

(i) section 4(2) (production, or being concerned in production, of controlled drug);

(ii) section 4(3) (supply of, or offer to supply, or being concerned in supply of, controlled drug);

(iii) section 5(3) (possession of controlled drug with intent to supply); or

(iv) section 20 (assisting in, or inducing commission of, certain drug related offences punishable under foreign law),

of the Misuse of Drugs Act 1971,

(b) in connection with a prohibition or restriction on importation and exportation having effect by virtue of section 3 of the said Act of 1971, an offence under section 50(2) or (3) (improper importation), 68(2) (improper exportation) or 170 (fraudulent evasion of duty etc.) of the Customs and Excise Management Act 1979;

(c) an offence under section 37 of the Criminal Law (Consolidation) (Scotland) Act 1995;

(d) an offence under section 38 of the said Act of 1995;

(e) an offence under section 12, 14 or 19 of the Criminal Justice (International Co-operation) Act 1990;

(f) an offence of conspiring, inciting or attempting to commit an offence mentioned in paragraph (a), (b), (c) or (e) above.

(6) For the purposes of this Act proceedings for an offence are instituted against a person—

(a) on his arrest without warrant;

(b) when he is charged with the offence without being arrested;

(c) when a warrant to arrest him is granted;

(d) when a warrant to cite him is granted;

(e) in summary proceedings, on the first calling of the case; or

(f) when a petition is intimated to him or an indictment or a complaint is served on him,

and, where the application of this subsection would result in there being more than one time for the institution of proceedings, they shall be taken to be instituted at the earliest of those times.

(7) Any reference in this Act to a conviction of an offence includes a reference to a finding that the offence has been committed.

Short title, commencement and extent

50.—(1) This Act may be cited as the Proceeds of Crime (Scotland) Act 1995.

(2) This Act shall come into force on 1 April 1996.

(3) Subject to subsections (4) and (5) below, this Act extends only to Scotland.

(4) Section 44 of and Schedule 2 to this Act and this section extend to England and Wales as well as to Scotland.

(5) Section 42 of this Act extends only to England and Wales.

SCHEDULES

SCHEDULE 1

ADMINISTRATORS

Appointment of administrators

1.—(1) On the application of the prosecutor the court may as regards property—

(a) affected by a restraint order or a suspended forfeiture order, appoint a person to manage, or otherwise deal with, the property; or

(b) where a suspended forfeiture order or a confiscation order has been made, appoint a person (or empower an appointee under paragraph (a) above) to realise the property,

in accordance with the court's directions and may (whether on making the appointment or from time to time) require any person having possession of the property to give possession of it to the appointee (any such appointee being in this Act referred as an "administrator").

(2) A requirement under sub-paragraph (1) above—

(a) subject to paragraph (b) below, may relate to the property generally or to particular such property and may be subject to such exceptions and conditions as may be specified by the court;

(b) shall relate to property mentioned in paragraph (b) of section 4(1) of this Act only if expressly stated so to do and then only in so far as the person in whom such property is vested is named in the requirement as being subject to it.

(3) On a requirement being imposed under sub-paragraph (1) above—

(a) the clerk of court shall forthwith notify—

(i) the person in respect of whom the restraint order, or as the case may be the suspended forfeiture order or confiscation order, has been made, and

(ii) any other person named in the requirement as being subject to it, and

(b) any dealing of or with such person in relation to the property shall be of no effect in a question with the administrator unless whoever dealt with the person had, at the time when the dealing occurred, no knowledge of the appointment.

(4) The court, at the instance of any person having an interest, may at any time—

(a) vary or withdraw a requirement imposed under sub-paragraph (1) above; or

(b) without prejudice to paragraph 4 below or to the powers and duties of an administrator pending a decision under this sub-sub-paragraph, on cause shown, remove the administrator from office.

(5) On the death or resignation of the administrator, or on his removal from office under sub-paragraph (4)(b) above or paragraph 5 below, the court shall appoint a new administrator.

(6) Such of the property (if any) as was, by virtue of paragraph 2(3) below, vested in the administrator who has died, resigned or been removed shall forthwith vest in the new administrator; and any requirement imposed under sub-paragraph (1) above shall, on the person subject to the requirement being notified in writing of the appointment by the appointee, apply in relation to the appointee instead of in relation to his predecessor.

(7) The administration of property by an administrator shall be deemed continuous notwithstanding any temporary vacancy in that office.

(8) Any appointment under this paragraph shall be on such conditions as to caution as the accountant of court may think fit to impose; but the premium of any bond of caution or other security thereby required of the administrator shall be treated as part of his outlays in his actings as such.

(9) Without prejudice to paragraph 5 below, section 6 of the Judicial Factors (Scotland) Act 1889 (supervision of judicial factors) shall not apply in relation to an appointment under this section.

Functions of administrators

2.—(1) Subject to paragraph 5 below, an administrator—

    (a) shall be entitled to take possession of, and if appointed (or empowered) under paragraph 1(1)(b) above where a confiscation order has been made shall as soon as practicable take possession of, the property as regards which he has been appointed and of any document which both—

        (i) is in the possession or control of the person (in this paragraph referred to as "A") in whom the property is vested (or would be vested but for an order made under sub-paragraph (3) below); and

        (ii) relates to the property or to A's assets, business or financial affairs;

    (b) shall be entitled to have access to, and to copy, any document relating to the property or to A's assets, business or financial affairs and not in such possession or control as is mentioned in sub-sub-paragraph (a) above;

    (c) may bring, defend or continue any legal proceedings relating to the property;

    (d) may borrow money in so far as it is necessary to do so to safeguard the property and may for the purposes of such borrowing create a security over any part of the property;

    (e) may, if the administrator considers that to do so would be beneficial for the management or realisation of the property—

        (i) carry on any business of A;

        (ii) exercise any right of A as holder of securities in a company;

        (iii) grant a lease of the property or take on lease any other property: or

        (iv) enter into any contract, or execute any deed, as regards the property or as regards A's business;

    (f) may, where any right, option or other power forms part of A's estate, make payments or incur liabilities with a view to—

   (i) obtaining property which is the subject of; or
   (ii) maintaining,

the right, option or power;

(g) may effect or maintain insurance policies as regards the property on A's business:

(h) where he has been appointed under paragraph 1(1)(b) above may, where A has an uncompleted title to any heritable estate, complete title thereto;
Provided that completion of title in A's name shall not validate by accretion any unperfected right in favour of any person other than the administrator;

(j) may sell, purchase or exchange property or discharge any security for an obligation due to A:
Provided that it shall be incompetent for the administrator or an associate of his (within the meaning of section 74 of the Bankruptcy (Scotland) Act 1985) to purchase any of A's property in pursuance of this paragraph;

(k) may claim, vote and draw dividends in the sequestration of the estate (or bankruptcy or liquidation) of a debtor of A and may accede to a voluntary trust deed for creditors of such a debtor;

(l) may discharge any of his functions through agents or employees;
Provided that the administrator shall be personally liable to meet the fees and expenses of any such agent or employee out of such remuneration as is payable to the administrator by virtue of paragraph 6(1) and (3) below;

(m) may take such professional advice as he may consider requisite for the proper discharge of his functions;

(n) may at any time apply to the court for directions as regards the discharge of his functions;

(o) may exercise any power specifically conferred on him by the court, whether such conferral was at the time of his appointment or on his subsequent application to the court in that regard; and

(p) may do anything incidental to the above powers and duties.

(2) Subject to the proviso to sub-paragraph (1)(j) above—

(a) a person dealing with an administrator in good faith and for value shall not require to determine whether the administrator is acting within the powers mentioned in that subsection; and

(b) the validity of any title shall not be challengeable by reason only of the administrator having acted outwith those powers.

(3) The exercise of a power mentioned in any of the sub-paragraphs (1)(c) to (k) above shall be in A's name except where and in so far as an order made by the court under this sub-paragraph (either on its own motion or on the application of the administrator) has vested the property in the administrator (or in his predecessor in that office).

Money received by administrator

3.—(1) Subject to sub-paragraph (2) below, all money received by an administrator in the exercise of his functions shall be deposited by him, in the name (unless vested in the administrator by virtue of paragraph 2(3) above) of the holder of the property realised, in an appropriate bank or institution.

(2) The administrator may at any time retain in his hands a sum not exceeding £200 or such other sum as may be prescribed by the Secretary of State by regulations made by statutory instrument.

(3) In sub-paragraph (1) above, "appropriate bank or institution" means a bank or institution mentioned in section 2(1) of the Banking Act 1979 or for the time being specified in Schedule I to that Act.

Application of proceeds of realisation and other sums

4.—(1) This paragraph applies only to an administrator appointed to realise property where a confiscation order has been made.

(2) Subject to sub-paragraph (3) below, sums in the hands of an administrator which are—

(a) proceeds of a realisation of property under paragraph 1 above, and

(b) other property held by the person in respect of whom the confiscation order was made, shall first be applied in payment of any expenses to the payment of which a person is entitled under paragraph 5(2) of Schedule 2 to this Act and then shall, after such payments (if any) as the court may direct have been made out of those proceeds and sums, be applied on the person's behalf towards the satisfaction of the confiscation order.

(3) If, after the amount payable under the confiscation order has been fully paid, any such proceeds and sums remain in the hands of the administrator, he shall distribute them—

(a) among such of those who held property which has been realised under this Act, and

(b) in such proportions,

as the court may, after giving such persons an opportunity to be heard as regards the matter, direct.

(4) The receipt of any sum by a sheriff clerk on account of an amount payable under a order shall reduce the amount so payable, but the sheriff clerk shall apply the money—

(a) first, in payment of any expenses to the payment of which a person is entitled under paragraph 5(2) of Schedule 2 to this Act but which were not paid to him under sub-paragraph (2) above;

(b) next, in payment of the administrator's remuneration and expenses;

(c) next, in reimbursement of any sums paid by the Lord Advocate under paragraph 8(2) below;

(d) next, in accordance with any direction given by the court under section 8(4) or 13(7) of this Act,

and the balance shall be payable and recoverable (or as the case may be disposed of) under section 211(5) or (6) of the 1995 Act (destination of fines) as applied by section 14 of this Act.

Supervision of administrators

5.—(1) The accountant of court shall supervise the performance by administrators of the functions conferred on them by Part I of this Act; and in particular an administrator proposing to exercise functions conferred by any of paragraphs 2(1)(c) to (p) above shall first obtain the consent of the accountant of court to such exercise.

(2) If it appears to the accountant of court that an administrator has, without reasonable cause, failed to perform a duty imposed on him by any provision of section 16 of this Act or of this Schedule, he shall report the matter to the court which, after giving the administrator an opportunity to be heard as regards the matter, may remove the administrator from office, censure him or make such other order as the circumstances of the case may appear to the court to require.

Accounts and remuneration of administrator

6.—(1) The administrator shall keep such accounts in relation to his intromissions with the property as regards which he is appointed as the court may require and shall lodge these accounts with the accountant of court at such times as may be fixed by the court in that regard; and the accountant of court shall audit the accounts and issue a determination as to the amount of outlays and, on the basis mentioned in sub-paragraph (3) below, remuneration payable to the administrator in respect of those intromissions.

(2) Not later than two weeks after the issuing of a determination under sub-paragraph (1) above, the administrator or the Lord Advocate may appeal against it to the court.

(3) The basis for determining the amount of remuneration payable to the administrator shall be the value of the work reasonably undertaken by him, regard being had to the extent of the responsibilities involved.

(4) The accountant of court may authorise the administrator to pay without taxation an account in respect of legal services incurred by the administrator.

Effect of appointment of administrator on diligence

7. Without prejudice to sections 32 and 33 of this Act—

(a) no arrestment or poinding of property executed on or after an appointment as regards the property under paragraph 1 above shall be effectual to create a preference for the arrester or poinder and any such property so arrested or poinded, or the proceeds of sale thereof, shall be handed over to the administrator;

(b) no poinding of the ground in respect of property on or after such appointment shall be effectual in a question with the administrator except for the interest on the debt of a secured creditor, being interest for the current half-yearly term and arrears of interest for one year immediately before the commencement of that term;

(c) it shall be incompetent on or after such appointment for any other person to raise or insist in an adjudication against the property or to be confirmed as executor-creditor on that property; and

(d) no inhibition on property which takes effect on or after such appointment shall be effectual to create a preference for the inhibitor in a question with the administrator.

Further provision as to administrators

8.—(1) Where an administrator takes any action—

(a) in relation to property as regards which he has not been appointed, being action which he would be entitled to take if he had been so appointed,

(b) believing, and having reasonable grounds for believing, that he is entitled to take that action in relation to that property,

he shall not be liable to any person in respect of any loss or damage resulting from his action except in so far as the loss or damage is caused by his negligence.

(2) Any amount due in respect of the remuneration and expenses of an administrator appointed under this Schedule shall, unless in a case where a confiscation order has been made there are sums available to be applied in payment of it under paragraph 4(4)(b) above, be paid by the Lord Advocate.

(3) Any disposal of property under paragraph 1 above to a person taking in good faith shall vest the ownership of the property in that person.

Discharge of administrator

9. After an administrator has lodged his final accounts under paragraph 6(1) above, he may apply to the accountant of court to be discharged from office; and such discharge, if granted, shall have the effect of freeing him from all liability (other than liability arising from fraud) in respect of any act or omission of his in exercising the functions conferred on him by this Act.

Compensation

10.—(1) Where the court, on an application made to it by a person other than the accused or the recipient of a gift caught by Part I of this Act or an implicative gift, is satisfied on the balance of probabilities that in relation to any property realised under paragraph 1 above he was the owner of, or a person otherwise having an interest in, the property immediately before such realisation, it shall make an order directing the Crown to pay to that person compensation of an amount equal to the consideration received for the property or, as the case may be, interest or the value of any such consideration at the time of such realisation, or, if no consideration was received, an amount equal to the value of the property or interest at the time of the realisation.

(2) An application under this paragraph shall be made not later than three years after the conclusion of the proceedings in respect of which the confiscation order was made.

(3) Subsection (6) of section 29 of this Act shall apply for the purpose of determining for the purposes of this paragraph whether proceedings are concluded as it applies for the purposes of that section.

Rules of court as regards accountant of court's supervision etc. of administrators

11. Without prejudice to section 5 of the Court of Session Act 1988 (power to regulate procedure etc. by Act of Sederunt), provision may be made by rules of court as regards (or as regards any matter incidental to) the accountant of court's powers and duties under this Act in relation to the functions of administrators.

Power to facilitate realisation

12.—(1) Without prejudice to any enactment or rule of law in respect of the recording of deeds relating to heritable property or the registration of interests therein, the court, to facilitate realisation under paragraph 1 above, may—

(a) order any person (in this paragraph referred to as "A") holding an interest in property, not being such person (in this paragraph referred to as "B") as is mentioned in paragraph (a) or (b) of section 4(1) or section 21 of this Act, to make such payment to an administrator appointed to realise estate comprising an interest of B in that property as the court may direct and may, subject to such payment being made—

    (i) authorise the administrator to transfer B's interest to A or to discharge it in favour of A; or

    (ii) itself by order transfer or discharge B's interest; or

(b) by order—

    (i) transfer A's interest to B; or

    (ii) discharge it in favour of B,

on the administrator making such payment to A out of that estate in respect of A's interest as the court may direct.

(2) The court may make such incidental provision in relation to any exercise of powers conferred on it by sub-paragraph (1) above as it considers appropriate; but it shall not exercise those powers without giving such persons as hold an interest in the property reasonable opportunity to make representations to it in that regard.

Section 44   SCHEDULE 2

SEQUESTRATION ETC. OF PERSONS HOLDING REALISABLE OR FORFEITABLE PROPERTY

Sequestration of person holding realisable or forfeitable property

1.—(1) Where the estate of a person who holds realisable or forfeitable property is sequestrated—

(a) property, other than heritable property situated in Scotland, for the time being subject to a restraint order made before the date of sequestration (within the meaning of section 12(4) of the 1985 Act) and heritable property situated in Scotland for the time being subject to a restraint order recorded in the General Register of Sasines or, as the case may be, registered in the Land Register of Scotland before such date of sequestration; and

(b) any proceeds of property realised by virtue of paragraph 1 of Schedule 1 to this Act for the time being in the hands of an administrator appointed under that paragraph,

is excluded from the debtor's estate for the purposes of that Act.

(2) Where an award of sequestration has been made, the powers on the court by sections 28 to 33 and 35 to 38 of and the said Schedule 1 to this Act or on an administrator appointed under paragraph 1 of that Schedule shall not be exercised in relation to—

(a) property comprised in the whole estate of the debtor (within the meaning of section 31(8) of the 1985 Act); or

(b) any income of the debtor which has been ordered, under subsection (2) of section 32 of that Act, to be paid to the permanent trustee or any estate which, under subsection (10) of section 31 of that Act or subsection (6) of the said section 32 of that Act, vests in the permanent trustee,

and it shall not be competent to a claim in relation to the confiscation order to the permanent trustee in accordance with section 48 of that Act.

(3) Nothing in the 1985 Act shall be taken as restricting, or enabling the restriction of, the exercise of the powers so conferred.

(4) Where, during the period before sequestration is awarded, an interim trustee stands appointed under section 2(5) of the 1985 Act and any property in the debtor's estate is subject to a restraint order, the powers conferred on the interim trustee by virtue of that Act do not apply to property for the time being subject to the restraint order.

(5) Where the estate of a person is sequestrated and he has directly or indirectly made a gift caught by Part I of this Act or an implicative gift—

    (a) no decree shall, at any time when proceedings as regards an offence to which Part I of this Act applies or, as the case may be, a drug trafficking offence have been instituted against him and have not been concluded or when property of the person to whom the gift was made is subject to a restraint order, be granted under section 34 or 36 of the 1985 Act (gratuitous alienations and unfair preferences) in respect of the making of the gift; and

    (b) any decree granted under either of the said sections 34 and 36 after the conclusion of the proceedings shall take into account any realisation under this Act of property held by the person to whom the gift was made.

Bankruptcy in England and Wales of person holding realisable or forfeitable property

2.—(1) Where a person who holds realisable or forfeitable property is adjudged bankrupt—

    (a) property, other than heritable property situated in Scotland, for the time being subject to a restraint order made before the order adjudging him bankrupt and heritable property situated in Scotland for the time being subject to a restraint order recorded in the General Register of Sasines or, as the case may be, registered in the Land Register of Scotland before the order adjudging him bankrupt was made; and

    (b) any proceeds of property realised by virtue of paragraph I of Schedule 1 to this Act for the time being in the hands of an administrator appointed under that paragraph,

is excluded from the bankrupt's estate for the purposes of Part IX of the Insolvency Act 1986.

(2) Where a person has been adjudged bankrupt, the powers conferred on the court by sections 28 to 33 and 35 to 38 of and the said Schedule 1 to this Act or on an administrator appointed under paragraph 1 of that Schedule shall not be exercised in relation to—

    (a) property for the time being comprised in the bankrupt's estate for the purposes of the said Part IX;

    (b) property in respect of which his trustee in bankruptcy may (without leave of the court) serve a notice under section 307, 308 or 308A of the Insolvency Act 1986 (after-acquired property and tools, clothes, etc. exceeding value of reasonable replacement and certain tenancies); and

    (c) property which is to be applied for the benefit of creditors of the bankrupt by virtue of a condition imposed under section 280(2)(c) of the Insolvency Act 1986.

(3) Nothing in the Insolvency Act 1986 shall be taken as restricting, or enabling the restriction of, the exercise of the powers so conferred.

(4) Where, in the case of a debtor, an interim receiver stands appointed under section 286 of the Insolvency Act 1986 and any property of the debtor is subject to a restraint order the powers conferred on the receiver by virtue of that Act do not apply to property for the time being subject to the restraint order.

(5) Where a person is adjudged bankrupt and has directly or indirectly made a gift caught by Part I of this Act or an implicative gift—

(a) no order shall, at any time when proceedings for an offence to which Part VI of the Criminal Justice Act 1988 applies or, as the case may be a drug trafficking offence have been instituted against him and have not been concluded or when property of the person to whom the gift was made is subject to a restraint order, be made under section 339 or 423 of the Insolvency Act 1986 (avoidance of certain transactions) in respect of the making of the gift, and

(b) any order made under either of those sections after the conclusion of the proceedings shall take into account any realisation under this Act of property held by the person to whom the gift was made.

Winding up of company holding realisable or forfeitable property

3.—(1) Where realisable or forfeitable property is held by a company and an order for the winding up of the company has been made or a resolution has been passed by the company for the voluntary winding up, the functions of the liquidator (or any provisional liquidator) shall not be exercisable in relation—

(a) property, other than heritable property situated in Scotland, for the time being subject to a restraint order made before the relevant time and heritable property situated in Scotland for the time being subject to a restraint order recorded in the General Register of Sasines or, as the case may be, registered in the Land Register of Scotland before the relevant time; and

(b) any proceeds of property realised by virtue of paragraph 1 of Schedule I to this Act for the time being in the hands of an administrator appointed under that paragraph.

(2) Where, in the case of a company, such an order has been made or such a resolution has been passed, the powers conferred on the court by sections 28 to 33 and 35 to 38 of and the said Schedule 1 to this Act or on an administrator appointed under paragraph I of that Schedule shall not be exercised in relation to any realisable or forfeitable property held by the company in relation to which the functions of the liquidator are exercisable—

(a) so as to inhibit the liquidator from exercising those functions for the purpose of distributing any property held by the company to the company's creditors; or

(b) so as to prevent the payment out of any property of expenses (including the remuneration of the liquidator or any provisional liquidator) properly incurred in the winding up in respect of the property.

(3) Nothing in the Insolvency Act 1986 shall be taken as restricting, or enabling the restriction of, the exercise of the powers so conferred.

(4) For the purposes of the application of Parts IV and V of the Insolvency Act 1986 (winding up of registered companies and winding up of unregistered

companies) to a company which the court has jurisdiction to wind up, a person is not a creditor in so far as any sum due to him by the company is due in respect of a confiscation order (whether under this Act or under and within the meaning of section 2 of the Drug Trafficking Act 1994 or any corresponding provision in Northern Ireland).

(5) Where an order for the winding up of a company has been made or a resolution has been passed by a company for its voluntary winding up and before the relevant time the company has directly or indirectly made a gift caught by Part I of this Act or an implicative gift—

(a) no order or, as the case may be, decree shall, at any time when proceedings as regards an offence to which that Part applies or, as the case may be a drug trafficking offence have been instituted against the company and have not been concluded or when property of the person to whom the gift was made is subject to a restraint order, be made under section 238 or 239 of the Insolvency Act 1986 (transactions at an undervalue and preferences) or granted under section 242 or 243 of that Act (gratuitous alienations and unfair preferences) in respect of the making of the gift; and

(b) any order made under either of the said sections 242 and 243 or decree granted under either of the said sections 242 or 243 after the conclusion of the proceedings shall take into account any realisation under Part I of this Act of property held by the person to whom the gift was made.

(6) In this paragraph—

"company" means any company which may be wound up under the Insolvency Act 1986; and

"the relevant time" means—

(a) where no order for the winding up of the company has been made, the time of the passing of the resolution for voluntary winding up;

(b) where such an order has been made and, before the presentation of the petition for the winding up of the company by the court, such a resolution had been passed by the company, the time of the passing of the resolution; and

(c) in any other case where such an order has been made, the time of the making of the order.

Property subject to floating charge

4.—(1) Where any property held subject to a floating charge by a company is realisable or forfeitable property and a receiver has been appointed by, or on the application of, the holder of the charge, the powers of the receiver in relation to the property so held shall not be exercisable in relation to—

(a) so much of it, not being heritable property situated in Scotland, as is for the time being subject to a restraint order made before the appointment of the receiver and so much of it, being heritable property situated in Scotland, as is for the time being subject to a restraint order recorded in the General Register of Sasines or, as the case may be, registered in the Land Register of Scotland before such appointment; and

(b) any proceeds of property realised by virtue of paragraph 1 of Schedule I to this Act for the time being in the hands of an administrator appointed under that paragraph.

(2) Where, in the case of a company, such an appointment has been made, the powers conferred on the court by sections 28 to 33 and 35 to 38 of and the said Schedule 1 to this Act or on an administrator appointed under paragraph I of that Schedule shall not be exercised in relation to any realisable property held by the company in relation to which the powers of the receiver are exercisable—

(a) so as to inhibit the receiver from exercising his powers for the purpose of distributing any property held by the company to the company's creditors; or

(b) so as to prevent the payment out of any property of expenses (including the remuneration of the receiver) properly incurred in the exercise of the receiver's powers in respect of the property.

(3) Nothing in the Insolvency Act 1986, shall be taken as restricting, or enabling the restriction of, the exercise of the powers so conferred.

(4) In this paragraph—

"company" has the same meaning as in paragraph 3 above; and

"floating charge" includes a floating charge within the meaning given by section 462 of the Companies Act 1985 (power of incorporated company to create floating charge).

Insolvency practitioners dealing with property subject to restraint order

5.—(1) Without prejudice to the generality of any enactment contained in the Insolvency Act 1986 or in the 1985 Act, where

(a) any person acting as an insolvency practitioner seizes or disposes of any property in relation to which his functions are, because that property is for the time being subject to a restraint order, not exercisable; and

(b) at the time of the seizure or disposal he believes, and has reasonable grounds for believing, that he is entitled (whether in pursuance of a court order or otherwise) to seize or dispose of that property,

he shall not be liable to any person in respect of any loss or damage resulting from the seizure or disposal except in so far as the loss or damage is caused by the insolvency practitioner's negligence; and the insolvency practitioner shall have a lien on the property, or the proceeds of its sale, for such of his expenses as were incurred in connection with the liquidation, sequestration or other proceedings in relation to which the seizure or disposal purported to take place and for so much of his remuneration as may reasonably be assigned for his actings in connection with those proceedings.

(2) Any person who, acting as an insolvency practitioner, incurs expenses—

(a) in respect of such realisable property as is mentioned in sub-paragraph (1)(a) above and in so doing does not know and has no reasonable grounds to believe that the property is for the time being subject to a restraint order; or

(b) other than in respect of such realisable property as is so mentioned, being expenses which, but for the effect of a restraint order might have been met by taking possession of and realising the property, shall be entitled (whether or not he has seized or disposed of that property so as to have a lien under sub-paragraph (1) above) to payment of those expenses under paragraph 4(2) or (4)(a) of Schedule 1 to this Act.

(3) In the foregoing provisions of this paragraph, the expression "acting as an insolvency practitioner" shall be construed in accordance with section 388 (interpretation) of the said Act of 1986 except that for the purposes of such construction the reference in subsection (2)(a) of that section to a permanent or interim trustee in a sequestration shall be taken to include a reference to a trustee in a sequestration and subsection (5) of that section shall be disregarded: and the expression shall also comprehend the official receiver acting as receiver or manager of the property.

Interpretation

6.—(1) In this Schedule "the 1985 Act" means the Bankruptcy (Scotland) Act 1985.

(2) References in this Schedule to the conclusion of proceedings, except for the purposes of paragraph 2(5) above, shall be construed—

   (a) as regards property subject to a restraint order under section 28(1)(a) of this Act, in accordance with section 29(6) of this Act; and

   (b) as regards property subject to a restraint order under section 28(1)(b) of this Act, in accordance with section 30(5) of this Act.

(3) References in this Schedule to property held by a person include a reference to property vested in the interim or permanent trustee in his sequestration or in his trustee in bankruptcy or liquidation.

Index